# Educational Leadership

British Educational Leadership, Management & Administration Society

Published in Association with the British Educational Leadership, Management and Administration Society

This series of books published for BELMAS aims to be directly relevant to the concerns and professional development needs of emergent leaders and experienced leaders in schools. The series editors are Professor Harry Tomlinson, Leeds Metropolitan University and Dr Hugh Busher, School of Education, University of Leicester.

Titles include:

# Educational Leadership

## Personal Growth for Professional Development

Harry Tomlinson

**SAGE Publications**
London • Thousand Oaks • New Delhi

First published 2004

SAGE Publications Ltd
1 Oliver's Yard
55 City Road
London EC1Y 1SP

SAGE Publications Inc
2455 Teller Road
Thousand Oaks, California 91320

SAGE Publications India Pvt Ltd
B-42 Panchsheel Enclave
Post Box 4109
New Delhi-110 017

**British Library Catalogue in Publication data**

A catalogue record for this book is available from the British Library

ISBN 0 7619 6776 1
ISBN 0 7619 6777 X

**Library of Congress Control Number: 2002115859**

Typeset by Dorwyn Ltd, Hampshire
Printed in Great Britain by the Athenaeum Press, Gateshead

# Contents

# Series Editor's Preface

I am delighted to celebrate the arrival of another book by Harry Tomlinson, for the BELMAS series of books. In it he discusses how important it is that leaders of educational organizations know themselves in order to be successful. How that process of self-knowing can be undertaken is carefully developed in the first six chapters through discussion of a variety of approaches for this. Clearly the pagan oracle at Delphi was sharper at developing resourceful humans than have been many modern secular perspectives on leadership and management. It, too, recognized the importance of people understanding how they related to the cultures and systems of the communities in which they worked, especially if they wanted to be successful leaders. It, too, encouraged people to understand themselves, their emotions, their strengths and weaknesses, and their values and the quality of their communications with other members of their communities, in order for them to be successful as leaders.

Harry, however, uses a different process from the smells and incantations of the oracle to gain and offer insight into the complexities of human interactions in educational organizations although he, too, recognizes the importance of leaders offering counselling, coaching and mentoring to help their colleagues develop creativity. This, he argues, is necessary to support the quest of staff for innovation and change to cope with the impact of alterations in the contexts of their schools and colleges on the ways in which they work. Six chapters consider ways in which leaders can support the professional development of their colleagues. In drawing on an extensive and up to date literature from business management as well as from educational management on personal and professional development and the implementation of change in schools and colleges, he shows how the priestly class of leaders at institutional and middle level can develop particular organizational cultures and sub-cultures to project their core values and shape the working environments of a school or college for staff and students. These values he argues are particularly visible in the visions projected by leaders to guide the missions of their schools and colleges, and in the systems and organizational structures that are established and maintained in them.

Learning is placed at the centre of personal and professional development and so at the fulcrum of organizational development: processes of individual and institutional change require participants to learn and to act within consciously rather than tacitly understood value frameworks and social, economic and polit-

With thanks for personal support from Berry, Kate (and Nodd), and Bob for keeping asking.

ical contexts. Those cultures (value systems and their manifestations) and practices that are more able to cope with ambiguity seem to help their participants accommodate to change more smoothly. Seven chapters consider the processes of change as they have been debated by a variety of recent scholars. Implicit in these and in some of the other chapters are the asymmetrical power relationships in schools and colleges between leaders at all levels and other staff and students, and the ability of successful leaders to project power effectively in order to bring about change.

This learning is, however, of a self-reflective nature that invites the actors in schools to consider their actions in their current contexts in order to resolve how to improve the quality of schooling to benefit all participants. The structure of the book reflects this concern with active learning, spattering the text with a series of questions as well as lists of actions which readers might undertake, to encourage readers to juxtapose critically their learning from engaging with the text with current practices in their schools and colleges.

It is perhaps fitting that the book should close with a chapter on one of the great conundrums of working life: sustaining a balance between work and life. And it is intriguing that the chapter places these notions in contradiction with each other rather than considering work as part of life. This chapter seems peculiarly apt, but offers no solutions except for people to tune into their values, at a time in English society when the importance of people's dedication to the pursuit of organizational goals has been emphasized by central government and private industry, heedless of people's personal and social needs or of the needs of others in their role sets outside the compass of the organizations for which they work. We have all suffered in this period from the impact of this individualist neo-liberal ideology destroying notions of community and social life and replacing values of collaboration and shared decision-making in pursuit of agreed common goals with ones of aggressive competition to generate increasing individual wealth regardless of the needs of those people lacking in sufficient social, personal or intellectual capital to compete effectively.

So it is of great value that this book reminds readers that there is more to living than work and that successful adaptation to changing circumstances, at least in educational organizations, depends more on cooperation and teamwork in pursuit of shared values and goals, developed through self-awareness, emotional understanding and collaborative learning, than it does on competitive cutting edge strategies that promote the aggrandizement of the implementer and the destruction of the opposition, be that construed as the neighbouring producer, neighbouring school or neighbouring classroom.

*Hugh Busher*
School of Education, University of Leicester

# Biographical Note

After 18 years as headteacher and college principal in Manchester and Stockport, Harry Tomlinson went to Leeds Metropolitan University where he was initially responsible for the International MBA in Educational Leadership. Later he became responsible for managing the NPQH for the Yorkshire and Humber Region, and project director for the LPSH for one of seven national consortia for the NCSL. He was also responsible for managing the Performance Management Contract for the Yorkshire and Humber Region for the DfES. He has been Treasurer for the Secondary Heads Association and Chair of BELMAS. Edited books for which he has had major responsibility have included *Performance-Related Pay in Education*, *The Search for Standards*, *Education and Training 14–19*, *Living Headship – Voices, Values and Vision*, and *Performance Management in Education*. He has more recently been a consultant for the Lithuanian Ministry of Education on contracts for School Reorganisation and Leadership and Management Development. He has an individual National Training Award, and has recently achieved an MBA and qualifications in performance coaching and life coaching.

# Introduction

There have been a significant number of books published which have focused on professional development for leaders in schools and teachers, particularly in the context of performance management. Though this book takes account of these, the focus is initially very much on personal development through self-understanding and self-management because this has to be the basis for profound professional development. These provide a context for a distinctive understanding of the emotional intelligence which it is now widely recognized is central to leadership effectiveness. The case is made for greater use of 360-degree feedback to provide a fuller self-understanding than more traditional feedback processes. The increased understanding of the significance of functioning of the brain and mind and its application to accelerated learning, increasingly used with children in schools, takes the argument forward. Neurolinguistic programming, a means of personal development widely used in business but less widely in schools is recommended as a means of modelling excellence. Creativity is now understood as essential to school leadership and this chapter presents an alternative exploration of what this means from a wider practical and theoretical context. Personal effectiveness depends on managing your own stress and time but this does take place in a more complex and intense context where careers are changing and require new competencies. These can be provided by training, coaching and mentoring, which are practised in schools, but the suggestion here is that they should be developed much more widely. Teams, groups and working parties are contexts for decision-making but provide opportunities also for insightful learning. The chapter on leadership explores leadership outside the educational context to provide a different challenge for learning. The chapter on performance management explores rewards, both psychological and financial, the latter using evidence from educational contexts in the USA where there is experience to provide high-quality evidence. The ethical and values dimension, with implication for vision and mission, particularly focuses here on the practice associated with gender issues. At the school level the concluding chapters again seek challenging evidence from outside education to clarify practice that can be improved. Good schools are working in these areas but the concluding chapters, like the whole book, are exploring areas outside the traditional for educational leadership books and are offering encouragement to carry out practical activities. Profound educational leadership will consistently develop further skills in improving the school's organizational health, focusing strategy, enhancing quality, achieving knowledge management, and radical change as well as a healthy work–life balance. The complexity of the demands on educational leaders should not be underestimated but should be enjoyed. These are new competencies for school leaders, and working through this book, and carrying out the reflective opportunities presented, will enhance the learning of all educational leaders. I have taken ideas from many sources. If, inadvertently, any of these are not acknowledged, I apologise.

# 1

## Self-Management and Personal Development

This opening chapter explores three issues. There is an introductory consideration of the self, an exploration of a model of effective teaching which is different from those we normally access, and a preliminary consideration of the Hay McBer (2000) *Research into Teacher Effectiveness* which has been important in developing government and National College for School Leadership (NCSL) policies for professional development.

Personal effectiveness is a precondition of professional excellence. This assertion provides a starting point and theme for this book intended for those working in schools. Improved self-management increases an education leader's ability to cope with stress, resolve conflict, manage change and manage to change, achieve sustainable peak performance, build and lead effective teams and influence organizational cultures. We will explore all of these in greater depth. It will be useful at this stage to carry out a preliminary self-audit of your recent professional growth in your current school.

1) Have you, in the last three years, progressed in your responsibilities, influence and performance?
2) What were your personal ambitions for this period, and did you achieve them?
3) Do you have clear aspirations for the next three years? Does the school have any plans for you? Are these fully aligned?
4) What new skills have you acquired recently? What opportunities have you taken to improve your existing skills?
5) How confident are you of progress within your current school?
6) How do you get on with colleagues and senior management?

*Reflect on the implications of this self-audit for your future.*

### MANAGING YOUR SELF-DEVELOPMENT

In order to achieve self-development, Parikh (1991) showed that the 'master manager' has knowledge, skills, attitudes, creativity and consciousness elements.

1) *Knowledge* – starts with in-depth insights into the five elements of your own inner dynamics, your body, mind, emotions, neurosensory system and states

of consciousness. Insights into the inner personal dynamics of other people, into ideas and current developments in the education service, and wider insights into environmental forces and trends enhance this.

2) *Skills* – personal skills enable you to achieve an inner balance of these five elements. Team skills involve motivating the team and linking individual interests and ideas into a common vision. Communication skills are two way, developed through active listening and creating clear messages for others. Facilitation skills enable everyone to perform at their peak level. A skill in managing the cultural level is about ensuring alignments within the organization and attunement within the individual.

3) *Attitudes* – changing from power and problem driven attitudes to vision driven because of a commitment to purposes and values. This involves a shift to management based on caring and connection. Your thoughts, feelings and actions are proactive and self-reliant.

4) *Creativity* – the capacity for envisioning and understanding intuition; the capacity for a wider and deeper perception; to see deeper significances and connections and to be able to break old connections; and to convert such connections into concrete applications.

5) *Consciousness* – based on your concept of the self, you develop the capacity to access the different states of consciousness. This is what, in the subtitle to the book, Parikh describes as 'management by detached involvement'. This process enables you to achieve your potential. This is the sustainable peak performance which inspires others.

*Using your own words reflect on your understanding for personal development of your knowledge, skills, attitudes, creativity and consciousness.*

## SELF-ACCEPTANCE

We are not always secure in our 'identity', particularly when there is some challenge to its integrity. What is central as the basis for professional and personal development is the willing acceptance of the self. The self has an existence with distinctive traits or characteristics and is related to your identity, a basis for your self-esteem, self-confidence, self-respect and self-regard. Self-affirmation is important for personal success. Irrational and negative beliefs are damaging. The belief that you should be liked by everyone for everything, or that you can be highly competent in all activities is irrational. You should not think there is a problem when things do not go as you want, believe you can necessarily have significant control over the future, or that external events or other people determine your happiness. There is always the opportunity to remake the past and not be trapped by the belief that something that once affected you always will. If some obstruction has stopped your progress, you could interpret this obstacle as irrational and impossible to challenge, or you could work round it. If you have negative feelings about yourself you will act less effectively, but you can also learn to change these feelings.

*How fully do you accept yourself?*

## SELF-MANAGEMENT IN A NEW JOB

There are stages that many people go through when starting a new job. The initial excitement is accompanied by remembering what you are missing from the last job, in particular the security. In coming to terms with the scope of new job, there may be questioning and self-doubt about your capacity to succeed. You will be trying out new ways of working, as you gain confidence in your performance and grow into the job. On entry into a new role or a new environment you will need to recognize the need to understand and manage new networks and relationships. In teaching it is common to explore the interview process with those who have not been offered the job. It is particularly important, however, for those who are appointed to understand what were the strengths that resulted in their being offered the job and areas where there may have been concerns if these can be accessed.

In the new post it is essential to explore the new context in depth. Your strategic planning of the entry process will be crucial. You should signal your broad agenda early but avoid promises and commitments until you are certain these are appropriate. The first three or four key questions to which you seek answers will convey your values. Give time to explore for learning, but with that exploration process highly structured. If there are problems, try out new behaviours and approaches, ensuring you are not limiting yourself to styles acquired in previous contexts. Remember your life outside work, in particular your family and friends, in the new circumstances. They may notice changes in you which you need to understand. Finally, review and reflect, and in particular seek detailed feedback at the end of each of the first three months which you should record to evaluate your progress.

*Reflect on your entry into your last new job.*

## PROFESSIONAL DEVELOPMENT AND PERSONAL DEVELOPMENT

In recognizing the competencies that have to be managed it is important to distinguish between professional development, that is, occupational role development; staff development which is about development in the particular school context; and personal development, which is the development of the whole person. Waters (1998, p. 30) makes similar distinctions arguing that the 'change of self by self' has to be recognized as the only basis for profound change. This is about 'changes in self-awareness' which has not been a major focus of teacher development. The focus has been on learning new technical skills – how to implement the numeracy hour, how to teach the new GCSE syllabus. Without underestimating the importance of these, the process of 'getting into closer contact with ... (your) inner intelligence, (your) higher self' and (your) 'personal capabilities' (Waters, 1998, p. 30) has not been the focus of professional learning. There has been some focus on the 'interpersonal-listening, assertiveness' work with fellow professionals. What is being suggested here is a central focus on 'the concepts of self-image (how we see ourselves), self-esteem (the value we place on ourselves), and self-efficacy (our beliefs about being able to bring about successful results)'.

(Ibid., p. 32) These are what will make the long-term difference. School perform-ance and pupil performance will improve when we concentrate on these central professional learning processes.

*Consider one example of each of professional development, staff development and personal development that you have been involved in recently.*

It is recommended that you keep a personal journal and develop a professional portfolio. These might provide an opportunity for developing skills in online recording and presentation. The personal journal is based on the reflective practi-tioner model of professional development which allows you to explore your feel-ings, your thoughts and ideas and your action-tendencies, but linked to research and theory. The professional portfolio encapsulates the most significant elements of that journey in a way representing who you are personally and professionally; essentially it is an elaborated and sophisticated CV. It can be anticipated that the professional portfolio will provide the most appropriate evidence you can present when you are seeking to further your development or a new appointment.

## CHARTERED INSTITUTE OF PERSONNEL AND DEVELOPMENT

Depending on your career aspirations, and your focus on people development, you may wish to consider membership of an organization such as the Chartered Institute of Personnel and Development (CIPD) which provides its members with a Continuing Professional Development (CPD) Record and Development Plan. Their essential CPD principles are:

- Development should be continuous in the sense that the professional should always be actively seeking improved performance.
- Development should be owned and managed by the individual learner.
- CPD is a personal matter and the effective learner knows best what he or she needs to learn. Development should be from the individual's current learning state.
- Learning objectives should be clear and wherever possible should serve orga-nizational or client needs as well as individual goals.
- Regular investment of time in learning should be seen as an essential part of professional life, not as an option (IPD, 1998).

This changing perception of what it means to be a professional is now becoming central for the teaching profession for all teachers but also for all other staff. The CIPD has only recently attained chartered status and in Scotland there are explo-rations of the Chartered Teacher approach. There is no prescribed formula for the CIPD development plan but it is recommended that there should be clear devel-opment objectives, which in turn can be divided into short-term requirements, and long-term career and development needs. There should be a clear action plan – exactly what is planned to do to meet the development objectives, with suggested headings including on-the-job opportunities, formal training and informal/self-directed learning.

*Do you have a personal/career development plan? Has your school developed plans for professional portfolios for all staff?*

## ACCOMPLISHED TEACHING

In this book you will be encouraged to explore outside the educational context. Here you are asked to compare Threshold Standards with an American model based on research. We do need precise definitions of effective or accomplished teaching, and these are emerging. The Hay McBer *Research on Teacher Effectiveness* uses a very different approach. It is suggested that you evaluate how fully as a teacher you match up to the five propositions of accomplished teaching. These are based on research which is not the case with standards in the UK.

*The Five Propositions of Accomplished Teaching*
(National Board for Professional Teaching Standards, USA)
1. Teachers are committed to students and their learning
2. Teachers know the subjects they teach and how to teach those subjects to students
3. Teachers are responsible for managing and monitoring student learning
4. Teachers think systematically about their practice and learn from experience
5. Teachers are members of learning communities

*The Five Propositions of Accomplished Teaching*
1. Accomplished teachers are dedicated to making knowledge accessible to all students. They act on the belief that all students can learn. They treat students equitably, recognising individual differences that distinguish one student from another and taking account of these differences in their practice. They adjust their practice based on observation and knowledge of their students' interests, abilities, skills, knowledge, family circumstances and peer relationships ... They incorporate the prevailing theories of cognition and intelligence in their practice. They are aware of the influence of context and culture on behaviour. They develop students' cognitive capacity and their respect for learning. Equally important, they foster students' self-esteem, motivation, character, civic responsibility and their respect for individual, cultural, religious and racial differences.

*Evaluate how fully you achieve this proposition and whether your school reflects this in its policies and practice.*

2. Accomplished teachers have a rich understanding of the subjects they teach, and appreciate how knowledge in their subject is created, organised, linked to other disciplines and applied to real-world settings. While faithfully representing the collective wisdom of our culture and upholding the values of disciplinary knowledge, they also develop the critical and analytical capacities of their students ... Accomplished teachers command specialised knowledge of how to convey and reveal subject matter to students ... They understand where difficulties are likely to arise and modify their practice accordingly. Their instructional repertoire allows them to create multiple paths to the subjects they teach, and they are adept at teaching students how to pose and solve their own problems.

*Evaluate how fully you achieve this proposition and whether your school reflects this in its policies and practice.*

3. Accomplished teachers create, maintain and alter instructional settings to capture and sustain the interest of their students and to make the most effective use of time. They also are adept at engaging students and adults to assist their teaching and at enlisting their colleagues' knowledge and expertise to complement their own ... Accomplished teachers command a range of generic instructional techniques, know when each is appropriate and can implement them as needed. They are as aware of ineffectual or damaging practice as they are devoted to elegant practice.

*Evaluate how fully you achieve this proposition and whether your school reflects this in its policies and practice.*

4. Accomplished teachers are models of educated persons, exemplifying the virtues they seek to inspire in students – curiosity, tolerance, honesty, fairness, respect for diversity and appreciation of cultural difference – and the capacities that are prerequisites for intellectual growth: the ability to reason and take multiple perspectives to be creative and take risks, and to adopt an experimental and problem-solving orientation ... Accomplished teachers draw on their knowledge of human development, subject matters and instruction and their understanding of their students to make principled judgements about sound practice ... Striving to strengthen their teaching, accomplished teachers critically examine their practice, seek to expand their repertoire, deepen their knowledge, sharpen their judgement and adapt their teaching to new findings, ideas and theories.

*Evaluate how fully you achieve this proposition and whether your school reflects this in its policies and practice.*

5. Accomplished teachers contribute to the effectiveness of the school by working collaboratively with other professionals on instructional policy, curriculum development and staff development. They can evaluate school progress and the allocation of school resources in light of their understanding of state and local objectives. They are knowledgeable about specialised school and community resources that can be engaged for their students' benefit, and are skilled at employing such resources as needed ... Accomplished teachers find ways to work collaboratively and creatively with parents engaging them productively in the work of the school.

*Evaluate how fully you achieve this proposition and whether your school reflects this in its policies and practice.*

It is important to have your model of what accomplished teaching is. Ingvarson (Middlewood and Cardno, 2001) explores the relationship between the accomplished teaching standards (USA) and threshold standards (England), particularly in examining the rationale for the standards and the depth, quality and professionalism of the judgements that are required. The National Board for Professional Teaching Standards (NBPTS) provides rich evidence justifying the procedures and research it undertakes to ensure the validity of each set of standards. Ingvarson suggests that the generic behaviours and student outcomes used by Hay McBer, considered below, do not take account of the extensive evidence that what expert teachers know and do is fundamentally subject and level specific. The NBPTS is working with teacher associations, educational researchers and unions to develop standards in 30 different fields. These standards represent the profession's conception of the standards that most teachers should be able to attain after ten years' teaching. Ingvarson notes that in the UK there has been little work on determining what level of performance is good enough to meet the standard, and suggests that with 97 per cent passing the assessment has gained no respect, and that this has inevitably led to problems associated with the Upper Pay Spine.

For National Board certification teachers prepare evidence of their teaching in a portfolio containing six 'entries' of three types. Two are based primarily on student work samples, two on video clips of class discussions, and two on documentation of professional accomplishments outside the classroom, one focused on contributions to the professional community and one illustrating commitment to the families and communities of their students. Each entry takes 20 to 30 hours to prepare and is about 12 pages long. In addition to the demonstration of the rich understanding of how knowledge in their subject is created, organized, linked to other disciplines and applied in real world setting, there is an assessment centre for one full day with four 90-minute sessions based on materials sent in advance. These processes have been selected because they demonstrably relate to accomplished teaching – based on research. Across the six entries and four exercises 20 teachers may be involved in the assessment of one teacher, and all will have needed to demonstrate high levels of reliability in their assessments. There has been research on both the reliability of the assessment process and on how the highly accomplished teachers differ significantly from others in classroom practice. In the US system, which is voluntary, nearly 10,000 applied for certification in 2000, of whom about 40 per cent passed. However there is a commitment to the process because the profession is building its own infrastructure for defining teaching standards, an opportunity that has been lost in England (Ingvarson, 2001).

*How do you respond to the accomplished teaching model?*

## Research into Teacher Effectiveness. Phase 2 Report: A Model of Teacher Effectiveness

This Hay McBer Report, with the title above, was published on 12 June, 2000 and presents the evidence for what is becoming understood and accepted as received wisdom about effective teaching. The DfEE invested an enormous amount into the model for teacher effectiveness which is based on the headteacher effectiveness model that underpins the Leadership Programme for Serving Headteachers (LPSH). What has to be determined now, if the quality of the evidence presented by Hay McBer is accepted, is what use is to be made of the evidence for the teaching profession. Hay has developed a commercial programme which is available for schools (www.transforminglearning.co.uk) for teacher development. The research process would seem to be unexceptionable in its own terms, though the British Educational Research Association (BERA) is concerned that the research evidence, for commercial reasons according to Hay, cannot be accessed. The *Research into Teacher Effectiveness* report itself concentrates on presenting the rationale for the conclusions. You may wish to consider the report itself if you wish to understand the evidence for what is likely to remain the most important basis for your professional development for the next few years. The conclusions are accessible on the National College for School Leadership (NCSL) website (www.ncsl.org.uk). This model presents the characteristics of superior performers to crystallize the nature of the key competencies that create the climate that impact on performance. The Hay McBer model is derived from the work of McClelland (1989) who provides one basis for understanding human motivation and its links to behaviour. Hay McBer has developed psychometric instruments, as have others, which examine the motive profile of individuals to present the relative strengths in the three McClelland social motives (see below). It is possible to access your motive profile through Hay McBer.

1) *Achievement* – the desire to accomplish a performance more effectively than in the past and than others. Those with this motive want immediate and specific feedback on performance. They assume personal responsibility for getting things done and are preoccupied with their work, so are task oriented and want to accomplish concrete goals. They prefer situations involving moderate levels of risk or difficulty. These qualities mean that they often make significant career progression and are successful, but they do not achieve senior leadership positions.
2) *Affiliation* – the need for human companionship. Those with this motive want reassurance from others and are genuinely concerned with others' feelings. They are likely to act as they think others want them to, especially those with whom they identify and desire friendship.
3) *Power* – the need to control one's environment. People vary significantly along this dimension, some seeking power, others avoiding it at all costs. Those with a high score in this motive can be successful managers if three conditions are met. They must seek power for the betterment of their organization rather than their own interests, they must have a fairly low need for affiliation, and they need plenty of self-control so that they can curb their desire for power when it threatens to interfere with effective organizational or interpersonal relationships (Baron, 1986; Moorhead and Griffin, 1995).

The Hay McBer model explores the links between the characteristics of effective teachers grouped as shown below. The report shows the links between characteristics, and how levels of performance in a characteristic can be described and recognized, and why each matters. It is the combination of characteristics that determines a teacher's effectiveness.

1) *Professionalism*
   (a) Challenge and support – a commitment to do everything possible for each pupil and to enable all pupils to be successful.

(b) Confidence – the belief in one's ability to be effective and to take on challenges.

(c) Creating trust – being consistent and fair. Keeping one's word.

(d) Respect for others – the underlying belief that individuals matter and deserve respect.

2) *Thinking*

(a) Analytical thinking – the ability to think logically, to break things down, and recognize cause and effect.

(b) Conceptual thinking – the ability to see patterns and links, even when there is a lot of detail.

3) *Planning and setting expectations*

(a) Drive for improvement – relentless energy for setting and meeting challenging targets for pupils and the school.

(b) Information-seeking – a drive to find out more and get to the heart of things, intellectual curiosity.

(c) Initiative – the drive to act now to anticipate and pre-empt events.

4) *Leading*

(a) Flexibility – the ability and willingness to adapt to the needs of a situation and to change tactics.

(b) Holding people accountable – the drive and ability to set clear expectations and parameters and to hold others accountable for performance.

(c) Managing pupils – the drive and the ability to provide clear direction to pupils, and to enthuse and motivate them.

(d) Passion for learning – the drive and ability to support pupils in their learning and to help them become confident and independent learners.

5) *Relating to others*

(a) Impact and influence – the ability and the drive to produce positive outcomes by impressing and influencing others.

(b) Teamworking – the ability to work with others to achieve shared goals.

(c) Understanding others – the drive and ability to understand others, and why they behave as they do.

The Hay McBer approach explores how teaching skills, professional characteristics and classroom climate are linked together to substantially determine pupil progress. The characteristics are presented in relation to national standards at main professional grade, threshold and Advanced Skills Teacher levels. Teaching skills, professional characteristics and classroom climate can all be measured. There are issues about whether the model is acceptable to the profession, and the use that is to be made of it in professional development, but more particularly in the evaluation of teacher performance within the new performance management framework. The success of the diagnostic instruments and the learning process within the Leadership Programme for Serving Heads is achieved because evidence remains confidential to the headteacher.

*How do you respond to the work of Hay McBer and its implications for teachers?*

## CONCLUSION

Hopson and Scally defined the key assumptions about self-development 20 years ago. They have been refined to provide a basis for your personal and professional development.

1) Each person is a unique individual worthy of respect.
2) Individuals are responsible for their own actions and behaviour.
3) Individuals are responsible for their own feelings and emotions and their responses to the behaviour of others.
4) New situations, however unwelcome, contain opportunities for new learning and growth.
5) Mistakes are learning experiences and are seen as outcomes rather than failures.
6) The seeds of our growth are within us. Only we ourselves can activate our potential for creativity and growth.
7) We can all do more than we are currently doing to become more than we currently are.
8) Awareness brings responsibility and responsibility creates the opportunity for choice.
9) Our own fear is the major limiter to our growth.
10) Growth and development never end. Self-empowerment is not an end to be achieved but a constant process of becoming.

## REFERENCES

Baron, R.A. (1986) *Behaviour in Organizations: Understanding and Managing the Human Side of Work*, Boston, MA: Allyn and Bacon.

CIPD (1998) Continuing Professional Development documents.

Hay McBer (2000) *Research into Teacher Effectiveness. Phase 2 Report: A Model of Teacher Effectiveness*, London: DfEE.

Ingvarson, L. (2001) 'Developing standards and assessment for accomplished teaching' in D. Middlewood and C. Cardno (eds), *Managing Appraisal and Performance*, London: Routledge, pp. 160–79.

McClelland, D.C. (1989) *Human Motivation*, Cambridge: Cambridge University Press.

Moorhead, G. and Griffin. R.W. (1995) *Organizational Behaviour*, Boston, MA: Houghton Mifflin.

National Board for Professional Teaching Standards (1997) *The Five Propositions of Accomplished Teaching*

Parikh, J. (1991) *Managing Your Self: Management by Detached Involvement*, London: Basil Blackwell.

Waters, M. (1998) 'Personal development for teachers', *Professional Development Today*, 1(2), pp. 29–37.

# 2

## Self-Understanding, Personality and Psychometric Instruments

In this chapter we will consider three psychometric instruments and how they can inform self-understanding as a basis for personal and professional development. The Myers-Briggs Type Indicator presents information about your personality type. FIRO-B presents information about your interpersonal orientation. The Team Management Profile presents information about your work preferences. They have been selected because they have a widely acknowledged credibility and because they illustrate the opportunities available for self-understanding as a basis for self-development. They are recommended because they have been found to be particularly useful.

### MYERS-BRIGGS TYPE INDICATOR (MBTI)

The Myers-Briggs Type Indicator is one of the oldest and most respected psychometric instruments. It is based on the theories of Jung and all 16 personality types have equal value derived from eight possible preferences organized from four bipolar scales.

Extroversion (E)——— (I) Introversion
Sensing (S)     ——— (N) Intuition
Thinking (T)    ——— (F) Feeling
Judging (J)     ——— (P) Perceiving

- The *extrovert's* essential stimulation is from the environment – the outer world of people and things.
- The *introvert's* essential stimulation is from within – the inner world of thought and reflection.
- The *sensing* function takes in information by way of the five senses – sight, sound, feel, taste and smell.
- The *intuiting* function processes information by way of a 'sixth sense' or hunch.
- The *thinking* function decides on the basis of logic and objective consideration.
- The *feeling* function decides on the basis of personal subjective values.
- A *judging* lifestyle is decisive, planned and orderly.
- A *perceptive* lifestyle is flexible, adaptable and spontaneous.

The four preferences that you identify are combined into one of 16 personality

11

types. You will normally have skills in all areas but one will be significantly stronger. The MBTI type does not predict behaviour or skill. The characteristics below are edited from some MBTI documentation.

*As you fully consider these consider how the personality types relate to colleagues and friends. Which type do you think is you?*

| ISTJ | ISFJ | INFJ | INTJ |
|---|---|---|---|
| Thoughtful, courteous, responsible and perfectionist, needs to be in charge and wants efficiency. May feel never off duty. Pays meticulous attention to systems and processes. Likes the clarity of sensible rules. Can be stubborn. May over-rely on detail and tend to dismiss the importance of other people's feelings. | Cordial, charming, patient, modest style fuelled by wish to help others through strong sense of loyalty to duty and liking for tradition. Observant of how others feel. Detail conscious, steady and serious; delivers on promises. May need to guard against being exploited and feeling responsible. | Sensitive, patient, insightful and hardworking; willing to put effort into understanding the complexity of human relationships. Wants to contribute decisively to ideas that will affect people in important ways. Can be dreamy and enigmatic and may find it difficult to put self first. | Inner energy, fierce independence and a preference for big-picture thinking Has a calm and unflappable public face, which disguises ardour for competence – for self and others. Impatient for improvement. Likes to organize. May have air of critical detachment which creates sense of being impossible to please. |

| ISTP | ISFP | INFP | INTP |
|---|---|---|---|
| Socially reserved; cool observer; needs variety; can come into own when the need is for quick thinking, practicality and coping calmly with a crisis. Needs to feel can meet the unexpected with ingenuity. Detachment, need for privacy and reluctance to communicate may create problems with others. | Kind, modest, attentive to others, with little need to impress or control. Loathes conflict. Needs to give service, but on own terms. Deeply loyal with quiet sense of fun; likes to offer practical support without judging. May make an art out of economy of effort and may annoy through holding back from communicating or explaining. | Gentle, loyal and apparently pliant style may hide intensely idealistic and driven interior. Wants to live in harmony with values and expand potential of self and others. Has little interest in worldly possessions or controlling others. Endless quest for the perfect may lead to perpetual dithering or unnecessary guilt. | Analytical, sceptical, cool seeker after truth. Tends to love the complex, theoretical and novel; resists authority and dislikes being in authority; constantly challenges the status quo through experiment; always ready to rethink. May need to learn that passion for the exact truth as sees it could alienate others. |

| ESTP | ESFP | ENFP | ENTP |
|---|---|---|---|
| Straightforward, cheerful, inventive, practical; has zest for life and loves a challenge as long as it results in immediate tangible action. Sees | Open, modest, generous and tactful; commitment to active fun, practicality and to valuing people creates disarming realism about self and others. | Enthusiastic, versatile innovator. Likes to improvise and help other people solve problems through creativity and insights into how people tick. | Energetic, brash, original; wants to be where the action is. Needs to be right and to be first. Loathes routine and detail. Likes to challenge |

self as an adaptable realist who gets round the rules. Has accepting attitude to others. Enjoys trouble shooting. May need to take care that expediency does not dominate.

Sociable, gracious, flexible and enjoys the limelight. Relishes the good things of life without apology. May need to take care that is not seen as frivolous or unfocused.

Must give and receive personal authenticity. Builds bridges and 'walks the talk'. May need to guard against 'butterfly' approach which exhausts self and others.

conventional wisdom and values independence. May need to be aware of unintentionally hurting others through love of argument and having the last word.

| ESTJ | ESFJ | ENFJ | ENTJ |
|---|---|---|---|
| Crisp, decisive, courageous; wants to get things organized now. Needs to maintain stability and order through care with detail; has robust often hearty style with people. Down-to-earth practical approach. May need to take care that in concern to get things done, does not overlook the need for tact and sensitivity. | Friendly, brisk, talkative, loyal and practical; brings common sense and warmth to dealings with people. Needs approval from others. Likes busyness, organizing and socializing. Values working systematically and co-operatively. Sensitive to indifference. May need to give and take criticism in a more detached way. | Tactful, diplomatic; natural facility with words and commitment to good causes that will make a difference to the world and can inspire others. Loves encouraging others; believes passionately in equality. Sensitive to disharmony. May need to watch tendency to 'rescue' others or to allow idealism to become rigid. | Energetic, clear-sighted, decisive, analytical; needs to turn ideas into action; loathes illogicality; needs to feel authoritative. Confident and articulate. Insists on looking at the big picture and enjoys robust discussions on improving standards and implementing change. Direct style can seem abrasive and may intimidate. |

The profile those being assessed receive shows how they typically think and behave. The profile presented below provides a fuller extension of the type description above, exploring in detail the implications for the style with people, work style, leadership and management style, style with subordinates, style with bosses, communication, thinking and decision style, work and home, stress, and development recommendations.

To illustrate the kind of information that might be provided, extracts from a report on an ENTP are presented (Cambridge Management Centres, 2000). The individual preference scores which led to this particular report are shown below. It is useful to note that there are both supportive and challenging comments. You are asked to think what the implications are for the individual, and whether you should seek such guidance for yourself.

## Case study 2.1

| Reported Type | E | N | T | P |
|---|---|---|---|---|
| Preference Score | 31 | 47 | 13 | 7 |

*Style with People*
ENTP ... charisma, articulacy and humour often attract others. Normally ENTPs can quickly shed any reticence, straightforwardly seeking and enjoying the limelight. Sometimes this gives the impression that the ENTP is readier for a closer relationship than is the case, leading to confusion and disappointment. Real intimacy can be an issue for some ENTPs: they need people and are sensitive to being ignored, but also need to guard their inner private person. ...

*Work Style*
Work has to be fun to hold the ENTP's interest. Commitment to self-defined high standards in everything they undertake drives the ENTP approach to work. ENTPs are attracted to work environments that allow maximum independence with a strong emphasis on novelty, creativity, experiment and the exchange of ideas ...

*Leadership and Management Style*
Leadership attracts ENTPs, as long as they can use it to develop their entrepreneurial skills. Direct, forceful and articulate, the ENTP's conviction that he or she is right, often draws the fierce loyalty of their followers. ENTPs lead through their belief that the impossible is within reach ...

*Style with subordinates*
The ideal subordinate for an ENTP is someone who is an expert in their field, needs little day-to-day direction and does not hold back the flow of ideas and activities. When an ENTP leads a team of this sort it is a powerful engine for growth and creativity ...

*Style with bosses*
... (On receiving feedback) To be criticised can therefore be a painful experience. If the feedback is sensitively handled by someone who the ENTP respects, ENTPs can usually accept it as a valuable process which will trigger learning and growth. If insensitively handled, ENTPs can become loud, arrogant and defensive, and may defiantly continue the complained-of behaviour.

*Communication*
... ENTPs are not always careful listeners: their minds are racing ahead and they want to make their own contribution so badly that they do not always note how much they interrupt or go on speaking at such length and with such enthusiasm that others cannot get a look in. ...

*Thinking and Decision Style*
ENTPs think broadly and strategically: their whole focus is on the future. Their strength is in generating possibilities which they can quickly synthesise, analyse and explain. They may also be attracted to grand ideas and theoretical models ...

*Work and Home*
Juggling work and home is in itself often an enjoyable task to ENTPs. They take work seriously, but play and rest are also important. ENTPs can sometimes be unpredictable: there will be phases in their lives when career is all important and they are hardly ever at home, and other phases when personal issues or some all-absorbing hobby suddenly assumes prime place ...

*ENTPs and Stress*
Stressful situations tend to be those where ENTPs
● feel constrained by rules they consider petty and ridiculous

- have to expend a lot of energy on routine, paperwork, form-filling or detail
- have no opportunity to turn creative ideas into action
- have to spend too much time in their own company

*Development Suggestions for ENTPs* (this section is presented in full)
Development intrigues ENTPs: they are open to any interesting suggestion that may improve their competence. ENTPs can learn to become even more effective if they try the following:

- assessing and concentrating on priorities, whether this is in the use of their time or the development of ideas; sometimes reining in their ideas by subjecting them to practical scrutiny
- learning to conserve their physical energy; making sure they get enough exercise and rest
- completing one project before springing off onto another
- practising and improving their listening skills; not wanting to have the last word on everything in every encounter
- being more sensitive to their impact on others, being alert to the possibility of being perceived as abrasive
- extending the range of techniques they use for dealing with conflict – accepting that there is often a desirable middle path between capitulation and confrontation
- getting in closer touch with their own feelings; learning to express them; being willing to ask for help
- taking longer to make decisions; consulting others, learning to take a moment in quiet reflection before jumping into action
- realizing that competence at absolutely everything is impossible, learning to relax and concentrate effort on the areas where it is really important to excel and to let the others go.

*If you were working with someone who received such a report how would you support him or her?*

The MBTI reflects preferences; it does not mean that you do not ever use the other half of the bi-polar scale. It does not describe skills, ability or intelligence. All preferences are equally important and valuable and have potential pluses and minuses. Each Type has its potential strengths and its potential blind spots. The Myers-Briggs Type Indicator is recommended as a basis for self-understanding for personal and professional development.

## FIRO-B

The FIRO-B (Fundamental Interpersonal Relations Orientation – Behaviour) examines how you typically interact with other people. Developed by Will Schutz during the 1950s, this questionnaire is based on the theory that the way we interact with others is determined by three interpersonal needs, Inclusion, Control and Affection.

FIRO-B provides you with feedback on how strong your needs are in each of these three areas and helps you to:

- understand your interactions with others;
- recognize where you may need to adapt your style to work more effectively with people;

- identify the value of different contributions within your team.

## The three interpersonal needs

### Inclusion (I)

Inclusion is about making contacts and associating with others. Our need for Inclusion determines how much we involve others and the degree of prominence we seek. There is no neutral ground with respect to Inclusion. You are either 'in' or 'out', 'one of us' or 'one of them'. As a result it can evoke strong reactions. Even if you do not want to be included, to be told you are being excluded feels bad.

*Positive aspects of Inclusion:*
Belonging, membership, togetherness, acceptance, involvement, significance.

*Negative aspects of Inclusion:*
Isolation, being an outsider or outcast, loneliness, detachment, being withdrawn/ignored/insignificant.

### Control (C )

Control is about making decisions and influencing others. Our need for Control determines how comfortable we are with power and the degree of dominance we seek. Many of the struggles within groups centre round Control – who is in charge? Who can make a decision? Who determines the direction we take?

*Positive aspects of Control:*
Influence, responsibility, power, leading, managing, competence.

*Negative aspects of Control:*
Aggression, resistance, rebellion, being submissive, anarchy, incompetence.

### Affection (A)

Affection is about making personal, emotional contact with people. Our need for Affection determines the degree of closeness we seek with others. Affection can occur only between pairs of people at any one time, whereas both Inclusion and Control may occur one-to-one, one-to-few and one-to-many.

*Positive aspects of Affection:*
Liking, warmth, friendship, closeness, feeling positive, love.

*Negative aspects of Affection:*
Being cool, distant, dislike.

## Expressed and wanted behaviours

Our interpersonal needs determine how much Inclusion, Control and Affection behaviour we initiate and how much we like others to initiate. Those behaviours that we push out in the direction of others are *expressed behaviours,* and those behaviours that we would like others to push in our direction *wanted behaviours.*

The FIRO-B questionnaire gives you some indication of your current preferences for expressed and wanted Inclusion, Control and Affection on 0–9 scale where 9 is high.

The combination of scores such as that which follows will have a specific inter-

t a fundamental interpersonal orientation and the
vide an alternative basis for personal and profes-
ssment centres used FIRO-B for the National
leadship initial needs assessments in the original

*model for analysing behaviour in groups? Reflect*
*ctions as demonstrated by your expressed and*
*groups.*

### Case study 2.2

below relate to responses to the questionnaire
attern of scores.

| on | Control | Affection | Total |
|---|---|---|---|
| 3 | 3 | 3 | 10 |
| | 3 | 5 | 12 |

Total e + w = 22

Inclusion
Your inclusion scores suggest that your self-contained, introspective, private and loner
profile belies a greater desire to be involved with others ... You will not always push
your desire for more contact or involvement with people, for you may fear rejection. ...
Control
Your control scores suggest you are self-confident and work well and realistically
within the limits of your ability ... You will like to lead and manage people; you can
be dominant but you are unlikely to be domineering. You will manage and develop
individuals well and you will foster respect in others. ...
Affection
Your affection scores suggest you are cautious about opening yourself to others at a
more personal, intimate and emotional level. ... You will be able to tolerate hostility
and interpersonal difficulty, but you will prefer people to be warmer and closer,
although ... you will prefer others to initiate such closeness and openness.

FIRO-B is used to provide evidence for relationship development and team development. You could more cheaply and easily access FIRO-B than the other two
models explored here.

*Could you use FIRO-B feedback for your professional development?*

## TEAM MANAGEMENT PROFILE

Though the Myers-Briggs Type Indicator and FIRO-B are widely available through occupational psychologists, the Team Management Profile explored below is commercially available from TMS Development International (see References).

The Team Management Profile Questionnaire (TMPQ) measures how people prefer to relate with others, to gather and use information, to make decisions and to organize themselves and others. The responses are fed into a Team Management Systems (TMS) software programme which identifies your highest scoring preferences and leads to a profile of some 4,000 words describing your key work preferences. The Team Management Wheel is also developed from the work of Jung and presents the major roles that need to be covered in any work team. There are eight key team roles: Reporter–Advisers, Creator–Innovators, Explorer–Promoters, Assessor–Developers, Thruster–Organizers, Concluder–Producers, Controller–Inspectors and Upholder–Maintainers. This instrument is widely used commercially and clearly would be more supportive and constructive if used with a team which could involve a whole primary school staff as well as teams within secondary schools including senior management teams. The focus is both on the individual and the team. The way that TMPQ is scored means that preferences can range from 0 to 30 in the raw scores as exemplified below.

### Case study 2.3

|  | | *Relationships* | | |
|---|---|---|---|---|
| E – Extrovert | 28 | | 9 | Introvert – I |
| | | *Information* | | |
| P – Practical | 6 | | 30 | Creative – C |
| | | *Decisions* | | |
| A – Analytical | 14 | | 27 | Beliefs – B |
| | | *Organization* | | |
| S – Structured | 22 | | 19 | Flexible – F |

This results in the major role being the Explorer–Promoter, and the two related roles of Creator–Innovator and Assessor–Developer.

In all there are 208 possible profile combinations. The report presented explores the major role preference and two related roles, which are frequently in adjacent sectors of the wheel. The profiles have been designed for use in industry, commerce and the public service for recruitment, selection, management development, career planning, team development and self-development. It is recommended that you explore this world of personal profiles in your leadership and professional development.

All work teams need to consider the eight key activities essential for high performance and the link with Belbin (1981) who concentrates on roles is clear. The activities are:

1) Advising – gathering and reporting information.
2) Innovating – creating and experimenting with ideas.
3) Promoting – exploring and presenting opportunities.
4) Developing – assessing and testing the applicability of new approaches.
5) Organizing – establishing and implementing ways of making things work.

6) Producing – concluding and delivering outputs.
7) Inspecting – controlling and auditing the working of systems.
8) Maintaining – upholding and safeguarding standards and processes.

When there is a good match between your preferences and the demands of the job, you are more likely to enjoy work, develop skills and perform well. When a team is made up of individuals with complementary work preferences, the team has a higher chance of being effective.

For the Explorer–Promoter with the scores above, extracted comments that appear in a very substantial report of 4,000 words are:

*Work Preferences*
As an Explorer–Promoter you will find it easier than many others to establish good relationships with colleagues. Indeed, it is probable you will value a work environment where people are friendly and considerate, and appreciative of the work you are doing. You do not like sitting in an office for long periods by yourself, thinking about the situation and planning in a detached analytical way ...

*Leadership Strengths*
It is your outgoing approach, combined with your creative insight, which has a major influence on your leadership style. You can sometimes, therefore, be enthusiastic and somewhat impulsive, particularly when you believe strongly in the issues at stake ...

*Decision-making*
You will tend, to a large extent, to judge issues on your creative ideas, personal beliefs and values. This is a powerful combination. While you go out and gather facts and opinions, you will be guided by your inner convictions. Where your beliefs and the requirements of the situation coincide, this is fine, but you may find personal conflicts when your principles tell you to do one thing and the situation demands other behaviour ...

*Interpersonal Skills*
You will usually find it easy to meet others in a variety of work situations. Indeed you will probably seek out various opportunities to meet and discuss ideas and developments. You will usually avoid the situation where you are a 'back room' person working on your own ...

*Team Building*
You can develop an effective work team, because of your ability to communicate easily with a wide variety of people and indicate to them a vision of where the team should be going. You can also draw out the best in people through your recognition of their abilities and your willingness to help on an individual basis. For you, everyone in the team has assets which can be developed, even if they are currently liabilities ...

Areas for Self-Assessment
(a) You often tend to speak as you feel. There may be a need to think things through more carefully before you give your views on a number of issues, particularly those with 'political' implications ...
(b) You may also take on too many projects at once and will sometimes have to reduce these in order to make sure certain things happen on time ...
(c) When it comes to decision-making, you tend to judge things on the basis of your ideals and beliefs. There are occasions when it is equally important to be more detached and work out in detail the costs and benefits ...

(d) You can sometimes be a little impulsive and rush into judgements too quickly ...

The report is much more substantial than this as indicated above. This approach is probably most appropriate for a whole-school approach. What is clear from the areas for self-assessment is that there is a clear focus on both the positive and areas for development.

## The Opportunities–Obstacles Quotient

TMS Development International have more recently developed a new instrument that taps into the fifth dimension of the human psyche which is widely used in clinical psychology to distinguish between normal and abnormal behaviour. This new instrument focuses on that portion of the fifth dimension considered as normal and gives people feedback on whether they are likely to focus on seeing the *opportunities* or *obstacles* at work. Those who focus on seeing opportunities will be positive when new ideas are presented and will look optimistically at most situations. They do not always see potential difficulties and this can cause them to misjudge situations and take unnecessary risks. Those who focus on seeing obstacles put a lot of effort into looking at all the things that might go wrong. When faced with potential opportunities they may well ignore them, presenting cogent arguments to support their view that the risks are too great.

*Do you tend to seek opportunities or see obstacles at work?*

## Case study 2.4

A score of 84.5 per cent for Seeing Opportunities, and 16.7 per cent for Seeing Obstacles results in a quotient of 5.1. A low score for seeing obstacles means that the subject may not always focus sufficient effort on looking for problems in the projects being worked on. The median score is 2.2.

A score >5 shows a tendency towards Pollyanna-ism, 3 to 5, a main focus on opportunities, 1.6 to 3, a balance between opportunities and obstacles, 1 to 1.6, a main focus on obstacles, and <1 a tendency towards Eeyore-ism.

The model suggests that balance is more appropriate across the Opportunities–Obstacles scale, based on the Zen wisdom, 'Nothing is possible without three essential elements: a great root of faith, a great ball of doubt and a fierce tenacity of purpose'. The TMS Development International report contains comment on the Opportunities–Obstacles Quotient and five subscales. Illustrative short extracts are:

> *Moving Towards Goals* ... you will probably expend a considerable amount of energy in trying to achieve the goals that you set for yourself. When problems arise which seem likely to prevent you from attaining your goals, you are likely to push even harder to get where you want to go.
> *Multi-Pathways* ... By putting energy into the generation of alternative pathways, you are likely to be successful in attaining your goals and finding solutions to problems.
> *Optimism* ... You are a person with an optimistic outlook on life ... when things go wrong you are less likely to attribute the cause of any problems solely to yourself.

*Fault Finding* ... At work, you will be considered to be a positive person who always looks for the best in others ... However, your positive approach may need to be balanced with a stronger focus on looking for faults in any proposals or projects.
*Time Focus* ... You enjoy looking to the future because you tend to see it in a positive light. However, you are also aware of the 'here and now', and are very realistic.

*You have explored instruments which explore personality, interpersonal skills and individuals within teams. Will you seek such feedback for your professional development?*

## CONCLUSION

There are many psychometric instruments available. The three discussed here are useful and productive and recommended. These recommendations may be idiosyncratic. What this chapter will hopefully have demonstrated, however, is that, if you are to concentrate on your own personal and professional development, there are instruments which you can use to provide a foundation for your growth. What should be recognized is that they are simply a start.

## REFERENCES

Belbin, R.M. (1981) *Management Teams: Why They Succeed or Fail*, London: Heinemann.
TMS Development International, 128 Holgate Road, York YO2 4FL.

# 3

## Emotional Intelligence

Emotional intelligence is the ability to perceive, integrate, understand and reflectively manage your own and other people's feelings. It is allied with many of the other personal characteristics and skills which this book deals with as a basis for professional development and personal integrity. This chapter explores the characteristics and capabilities of those who think intuitively about emotion at a high level so that you can develop and enhance your emotional intelligence.

For the career management of staff (Chapter 9) the emotionally intelligent school enables:

- the identification of potential, in each individual and the staff as a team, to encourage effective career management;
- understanding the importance of aligning school and individual objectives to maximize the benefits for both parties;
- translating success in career development into resilient loyalty to the school to retain the key players;
- acknowledging and rewarding people's strengths, achievements and successes.

For change management (Chapter 15) the application of emotionally intelligent leadership can:

- adapt to changing circumstances and lead others through the personal discomfort of change;
- offer innovative solutions, identify key issues, simplify problems and find a way through unclear situations;
- have confidence in their own abilities to enable them to encourage the team and keep them motivated and productive;
- remove barriers to change as others are enabled to overcome the fear of risk and failures which can produce defensive and cautious behaviour.

This chapter is developed from a presentation at the Institute of Personnel and Development (IPD) HRD conference (1998) on 'Emotional Intelligence: Its Value and Application in Leadership and Organizations' by Robert K. Cooper, author of *Executive EQ: Emotional Intelligence in Leadership and Organizations* (1997) and *21st Century Leadership* (2000). Cooper argues that emotional intelligence has clear benefits in life and work. It is built on three driving forces for competitive advantage – *building trusting relationships*, that is, values in action, *creating the future*, that is, vision in action, and *increasing energy and effectiveness under pressure*, that is, vitality in action. These combined create capacity, character, initiative and consequently success. Cooper defined emotional intelligence in leadership as the ability to sense, understand and effectively apply the power of and acumen about emotions as a source of energy, drive, information, trust, influence and creativity. It is accessing untapped individual, team and organizational capacity under pressure that leads to improved performance.

Cooper asserts that there is a massive untapped human capacity at work when people's emotions are not involved. Building increased trust, loyalty and commitment comes from bringing out the best in people through respecting them as individuals, valuing them as people, and accountability, that is, in creating a challenging working environment, which acknowledges emotions. Increasing people's energy and effectiveness under pressure at work is about mobilizing the best in people through their increased alertness, stamina and exceptional attentiveness. The productive use of emotional intelligence results in all those in a school being committed emotionally to greatly improved learning for children.

The 'Four Cornerstones of Emotional Intelligence' (Cooper and Sawaf, 1997) are as follows:

1) First cornerstone – *emotional literacy* – being real and true to yourself: builds awareness, inner guidance, respect, responsibility and connection.
2) Second cornerstone – *emotional fitness* – being clear and getting along: builds authenticity, resilience and trusting relationships.
3) Third cornerstone – *emotional depth* – reaching down and stepping up: builds core character and calls forth your potential, integrity and purpose.
4) Fourth cornerstone – *emotional alchemy* – sensing opportunities and competing for the future: builds intuitive innovation, situational transformation, and fluid intelligence.

There is a useful questionnaire at the end of their book to help with a self understanding of your emotional intelligence which can be followed through at http://www.eq.org

*Consider occasions when you have successfully used the four cornerstones of emotional intelligence.*

'The Emotional Side of Leadership' (Ginsberg and Davies, 2001) and 'The Paradox of Emotion and Educational Leadership' (Beatty, 2000) illustrate the growing recognition of the importance of emotions for leadership. Ginsberg and Davies carried out research with leaders from community colleges, school districts and schools/colleges of education in the USA. Their first question asked what kinds of decisions evoked an emotional response. Approaching two-thirds of the responses were related to dismissal for either a poor fit with current job responsibilities, financial reasons, sexual harassment or poor job performance. A quarter of these cases were with personal friends. Others were associated with particular situations: a shooting, being the first non-white female leader in the organization. These all took an emotional toll on the leader. There were five themes in the stories:

- The agony of decision-making – from the high levels of stress and anxiety, the circumstances involved and the impact on the lives of others. The depth and intensity of the emotions were frequently extreme

    I am in the middle of this excruciating process, dismantling pieces of the college, perhaps risking the position to which I aspired for so long. For several weeks I tossed and turned at night, rising to make notes to myself about points I should make. I cannot escape the heaviness of heart that I feel. I exercise each morning to try to take care of myself, but I talk less about my work with my husband, as I am just emotionally spent.

- Finding order out of chaos – despite all the pain, something good came, including a great deal of personal growth and learning. The characteristics of complex systems take on almost human qualities in their non-linear and non-predictable reaction to inputs and this can lead to incredible learning.

    At each level, I learned and I grew and I benefited. One of the things that I say to people all the time – as a leader, don't be afraid to learn. Because you constantly will be faced with obstacles or situations you have not faced before. You are going to be facing people who don't believe in you, don't trust you, or for whatever reason are trying to tear you down.

- Communication is the key – being as open as possible in communication is important for organizational health and individual success in dealing with the specific. This may be self-protective since their own position could be compromised by what is unfolding. Open communication can contain the potential damage to the organization and the leader to some extent.

    How to handle the media becomes critical in traumatic situations – because you can be sure the media will be there. You must be fast, and you must be the initiator or it puts you in a vulnerable situation ... There are services available in any kind of crisis situation, any kind of jeopardy, for any kind of problem.

- Follow your heart – in about half the stories leaders felt good about their decisions, because they had a clear belief that they had acted to benefit the institution.

    As I was wont to do in those days I took a long weekend alone and went to the ocean. I wanted to reconnect with my soul. It didn't take long to realize how incredibly saddened I was by what we were doing and what was going to have to take place. I felt angry and resentful that previous leaders had dropped the ball and had let the faculty down. They didn't have the courage it took to make tough decisions along the way.

- Showing the right face – occasionally there was a need to wear a leadership mask to serve the organization and to maintain and convey their stature as leader.

    There is no question that I felt great grief during this situation ... one must steel oneself, because you must act on behalf of others, making sure of their well-being and safety. You cannot do this if you abdicate your leadership by indulging your emotions. If and when you decide to do this you must do it someplace else, later on.

Emotional decision-making is hard work for leaders who are dedicated to their positions and are feeling and caring individuals, partly because they are rarely prepared for the emotionally intense experiences. Many had a sense of being alone in this journey throughout the emotional experience and frequently cut themselves off in an unhealthy and counter-productive way.

For Beatty (2000) the paradox of emotion and educational leadership is that emotional awareness can often lead to emotional control. The evidence came from an asynchronous online conversation involving school leaders in six different countries. In these conversations professionalism appeared to be about emotional control and professional detachment, and for the leader's own psychological protection. However, this avoidance of the expression of emotions, Beatty argued, was potentially dangerous and health-threatening. She was advocating the accessing of new energy sources through greater emotional authenticity. The emotional realities of life in schools demand authentic emotions, not settling for contrived collegiality. This authenticity assists in quelling the existential anxieties with which we all contend. Emotional labour involves knowing about and assessing as well as managing emotions, other people's as well as one's own. If leaders seek out and find the necessary support and develop critical relationships, this avoids the traditional conception of leadership as emotionally laborious with leaders often left holding the emotional baggage of others with no time or encouragement to consider their own. Beatty argues for:

- *the necessity of convergence ... and congruence* – particularly important in issues associated with teachers' careers. A culture full of silence and emotional subversion pervades too many school cultures, whose members, in the name of being professional and at the expense of deeper human understanding and authentic relationship, unquestioningly accept the need for 'control' and the pursuant demands of complex organizational processes;
- *commitment ... to connectedness* – educational leaders need to be emotionally accountable. Teachers need more connectedness and a commitment to professional relationships, more support and more courage to change the pattern of communication and the traditions that deaden expectations, allowing themselves to be authentic and human. It is time for breaking the silence.

*What situations have created the emotions explored above for you? How did you respond?*

In a submission to the QCA Review of the National Curriculum, *Learning by Heart: The Role of Emotional Education in Raising School Achievement*, McCarthy (1998) argued that young people have to cope with the rapid pace of change in society, the vast spread of information technology. In order to make meaning of their lives they need to think clearly, to cope with insecurity and to respond with creativity and resourcefulness to challenges that arise at every stage in their lives. They need to have and to develop their emotional intelligence, through an education that will enable them to have:

- a strong sense of self and an empathetic awareness of others;
- an awareness of the role and power of emotions in decision-making;

- a sound basis for their values and morality;
- a tolerance of diversity and difference;
- a sense of meaning and purpose in their lives.

Emotional learning matters for teachers as it does for the pupils discussed in this pamphlet and for precisely the same reasons.

- Understanding emotions is directly connected with motivation and with cognitive achievement.
- Dealing with emotions helps develop better relationships and a sense of psychological and mental well-being.
- Emotionally developed young people are better equipped to live with difference.
- Educating the emotions leads to a more effective workforce.
- Our moral outlook and value systems are deeply shaped by our attitudes and dealings.
- Our sense of meaning and purpose is derived as much from feeling as from understanding.

In a learning organization, the learning of teachers, their professional development, and the learning of children, their education, are inevitably complementary and mutually reinforcing. The place of emotional intelligence in this has recently been recognized in an excellent book, *The Intelligent School* (MacGilchrist, Myers and Reed, 1997), in which emotional intelligence is one of nine intelligences which are present in the intelligent school. Emotional intelligence is interpreted as the capacity of the culture within the school to allow feelings to be 'owned, expressed and respected'. The nine intelligences of the intelligent school are contextual intelligence, strategic intelligence, academic intelligence, reflective intelligence, pedagogical intelligence, collegial intelligence, emotional intelligence, spiritual intelligence and ethical intelligence. The authors are clearly committed to enhancing children's learning as a result of the application of corporate intelligence, the combination of the nine intelligences, by the school leadership.

In Gardner, Kornhaber and Wake (1995), there is an exploration of the origins of the application of scientific psychology to intelligence and the psychometric, developmental (Piaget), biological and cognitive perspectives on intelligence. Gardner was one of the first to recognize what is now called emotional intelligence. This changed focus provided a basis for considering, from the perspective of the school, its understanding and interpretation of the significance of newer forms of intelligence for learning. The final chapter of the book, focusing on the perspective of the workplace, considers intelligence in relation to the development of work-related skills, apprenticeship and the novice–expert continuum. The analysis of the advances in understanding which characterize the problem-solving expertise of the expert, and the ways in which they acquire this expertise focuses on a distinctive and wider interpretation of intelligence. This intelligence is that of the expert teacher professional and her/his capacity for further enhanced skill development.

Gardner's own theory of multiple intelligences questions the excessive emphasis on abstract reasoning. He asserted, by the early 1980s, that there were several relatively autonomous intelligences – linguistic intelligence, musical intelligence, logical–mathematical intelligence, spatial intelligence, bodily-kinaesthetic intelligence, intrapersonal intelligence and interpersonal intelligence. These intelligences are ways of describing capabilities which allow access to distinctive forms of thinking. He argued that there was an excessive emphasis on some of these at the expense of others.

Intrapersonal intelligence is how people distinguish their own feelings. It involves understanding the inner world of emotions and thoughts, and developing the ability to control and consciously work with them. At its highest level this capacity leads to a deep self-knowledge which allows the person to build an understanding of her/himself and to use distinctive abilities to operate effectively in life. Interpersonal intelligence applies similar skills to understanding the feelings, beliefs and behaviours of others. It involves understanding how to communicate and how to work collaboratively.

Barnes (1995) complements some of the more visionary approaches to emotional intelligence in a more developmental approach. The evidence is used more analytically to explore emotions in infancy; emotions, family relationships and social understanding; understanding emotion and a theory of mind; controlling emotions; and emotion and gender. Another chapter deals with the development of a sense of self from its early emergence, self-esteem, gender identity and reflecting on the self, focusing on self-descriptions and self-esteem. Gender identity is recognized as particularly important in secondary schools because adolescence accesses the development of emotional intelligence. Gender differences in emotional intelligence are important with the feminization of the teaching profession, and the stereotypical assumption that women will have greater emotional intelligence.

Basic human emotional needs and feelings are not always recognized and accepted. The invalidation of the individual feelings of teachers or pupils destroys the self-esteem which is a prerequisite for successful teaching and learning. Validation, one of the keys to emotional intelligence, allows a person to be her/himself. This is the key to high self-esteem. Psychological invalidation kills confidence, creativity and individuality. Within schools, bullying and sexual harassment can be tackled more effectively in a climate where all can express their feelings openly. Invalidation in this context in particular needs to be understood and taken seriously. Research by the NASUWT on the bullying of teachers, and the mistreatment of staff by other members of staff, shows it at an unacceptable level. Some schools have an excessively unhealthy environments.

The curriculum could involve staff (and children) developing skills in:

- *emotional self-awareness* – being able to recognize feelings as they happen and put a name to them; being aware of the relationship between thoughts, feelings and actions; considering why feelings have emerged in a particular instance; understanding the feelings that lie behind particular actions. This is the keystone to emotional intelligence.
- *managing emotions* – realizing what lies behind feelings; clarifying personal beliefs and their effect on the ability to act; recognizing the importance of hope; developing better frustration tolerance and the capacity to deal with

anger, fear, anxiety and sadness; learning how to comfort oneself; understanding how to control emotions when this is appropriate; being able to handle feelings and channel emotions; developing less aggressive or self-destructive behaviour; achieving more positive feelings about the self.

- *empathy* – being able to understand the feelings of others and act appropriately; learning to listen to others without being overwhelmed by personal emotions; distinguishing between what others do or say and personal reactions and judgements; having the skill of attuning to the signals which indicate what others want or need.

- *communicating* – achieving the capacity to communicate one's own feelings and to interpret the feelings of others; understanding the effects of the communication of enthusiasm and optimism and negativity and pessimism; being able to communicate personal feelings without anger or passivity.

- *co-operation* – knowing when to lead and when to follow; understanding leadership as the art of helping people work together and the feelings associated with this; recognizing the value of others and encouraging participation; making commitments and taking responsibility for decisions and acts, and understanding the feelings this creates.

- *resolving conflicts* – recognizing the underlying feelings behind the conflict; using the skills above to resolve conflicts; recognizing the self-perpetuating emotions which can be a major cause of conflict; managing of the emotions of others.

*Does the model above describe a curriculum for developing emotional intelligence for you?*

## DANIEL GOLEMAN

Goleman (1996) provides examples that demonstrate emotional intelligence in practice. The 4-year-old who achieves a perfect social map of her class, with no apparent effort, showing astonishing social perceptiveness; the problem of the brilliant, successful surgeon who has no capacity to articulate his feelings – alexithymia – and its profound impact on a partner; the terrifying incompetence of the angry parent, literally a slave of her passion, destroying her relationship with her own child, and her child's emotional intelligence. This is complemented by the emotional brilliance of the man who has the capacity to calm a drunk terrorizing passengers in a suburban train. If we are to sustain adult relationships then we need to have skills to avoid our partners, and others, becoming what Goleman calls intimate enemies. All these emotional encounters, or variants of them, exist in and around schools, in staffrooms as well as classrooms. Medical research shows how helping people better manage their destructive feelings – anger, anxiety, depression, pessimism and loneliness – is a form of disease prevention. Many patients benefit measurably when their psychological needs are attended to along with their purely medical ones. Emotional intelligence, which helps the survival of those with cancer, can help create healthy environments in schools also.

The meanness, ferocity and callousness of abused toddlers shown by Goleman demonstrate how the brain can be shaped by brutality. Temperament and experience is not, however, destiny. A survivor of five horrific years in a prison camp remakes herself and in old age is ebullient despite her stroke. All the concerns in schools of teachers and children, and the wider concerns of society, may be addressed by concentrating on developing emotional intelligence.

*Reflect on any occasions when you have observed astonishingly high levels of emotional intelligence and shockingly low levels of emotional intelligence.*

## HENLEY MANAGEMENT COLLEGE QUESTIONNAIRE

The Henley Management College has devised an emotional intelligence questionnaire which measures seven dimensions and is administered by ASE, a leading provider of assessment and training services (Dulewicz and Higgs, 1999). This presents scores in the dimensions outlined below:

- awareness of one's feelings and ability to control them. Belief in one's ability to manage emotions and control one's impact in the work environment;
- sensitivity to others' needs and perceptions when making decisions;
- influence: the ability to persuade others to change a viewpoint when necessary;
- motivation: drive and energy to achieve results, to make an impact and balance short- and long-term goals;
- decisiveness: the ability to arrive at clear decisions and implement them when presented with incomplete or ambiguous information, using both logic and emotion;
- conscientiousness and integrity: the ability to display clear commitment to an action in the face of challenge, and match words and deeds;
- emotional resilience: the ability to perform consistently in a range of situations under pressure and to adapt behaviour appropriately. Ability to stay focused in the face of personal criticism.

Henley provides training programmes for leaders to use the analysis. Self-awareness, sensitivity and influence, the *enablers*, can be more easily developed. The *drivers* (motivation and decisiveness) and the *constrainers* (conscientiousness and integrity and emotional resilience) are more enduring elements of an individual's personality. For these it is more a case of exploiting strengths in the characteristic and developing coping strategies where it is less strong. Those with low emotional resilience should try to avoid highly stressful situations. Those with low integrity should avoid temptation or delegate ethical issues to others higher on that scale.

*Evaluate yourself in these seven dimensions using evidence to demonstrate your emotional intelligence.*

## PERSONAL AND SOCIAL COMPETENCE

There are characteristics which show the competencies of the 'stars' (Goleman, 1998). Personal competencies determine how we manage ourselves, and social competencies how we handle relationships. Goleman has taken forward his emotional intelligence framework into practice to provide the structure for his most recent book (ibid., pp. 26–7):

Personal Competence

- Self Awareness (knowing one's internal states, preferences, resources and intuitions)
  Emotional awareness, accurate self-assessment, self-confidence
- Self Regulation (managing one's internal states, impulses, and resources)
  Self-control, trustworthiness, conscientiousness, adaptability, innovation
- Motivation (emotional tendencies that guide or facilitate reaching goals)
  Achievement drive, commitment, initiative, optimism

Social Competence

- Empathy (awareness of others' feelings, needs and concerns)
  Understanding others, developing others, service orientation, leveraging diversity, political awareness
- Social Skills (adeptness at inducing desirable responses in others)
  Influence, communication, conflict management, leadership, change catalyst, building bonds, collaboration and co-operation, team capabilities.

This map of emotional intelligence is defined and the competencies fully exemplified. *Self-control*, one element of one of six competencies, self-regulation, is about keeping disruptive emotions and impulses in check. People with this competence manage their impulsive feelings and distressing emotions well; stay composed, positive and unflappable even in trying moments; think clearly and stay focused under pressure. The ultimate act of personal responsibility at work may be in taking control of your own state of mind. The examples of self-control in action in Goleman (1998) can all be matched in schools. Those with self-control and reasonably high-level competencies in the 25 elements in the model above will enhance their performance. All of these can be recognized, measured, practised and enhanced.

*Explore your own strengths in some of the elements within this competence framework.*

## EMOTIONAL CAPITAL

The culture and relationships in school, the combination of emotions, feelings, beliefs and values make up what might be described as the emotional capital of the school. There is a need to attract and retain the best people, to provide higher standards of service for increasingly sophisticated and demanding customers, both pupils and parents, with greater levels of change and innovation, new management and career structures and more complex decision-making. Pride, commitment, excitement, trust and determination are elements of the emotional context in which leaders work and the capabilities of the staff in a school, including their emotional intelligence, are the only sustainable competitive advantage the school has.

The emotional capital of companies affects their profitability. An organization will enhance its emotional capital by effectively combining the emotional intelligences of the individuals in the organization. Each positive feeling provides potentially valuable information that ignites creativity, sustains honesty with the self, provides a compass for life and career, guides an individual to unthought of possibilities and may be crucial in providing solutions to the most complex problems. Highly effective organizations will release and build this emotional intelligence of its members. Intellectual capital is the alignment of knowledge and understanding to the organization's goals. Emotional capital is about engagement, and the commitment to apply knowledge and abilities to support the organization's goals.

Even strategic planning, Goleman (1998) suggests, is not a purely cognitive task. The outstanding strategic planners are not necessarily superior in analytic skills. It is their emotional competence that raises them above the average. They have an astute political awareness, the ability to make arguments with emotional impact and high levels of interpersonal influence. The effectiveness of strategic planners depends on knowing how to involve key decision-makers in the planning process throughout, making sure that these people are committed to the plan's assumptions and goals, and are therefore willing to adopt it. These champions require intellectual and emotional intelligence.

## SPIRITUAL INTELLIGENCE

Emotional intelligence is increasingly recognized and understood. Spiritual intelligence is based on the affirmation that your most important characteristic is the underlying passion or commitment which is derived from the profound values which are you, and which may or may not be evidenced within traditional religious beliefs (Zohar, 2000). Zohar argues that spiritual intelligence is about the fundamental 'why?' questions and that it provides a context within which the other intelligences operate. It is more important today in an uncertain world, when we are, in chaos theory terms 'on the edge', at the border between order and uncertainty. Spiritual intelligence, our deep intuitive sense of meaning, provides the deep sense of security, which allows the flexibility, imagination and inspiration that leaders need. It also gives the courage and security to ask and explore the difficult questions because it involves a more holistic approach. Zohar argues that if our spiritual intelligence is engaged we face the discomfort of challenging ourselves and changing our way of being.

*How important is emotional and spiritual intelligence for your personal growth and professional development?*

## REFERENCES

Barnes, P. (ed.) (1995) *Personal, Social and Emotional Development of Children*, Oxford: Blackwell.

Beatty, B. (2000) 'The paradox of emotion and educational leadership', paper presented at BELMAS Annual Conference.

Cooper, R.K. (1997) *Executive EQ: Emotional Intelligence in Leadership and Organization*, New York, NY: Grosset/Putnam.

Cooper, R.K. (2000) *21st Century Leadership*, New York: Advanced Excellence Systems.

Cooper, R.K. and Sawaf, A. (1997) *The Four Cornerstones of Emotional Intelligence*, New York, NY: Grosset/Putnam.

Dulewicz, V. and Higgs, M. (1999) *Making Sense of Emotional Intelligence*, London:

NFER-Nelson.

Gardner, H., Kornhaber, M.L. and Wake, W.K. (1995) Intelligence: Multiple Perspectives, Fort Worth, TX: Harcourt Brace.

Ginsberg, R. and Davies, T. (2001) 'The Emotional Side of Leadership', paper presented at AERA.

Goleman, D. (1996) Emotional Intelligence, London: Bloomsbury.

Goleman, D. (1998) Working with Emotional Intelligence, London: Bloomsbury.

MacGilchrist, B., Myers, K. and Reed, J. (1997) The Intelligent School, London: Paul Chapman Publishing.

McCarthy (1998) Learning by Heart: The Role of Emotional Education in Raising School Achievement, Brighton: Re:membering Education.

Zohar, D. (2000) SQ – The Ultimate Intelligence, London: Bloomsbury.

# 4

## 360-degree Feedback

360-degree feedback is now being practised in the education service and used imaginatively for professional development. Creissen (1999) presents his analysis of the value of the feedback and associated developmental processes in the Leadership Programme for Serving Headteachers (LPSH) that he has undertaken. The LPSH requires participants to complete a series of diagnostic questionnaires and to ask five others – ideally a governor, a senior colleague, a middle manager, a main scale teacher and a member of the support staff – to complete similar questionnaires. The relationship of the chair of governors to the headteacher is not easy to define in hierarchical terms but evidence elsewhere (Alimo-Metcalfe, 1998) suggests it is the upwards feedback that is particularly productive. What is interesting and perhaps significant in this context is that now there is a renewed formal appraisal system in schools, within the new performance management framework, that the line manager model, with the team leader, has been strengthened. The 360-degree feedback to headteachers on the LPSH is found particularly helpful because the methodology provides a more soundly based, challenging and therefore even more valuable feedback to raise awareness of areas for development and to assist in the analysis of performance. This helps define more accurately areas for professional growth and school improvement. Headteachers are willing and able to use 360-degree feedback as a means of gaining understanding of their professional characteristics, their leadership styles and the context for school improvement (the climate) in their schools. There is considerable trust in this process already embedded in the education service which is likely to be developed in the future as a process of 360-degree appraisal for teachers within schools.

*In principle would you prefer 360-degree feedback, the performance management process or both?*

### 360-DEGREE FEEDBACK AND TEAMS

360-degree feedback, a concept that is broader than 360-degree appraisal, provides a comprehensive indication of how successful an individual is in the totality of her or his relationships at work. It focuses on the skills and competencies which those working within organizations believe will improve organizational performance, rather than those that have been cascaded down, through and across the organization. This builds on the argument that subordinates, or those led and managed, and peers have more to contribute to an analysis of the performance of an individual than has been previously recognized. Some skills, such as leadership, are almost certainly best judged by subordinates and peers rather than by managers. These co-workers understand the quality of the performance in depth better than the manager does. They know the people who really make a positive contribution and perform, and they understand the living reality of the attitudes and beliefs and underpinning values of those to whom they are feeding back information (Bahra, 1996). In so far as schools are genuinely working through teams, where everyone's contribution is valued, peer feedback will also be particularly appropriate. Teamworking may be more common in principle than in practice in schools. The redefinition of team leader in the performance management framework will not necessarily lead to stronger teamwork. The team may exist in name only. In 'real' teams people genuinely contribute according to their skills and expertise rather than their status and the team works consistently together. The National College for School Leadership (NCSL) was planning to make a DVD available for newly appointed heads (2002) for those who wish to create a genuinely team-based school.

## 360-DEGREE FEEDBACK, PERFORMANCE AND PERSONAL DEVELOPMENT

360-degree feedback comes from the systematic collection and feedback of performance data on an individual, or possibly a group, derived from a number of stakeholders on their performance. This combined judgement gives a more accurate, objective and well-rounded view of the performance. It measures in detail behaviours and competencies and can be used for self-development and individual counselling, as well as for organized training and development. Arguably teachers, just as much as headteachers, need to be given the opportunity to learn from this process. Comments are difficult to ignore when they are expressed by a number of colleagues. The quality of evidence is such that it can be used for team-building for the team as a group of individuals or as a genuinely whole team. It is increasingly used in business as a form of appraisal for performance management, strategic or organizational development and for total quality management. We therefore need to consider whether and how this could be developed in the education service to support individuals planning their own personal development and to enhance performance. There will be associated professional and ethical issues. 360-degree feedback is used elsewhere, and more controversially, for remuneration but usually only after it has become firmly embedded in the organizational culture. This would not be appropriate in the education service, though those with evidence of highly skilled performance may well choose to present it in promotion applications. Headteachers are presenting LPSH data to their governing bodies to demonstrate their leadership effectiveness. The 360-degree feedback is normally presented by a skilled specialist and has a particularly powerful impact because of the anonymity and integrity built into the process. Almost always it shows that those receiving feedback have a mixture of strengths and areas for development.

*Would it be possible to implement a 360-degree feedback process in your school now?*

## PERFORMANCE MEASUREMENT

360-degree feedback has developed strongly recently because of changes in the expectations of employees in business, the increasing emphasis on performance measurement, changing management approaches and more receptive attitudes from staff. Performance measurement in schools may be perceived to be narrowly focused on pupil performance in tests and examinations but it is possible to develop more extensive measures. 360-degree feedback originally concentrated on individuals at more senior levels but it is being extended down organizations as its power for genuinely evaluating individual performance and supporting development becomes recognized and accepted. It would be hoped that this could be achieved in the education service because 360-degree feedback provides information of much greater value and depth than managerial appraisal. The new performance management system does allow and encourage the collection of additional evidence but this does not have the rigour of 360-degree feedback. The supporting evidence for the feedback in business comes from managers, staff, team members, peers, internal customers and external customers, and is more beneficial the broader the range of participants. There are equivalents to all these groups in schools. The *intentions* in behaviours of the individual being evaluated are much less significant than the *perceptions* about those behaviours of those who work with them. These perceptions are the reality. If there is no formal system of 360-degree appraisal and feedback in your school, and, if you are taking your career development seriously, you may wish to seek the views of those you work with and those you teach, as well as your team leader, to seek for a broader interpretation of your strengths and development needs. You may wish to develop a formal system within your school. There are many high-quality diagnostic instruments available.

## FEEDBACK AS A PRIVILEGE

The quality and quantity of data are significant. The LPSH uses only five respondents for cost reasons and because this is the minimum number for reliability and which is sufficient to provide high-quality information. The wider development of 360-degree feedback is an exercise in open management and, though the data is confidential, those who have the courage to share the results appear to benefit more from the opportunities presented. The process ensures that individuals can know exactly how they are perceived. This openness can result in clearer target-setting for development and growth. Receiving accurate and honest feedback is increasingly recognized as a privilege. Feedback normally has a morale-boosting effect for the individual. The feedback on current strengths is directly motivating. Those who succeed in achieving progress in their areas for development following the feedback have an even greater improvement in morale. The process can also be helpful in clarifying the roles of those receiving feedback. In particular it provides information for focusing the individual's contribution to strategic development at the organizational level. The performance management model being developed in schools recognizes the rationale presented here.

For teachers there would inevitably be the issue of how to use feedback from pupils, and possibly parents, as our most important internal and external customers. Morgan and Morris (1999) state that their research project, based on earlier evidence from rigorous experimental methods, shows that pupils are clearly competent to perceive teachers' behaviours accurately. This project, based in Welsh secondary schools, explored classroom pedagogy as interpreted by pupils and teachers. Pupils focused on the centrality of the teachers' methods of presentation, the range of learning experiences, the quality of feedback, classroom control and order, and interpersonal relationships. They were capable of making sophisticated judgements about the quality of teaching. If teachers are to have effective 360-degree feedback it would seem essential to incorporate pupils and parents in a way that teachers are willing to accept. This may require a confidence and trust in their pupils that teachers may not initially find easy to accept unless there are appropriate confidentiality arrangements.

*How do you know how pupils and parents evaluate your performance? Would you want to make this more rigorous?*

There is increased emphasis in 360-degree feedback on the measurement of particularly important aspects of personality such as attitudes, which cannot easily be accessed through line manager appraisal. If we are to find more complex measures of school performance to complement the academic results, even with the additional sophistication of added-value scores, that take account of a wide range of variables, measures of changed attitudes to learning could be partiularly significant. Communication in the classroom has to be two-way. The pupils in the study above saw the quality and individualizing of feedback as a characteristic of highly effective teachers. The LPSH analysis suggests this is also a skill of highly effective headteachers. Teachers may benefit equally from a similar process where they gain better information about the quality of their feedback from a broader constituency than they are likely to receive from a team leader observing perhaps only one lesson a year, or an Office for Standards in Education (OFSTED) inspector even if there are a number of visits in the week. The pupil knows about the continuing quality of feedback, and many other teaching skills, much better than those who make occasional visits. The concept of continuous improvement in performance applies to individuals as well as schools and this can be measured through improvements in 360-degree feedback data. The LPSH measures encourage headteachers to set targets for personal and school improvement in the softer areas and provide means for them to evaluate their success in achieving them The personal development needs of individuals need to be defined more precisely, and heads are finding that the LPSH process supports this. That does not take away individual responsibility however. Arguably it enhances it. Similarly teachers will need to respond constructively to feedback and themselves determine the implications of any evidence and to sustain the commitment to learning over many years. The responsibility for personal and professional development and performance has to remain with the individual teacher.

*Evaluate your own success in providing feedback in different contexts. How could this performance level be imporved?*

Over time it should prove possible to trust the pupils who would feel valued by being taken seriously if teachers responded to their feedback. 360-degree feedback fits in with other developments in schools such as team management, teacher empowerment and total quality management. The flatter organizational structures, which have emerged in business, and may well emerge within schools, would also be aligned with 360-degree feedback. The feedback process may sound intimidating but, when presented sympathetically and with skill, it has been shown to be effective in changing behaviour and improving performance. The individual who has the courage and professionalism to own the feedback can use it for her/his own purposes. The cultural change in schools, including the 'learning organization' concept, has led to a greater willingness of individuals to take responsibility for their own development and careers. There is a complementary recognition of the need to achieve greater balance between upward and downward flows of information, and the increased interdependency as a consequence of the co-ordination of performance evaluation. To take 360-degree feedback forward in education, the national standards at different levels which partially focus on competencies, might be broken down into detailed behaviours for evaluation.

## THE TECHNICAL PROCESS OF 360-DEGREE FEEDBACK

The technical processes are always questionnaire-based and can be on paper, disc or even, if anonymity could be guaranteed, on a network. It would be possible for a network model to be developed at relatively little cost, which could then fairly quickly provide a database against which teachers could evaluate their feedback. Questionnaire design for 360-degree feedback is a new and sophisticated process but it would be possible to design instruments which could be widely used in teaching, particularly if the initial focus was on classroom teaching. It will be important to agree what high-quality teaching is and not necessarily to accept those models most easily accessible. The information gathered could be of enormous value in understanding what is happening in the classrooms of the country. Open-ended questions can be used when this provides additional information of value. The questionnaires are normally sent out by the participant and collected externally or at a central internal point. Rating scales can be used to show perceptions of how effective particular behaviours are in relation to the behaviours of others and other behaviours. Concerns about confidentiality will need to be overcome.

The process normally requires that the individual feedback report is discussed with a trained facilitator. In schools, initially, this may need to be someone from outside the school. Where there are suitable relationships with the LEA this might be possible if the facilitator is not involved in current accountabilities. What will be important, if such an instrument can be developed for the benefit of the individual teacher, is how it will be aligned with other forms of professional and personal guidance and support. Even with the new performance management team-leader role, there is some anxiety from others who have responsibility for performance, not necessarily having access to the objectives. A 360-degree feedback model might increase this anxiety further if school leaders seek to exercise a more managerialist control. The new culture, with empowerment of teachers for their own development, will not be implemented easily.

*Above you considered whether this process would be culturally acceptable in your school now. If this is not the case, what could be done to make it so? Is it worth the effort?*

## PAY AND TRUST

Future applications of 360-degree feedback in the wider world are likely to focus on remuneration, strategic organizational analysis and as an aid to creating open cultures. Teachers at present may see these as contradictory. Since there is performance-related pay, it would seem important to ensure that the best possible information about performance is used to make judgements. There is some uncertainty about the validity of threshold and post-threshold processes. The use of 360-degree appraisal for pay would come at a much later stage of implementation when staff have become used to using the information for development, and certainly not within three years. There is, in addition, the problem that incorporating feedback into processes which have implications for pay may affect the trust which is at the heart of 360-degree feedback.

People may fear adverse consequences if they give negative feedback, or if the feedback may be misinterpreted by a manager. In any case people may be less ready to accept feedback if it has potentially damaging consequences. There is evidence that, when ratings become evaluative rather than developmental, up to a third of those giving ratings change their assessments. This means that the instrument is ceasing to measure the competencies it is supposed to. Line manager appraisal in the more traditional way is being used in business for any decisions about remuneration until the process is more culturally acceptable. The headteacher evaluation of threshold applications and upper pay spine decisions is the current equivalent. Even in business the appraisal link to pay is more successful if there is a significant time and situational gap between the feedback on performance for development and complementary decisions on pay.

## THE FUTURE IN SCHOOLS

A strategic analysis of future skill requirements within the school may show that there is an inadequate link between what teachers are good at now, and important parts of the job as it will evolve. 360-degree feedback may also show that a teacher's strengths are not being used fully in the current post. Planned training and development should be of value for the individual and the organization. Gaps in current skills and the skill requirements for possible future roles can be addressed. These issues can be addressed by feeding the whole-school evidence from 360-degree appraisal into the strategic planning process. Evidence from business shows that managers are frequently more competent in the task-centred rather than the person-centred areas of the job as has been measured in the 360-degree feedback (Ward, 1997). This has implications which are being addressed elsewhere in this book. We do not know whether this is the case in the education service but it may well be.

However difficult the feedback process, there is an argument that obtaining a fully rounded picture of yourself is a crucial first step towards building on your strengths and remedying weaknesses when that is appropriate. If 360-degree feedback is to be developed for teachers it will be important to decide which stakeholders will be asked for feedback. This may involve extending the range of stakeholders as confidence in the process grows. It will be important that any new project is planned, piloted and validated. Any questionnaires or diagnostic instruments will need to be designed or customised. The process of transferring the response data into effective reports and the presentation of the results to facilitate change will need to be carefully planned because of professional sensitivities. This provides a very strong reason for beginning the process of addressing the issues now. You will need to make your own decisions. What will be crucial will be maintaining momentum and confidentiality. This new approach to personal and professional development and performance, using 360-degree feedback, will be made acceptable in many schools.

## THE PROBLEM WITH THE TEAM LEADER MODEL

Alimo-Metcalfe (1998) explores the relationship between leadership and stress showing how, for 60–75 per cent of employees in all organizations, they find the most stressful aspect of their job is their immediate boss. Hence the problem with traditional line manager appraisal. The responses to inept leadership include insubordination, high turnover, sabotage and low morale. It would be helpful to know the significance of this among the many reasons for the apparently large numbers of teachers who leave teaching early in their careers. Information from 360-degree feedback in schools would reveal if this were also the case in schools. Transformational leaders realign the organization's culture with a new vision, and a revision of its shared assumptions, values and morale. Alimo-Metcalfe considers research which shows that subordinate ratings are in the upper echelons of predictors of managerial performance, and how subordinates are more satisfied when their perceptions match the managers' self-perceptions. Her evidence shows that managers who originally scored low improve and their self-ratings decrease whilst other ratings increase. There is a virtuous circle. Improvement occurs only in dimensions which are owned by the manager. However, these improvements were sustained over two years. Commitment to the organization and the performance of subordinates improved following feedback and the subsequent leadership development of their managers. Women managers were rated higher on the leadership factors that have been shown to predict individual, group and organizational performance. They were rated higher on both transformational and transactional factors. This may mean that 360-degree feedback might contribute to addressing gender issues in education.

## THE ROLES IN THE PROCESS

There are four roles in the 360-degree model which it is suggested should be addressed strategically, at a national level, rather than in schools, though some local education authority (LEAs) may be able to establish models which could be piloted (Farrell, 1999):

1) *The process manager* is the expert adviser on the use of 360-degree feedback. This is the policy adviser who project manages the scheme, and builds support for it. This role would also involve training the facilitators, and conducting the whole database analysis to generate strategic-level information. It will also involve ensuring that resources are accessible for developmental follow-up. The process manager will need to ensure that the process is aligned with the other professional development and performance management initiatives. Schools will need to consider commercial providers, value for money and trust in the process.

2) *The facilitator* will need the ability to interpret data in feedback reports, to communicate definitions of what is being measured and to build the recipient's awareness and understanding. She/he will need the skill of communicating feedback in a structured, time efficient and articulate fashion. More complex is the ability to assess the motives and temperament of the feedback recipient, and the complementary skill to adjust and individualize the feedback approach. The facilitator will need to pay as much attention to areas of strength as to areas of development need in the recipient. It will be important to understand how people respond to the need for change and to be able to address issues of denial. After the feedback it will be important to leave the recipient feeling positive and motivated. Many of these skills will be those of skilful facilitators in other contexts.

3) *The rater* carries the responsibility for generating accurate, valid and reliable observations. Raters may need to seek opportunities to observe the recipient's behaviour in job-relevant situations and to rate in an open and honest way, providing feedback the recipient can trust. They need to exercise discretion by respecting confidentiality and avoiding discussion of the ratings given. The number of raters within the school may need to be limited until trust in the process is developed. Those providing feedback need to have the courage and integrity to make honest rating evaluations.

4) *The recipient* needs to approach involvement in 360-degree feedback with an open mind and a willingness to respond to feedback. Recipients need to select raters who can provide useful insights into performance and whose views will be respected. After the event they need to seek ways of capitalizing on their strengths and addressing their own development needs. It is also important to provide the facilitator with feedback on the perceived quality of the process.

## THE FEEDBACK PROJECT

The Feedback Project (Farrell, 1999) builds on these definitions of those involved in the process to explore the current expansion of 360-degree feedback and the emerging new characteristics of the process. Though organizational culture has been identified as one of the significant factors that determines the effectiveness of implementing 360-degree feedback, there has been no detailed research on this that they are aware of. The findings from the those who have been using the process for more than four years were that:

- 360-degree feedback is mainly used as part of the development process. It also provides a framework for the assessment and development of poor performers. It is most effective where the senior management demonstrates a commitment to creating an environment that encourages individuals to take risks;
- 360-degree feedback is used in practice to inform strategic planning, to identify organization-wide strengths and weaknesses, and to inform resourcing as well as training development strategies;
- the organization must ensure that feedback givers remain anonymous and that feedback reports are totally confidential, if people are to trust the process;
- some organizations were developing internal less structured forms of 360-degree feedback. Those with flatter structures and more devolved forms of responsibility felt this provided a higher level of flexibility where there was individual and organizational maturity;
- effective communication about how the 360-degree feedback fits in with performance management systems is essential. People will only buy in if they can see a direct and overt link between 360-degree feedback and their individual objectives and the overall performance objectives of the organization;
- there can be considerable conflict between short-term business priorities and the time needed for effective feedback;
- visible and tangible involvement of senior management was critical initially to ensure sufficient resources to design and implement 360-degree feedback effectively. Senior management should also publicly demonstrate a commitment and act as role models in showing the courage to receive feedback form peers and subordinates;
- comprehensive training and ongoing support were essential at all levels of the organization to ensure that all individuals are comfortable with the process, and that incidences of negative feedback were handled competently.

### Will you take forward the 360-degree feedback process?

Research at Ashridge Management College suggests that success requires a number of factors: a clear strategic rationale; top management support and involvement; a culture geared towards behaviours and attitudes rather than simply towards performance; sensitivity; and a genuine willingness to discuss any issue. It would seem that 360-degree appraisal has potentially a great deal to offer the education service. The profession has the opportunity to develop this process to meet its own personal and professional development needs.

## REFERENCES

Alimo-Metcalfe, B. (1998) 'Leadership skills', presentation at the Institute of Personnel and Development Human Resource Development Week, 31 March–2 April.

Bahra, N. (1996) *360 Degree Appraisal: A Best Practice Guide*, Hitchin: Technical Communications.

Creissen, T. (1999) 'Follow my leader', *Professional Development Today*, 2(2) pp. 87–92.

Farrell, C. (1999) *Best Practice Guidelines for the Use of 360-degree Feedback*, The Feedback Project. Presented at Harrogate Conference.

Morgan, C. and Morris, G. (1999) *Good Teaching and Learning: Pupils and Teachers Speak*, Buckingham: Open University Press.

Ward, P. (1997) *360-Degree Feedback: Developing Practice*, London: IPD.

# 5

## Accelerated Learning, the Brain, Competencies and Interviews

Accelerated learning has developed from Georgi Lazanov's 'Suggestopedia', a technique for introducing positive suggestions and eliminating the negative in the learning process. Dynamic descriptions and key points of the materials to be learned were fixed into the subconscious using music during 'concert' sessions and later activated to provide the basis for in-depth learning. Lazanov discovered that the brain has an almost infinite potential for learning if the subconscious mind receives information in the right way. Accelerated learning is an effective method in certain contexts for increasing the absorption of knowledge – a key to the success of education. Learning can be accelerated if an appropriate preferred learning style is used. The creation of long-term memory through processing using multiple intelligences and subsequent activation of that memory in effective ways, is the way to unlocking the immense potential of the brain.

Accelerated learning is about acquiring new attitudes, skills and knowledge (*faster*) so that new information is retained (*longer*) and new information is assimilated at a (*deeper*) level. It is about unlocking the reserve capacity of the para-conscious mind. A simple working model of the mind suggests that the conscious mind can hold one unit of information, the pre-conscious 7 +/- 2 units, whereas the para-conscious has infinite storage and process capacity. Teachers are using accelerated learning techniques to achieve profound changes in quality of learning. Teachers as managers of accelerated learning sustain their own energy so the process is invigorating for them.

### UNDERSTANDING THE MESSAGE

The manager's tools for accelerated learning are explored in the MESSAGE model or template (McKee, 1998) which is one example of the application of accelerated learning which provides evidence of the neurological basis for accelerated learning.

M – *Mindset* – the achievement of success and learning comes from a mindset, specifically 'relaxed awareness', which can be developed and enhanced. It concentrates on the pacing of learning, for example including a two-minute break every 45 minutes. This mindset is about ensuring a clear focus, putting aside all distractions, planning the outcomes very clearly, creating a learning environment by relaxing the body yet encouraging the mind to be aware, and when working with people creating an atmosphere of low threat/high energy.

E – *Entrance* – the more different ways of 'teaching' that are provided, a multi-sensory input of fresh information, the more individual or team learning will be enhanced. This means using emotional enrichment establishing the benefits to all concerned, accessing the unconscious, and ensuring sensory enrichment in the learning or training context – visual portrayal, sonic portrayal, physical representation with peripheral visual, auditory and physical cues.

S – *Sequence* – this is the deliberate systematic stimulation of the seven intelligences in order to activate deep personal learning. The individual or team will only follow through on ideas that they own. They need to be allowed to activate the ideas using their own intelligence 'fingerprint', or combination of intelligences they use for learning, which is unique. The suggestions presented below are processes which would use the different intelligences:

   Mathematical–logical – prioritize, sort, calculate, reason, plan, evaluate, assess, research analyse;

   Musical – compose, rhyme, sing, recite;

   Linguistic – articulate, put in your own words, rewrite;

   Visual–spatial – arrange, map-out, draw, paint, colour, show connections, make a pattern, visualize, imagine, sketch;

   Physical – manipulate, build, construct, model, move, dance;

   Interpersonal – discuss, argue, present, share, exchange, empathise, solicit feedback, reach agreement, listen;

   Intrapersonal – reflect, review, consider, associate, extrapolate.

S – *Store* – even the best learning is lost without enough hooks to link to current knowledge and learning. Using the vowels of memory – association, exaggeration, imagination, order, unusual – all make the storage of new learning more fully embedded. Storing is making absolutely sure that the *key* ideas are memorized, encoding the 10 per cent memory triggers for recalling the learning. The rest is retrieved as a consequence of the brain's propensity towards linking information in its bio-database

A – *Action* – this presents the opportunity to demonstrate what has been learned, building confidence and competence through catching the group 'getting it right'. A team that recognizes its achievements will learn to get it right more often in the future. It learns from positive experiences as an individual does. The team and the individual need an opportunity to demonstrate the acquisition of new attitudes, skills or knowledge and for recognizing and rewarding the learning.

G – *Go-again* – unlocks and activates the para-conscious reserve capacity by reviewing the learned material in a brain state where theta brain waves predominate. It is important to give space for the para-conscious in the reinforcement of learning. Processes include a systematic sequential review, listening to baroque music with the largo movements at 60 bpm, retaining and considering forms of language such as metaphors or stories as part of the learning, and the use of reviewing at the individual level where the learner reviews and reflects on the learning journal with music thus accessing the theta dominant state where learning best occurs. The focus is on the unconscious mastery of the new material.

E – *Exit* – only the team that paints scenarios can visualize future potential applications of the new attitudes, skills and knowledge which have been learned. This applies also to the individual. The end of the first phase of learning is the doorway and key to the future. This can only be created through offering the many scenarios which might develop. The building of the memory maps for the future will provide opportunities for learning which can be recognized when they arise. Learners use the model with their focus on how they plan to immediately apply the learning. Exit is a time for reflection and review.

*How do you respond to this model for learning – in the classroom and for professional and personal development?*

The importance of research on the learning brain for pupil learning and teacher professional development has been increasingly recognized over the last ten years. The research on left brain/right brain and how the brain operates on many levels processing colour, movement, emotion, shapes, intensity, sound and taste underpins accelerated learning theory. Learners need to be positive and receptive. This can be enhanced by trainers using activities which increase curiosity and challenge. Using different learning styles ensures the potential of every learner is accessed. New productive rituals direct learning towards mutually agreed goals. We are perhaps more reticent than in the USA when planning opening rituals for training events or conferences. There is not the commitment to developing new organizational rituals, situational rituals or indeed closing or ending rituals, though most of these approaches can transfer directly to and be accessed in classrooms. Learners in all situations need a global overview of where the learning is leading and the sequence of steps to be followed to reach that goal. The rich positive-feeling learning environment that needs to be created can be enhanced not only by the accentuation of learning through all the intelligences but also by skilled use of more appropriate body language and of sensory elements contributing to that learning environment.

## BRAIN, MIND AND BEHAVIOUR

It is becoming important to have some understanding the links between brain, mind and behaviour (Bloom and Lazerson, 1988). The new techniques that allow direct study of brain mechanisms and processes also shed new light on the study of mind and behaviour. The complexity of the brain with the billions of nerve cells with each communicating with an average of 10,000 others, using chemical signals of which over 40 have been identified, means that for the purposes of personal and professional development it is necessary to understand the significance of this complexity and then to focus and determine the implications for learning. Knowledge of how the brain works is increasing rapidly. The two basic concepts of neuroscience are that the nervous system operates throughout the body and that the separate functions of the nervous system are carried out by subsystems organized according to the area of responsibility.

Study of the cellular and chemical machinery of the brain focuses on the basic elements of the nervous system, the individual nerve cells or neurons. The lifespan development of the brain is of particular importance to teachers in particular the elements relating to gender and ageing. The sensing and moving systems of the brain and spinal cord are also enormously complex but the associated sensory integration process and motor co-ordination processes feed into accelerated learning. The maintenance of the internal environment, homeostasis, through the autonomic nervous system, the endocrine system and the maintenance of physiological set-points such as temperature regulation, the control of blood pressure and eating behaviour are all related to the learning process. The rhythms of the brain and, in particular, the different levels in sleep cycles and the link to the alpha rhythms which occur just before sleep is important in some forms of learning. The link between emotion and motivation, in particular in this context how the brain functions to produce the visceral changes that accompany emotional arousal, remains problematic.

Here there is no detailed attempt to explore the brain structures that mediate emotion – the limbic system, structures in the brain stem, the cerebral cortex and the role of the autonomic nervous system. Ideally the links to cognition and emotion, aggression, pain, pleasure and stress and anxiety need to be understood in principle, because of the links to learning and memory. At its simplest, learning is about information acquisition, and memory is the aligned storage process. The different regions of the brain – the cerebellum, which may store some classically conditioned responses; the hippocampus, which seems to be vital in short-term memory or working memory; and the cerebral cortex – fulfil different and reasonably distinct and complementary roles in the learning and remembering process. The process of linking short-term and long-term memory, which is the function of the hippocampus, is particularly important in learning.

Consciousness is awareness of one's own mental and/or physical actions. Language is usually the vehicle that makes thought and action available to conscious awareness. One explanatory approach suggests that consciousness is a function of the columnar organization of the cerebral cortex. The column's intrinsic and extrinsic connections allow for dynamic and interchanging information flows through the system with different pathways according to needs. Information from the outside world and re-entrant information – memories, emotions, cognitive skills – are simultaneously processed allowing a continuous updating of perpetual images of oneself, which, when matched against external conditions, is the proposed mechanism for consciousness. Self-consciousness is central to the learning and professional development discussed in this book. This short section attempts to encapsulate some significant elements from *Brain, Mind and Behaviour* (Bloom and Lazerson, 1988). Arguably, for teachers it is important to have an increasingly sophisticated and rigorous understanding of the links briefly referred to here as a basis for teaching and learning in school and professional development.

*How do you respond to this information about the brain, mind and behaviour?*

## MAPPING THE MIND

A more recent book, which is about mapping the mind (Carter, 1998), shows how human behaviour and culture have been developed by the structure of the brain.

This focuses on how our personalities reflect the biological mechanisms underlying thought and emotion, and how behavioural idiosyncrasies are due to unique elements of the individual brain. An understanding of the shape and structure of the brain is increasingly recognized as linked to a conceptualization of the mind. The architecture of the brain can be understood as the hardware, and the mind the software which has links to thought, memory, consciousness and language. The discussion above implies that the better the understanding of the links between brain, mind and behaviour, the more the teacher will have a professional understanding of their significance for teaching and learning. Accelerated learning is a way of unlocking that potential.

*How important is your understanding of brain research for further professional development? Will you pursue it further?*

## TRAINING

Sloman (2000) states that given the new competitive pressures, the key source of competitive advantage is embedded in the skills and capabilities of knowledge workers within a resource-based strategy. This is sustained by appropriate policies on encouragement, involvement and commitment, and must affect the role, process and management of training. The critical influences are that capable individuals seek employability, there is a new psychological contract, the demise of the career, and that technology permits new approaches to delivery. The school needs to articulate a training strategy and plan with clear targets and to develop an appropriate training culture for the school in which staff at all levels embrace the role of training in achieving school objectives. In this context the balance between school and individual training needs has shifted and the targeting and monitoring of resources is more critical.

Schools need evidence that training is of value and is strategic. In order to evaluate the training it is essential to measure the responses, the learning and the effect on an individual's work performance, and to evaluate the impact on organizational performance.

*How is training evaluated in your school? How does it relate to other elements of professional development?*

## LEARNING

Honey (1999) presented a declaration on learning developed with other leaders in the world of learning. Learning is seen as the central issue of the twenty-first century, the most powerful, engaging, rewarding and enjoyable aspect of our personal and collective experience. School leaders need to harness the relevant knowledge and experience so that the school and the staff and pupils can learn more effectively.

Honey's learning cycle embeds learning through four distinct phases: the activist having an experience, the reflector reviewing the experience, the theorist concluding from the experience and the pragmatist planning the next stage. The individual learner selects learning opportunities that match their style preferences but can also become a more balanced learner by strengthening their underutilized preferences. The learning style preferences of individuals can become a basis for mixing and matching learning partners or teams. The learning process occurs inside the person, but making the outcomes explicit, and sharing them with others, adds value to the learning.

Learning is complex and covers knowledge, skills, insights, beliefs, values, attitudes and habits. Learning is a process and an outcome, it can be incremental or transformational, conscious or unconscious, planned and unplanned, it is a cause of change and a consequence of change. Teachers and children can learn to analyse how they learn, adopt discipline and routines to improve the way they learn, experiment and develop new ways of learning, learn from people around them and transfer learning to new situations. Learning to learn is the most fundamental learning.

For the individual, learning is the key to meeting the demands of change, for developing their potential. For schools, learning increases the capacity of all involved to contribute to the success of the school, and to be more effective in meeting its goals and achieving its purposes. It helps achieve a better balance between long-term organizational effectiveness and short-term organizational efficiency. Learning to learn should be included in all personal development. Learning must include dialogue about ethical and value issues. Processes and systems for capturing and sharing learning must be put in place. The opportunity to learn must be regarded as an intrinsic part of all work.

*You will have a deep understanding of learning. How can your training and development enhance this further?*

## SELF-MANAGED LEARNING

Self-managed learning is a process through which individuals determine what they learn and how they learn with others in the context of their unique situation. There are potential benefits in that the new knowledge, skills and abilities are defined in the learning contract as a basis for a personal development plan. The benefits include, for the individual, a better understanding of how they learn and a belief that they can, to a large extent determine their own future. For the organization this leads to a better matching of individual and organizational needs which can support broader organizational and cultural change. Self-managed learning is an approach 'owned' by the organization with a strong emphasis on the development of internal resources.

Professional development for teachers has traditionally focused on knowledge and skills development. Hargreaves and Fullan (1992) explore three phases of two complementary processes: teacher development as ecological change which concentrates on the importance of the context of the working environment, and teacher development as self-understanding.

First, there is development as a person – since personal maturity may affect professional development. Though maturity may be significant, it is arguably not necessarily a particularly central element in understanding the whole person. Indeed the word may have associations with age, having experience and being responsible, and be different from drive, enthusiasm and creativity. These may be more challenging and important than the more passive self-understanding and maturity.

Secondly there is development associated with the life cycle, where energy and commitment may depend on age, which may affect attitudes to change and improvement. There is a determinism in the Erikson model in which we are all partially creatures of our past. Erikson suggests that maturity is the result of developing all the ego qualities through the process of living the Eight Ages of Man (Erikson, 1950). Generativity, the mature stage of life, is about productivity and creativity. The wisdom and sustaining ego-integrity of the last phase may withhold the excitement and challenge that young teachers can bring.

Thirdly, the experience of the teaching career may bring positive or negative attitudes to further development. There seems to be an emphasis on the determinism of the context, though Hargreaves and Fullan warn of an overindulgence of this. This appears to imply that teachers may be victims of their circumstances and cannot take control. Self-understanding can focus on growing old and wise and what life has done to you.

*Are you professionally mature and what are the implications of your answer for personal growth?*

## THE CRANFIELD MODEL

The Cranfield University School of Management underpins its learning programmes by six competency sets. The first two are groupings of specific competencies associated with the management role – applied to teachers as managers as well as leaders in the classroom:

- *managerial knowledge* – for teachers this will involve keeping abreast of current developments in teaching methods in the context of the current policy environment;
- *influencing skills* – communication skills, assertiveness and dealing with conflict, persuading others, managing school politics, and developing others – delegating, coaching and counselling.

These two demonstrate how teachers need to be skilled managers and control and determine their lives.

- *Cognitive skills* are the thought processes required to understand situations and include intellectual capacity. Cognitive complexity is the ability to take varied perspectives and use conflicting concepts to change perspectives. Visionary ability is thinking long term and strategically. Achieving clarity is using the information effectively. Perceptual acuity is about understanding interpersonal interactions. These skills can be developed through practice.
- *Self-knowledge* is interpreted as including self-awareness and the awareness of how one impacts on others. Teachers can use such skills flexibly and see a range of behavioural, and therefore learning, options. This process allows teachers to understand their long-standing behavioural habits and the impact

of these on limiting their effectiveness. They can then do something with this knowledge.

- *Emotional resilience* is self-control and self-discipline, the ability to use emotions appropriately. Emotional intelligence is discussed elsewhere with here a focus on personal resilience and being balanced about one's self. For teachers this will accomplish better learning in the classroom.
- *Personal drive* is about personal achievement orientation and motivation. Personal ambition for responsibility is a basis for the capacity to motivate the self and others and to take risks. This is perhaps underemphasized at present.

These competencies are significant for teachers. This model might provide a basis for teachers who wish to develop strategies for managing their careers and their personal development. Education can learn from the strengths in people development that the most effective business schools achieve.

*Do these competencies provide a basis for your personal and professional growth?*

## INTERVIEWS FOR PROFESSIONAL DEVELOPMENT – EVALUATING THE TALENTED

The Gallup Organization has built a library of structured interviews over the last 30 years to measure 'life themes' in highly effective performers. These life themes focus on the intensity of the performer's drive for task completion, based on a thorough understanding of their strengths focusing on the underpinning values and their determination to help others achieve quality.

### Content analytical interviewing

This is the Gallup Organization model developed in the 1950s at the University of Nebraska by Don Clifton and others. The content analytical interviewing process is based on the discovery, 30 years ago, that talented people talk significantly differently from average performers. Since then a library of structured interviews has been developed. The focus is on the exact content of each candidate's response. Content analytical interviewing uses questions from the biographical, situational and behavioural interviewing traditions. Also included are questions on personal satisfactions and values, individual routines and previous work experiences. Some are based on motivation theory and explore how responses are invested with affect, intensity and frequency. Each question is a discrete item, scored separately before totalling. Trained interviewers tape-record the interview. The fairness and difficulty of each question has been built into the process. It is essential, with this technique, to comply strictly with pre-worded interview scripts. Highly skilled interviewers can and do build excellent rapport under such conditions, and score interviews as they progress. The questions in the interview are easy, open, bias-free and minimally stressful. The starting point is the recognition of talent, the tendency to do more of the right things each day, which leads to exceptional performance.

*Would you accept that skilled interviewers can provide an analysis of your strengths and development needs?*

### The Gallup process with headteachers

In a focus group, highly performing primary heads were encouraged to talk constructively about their work, prompted periodically by open-ended questions. The focus group led to the provisional identification of the thoughts, feelings and behaviours which characterize highly talented headteachers. When star performers recount and share their best moments with their colleagues, it approaches a video replay of their peak performances. The focus group was tape-recorded to explore how these exceptional achievers talked differently and to crystallize their work experience more vividly. The transcript of the focus group provides a basis for a model of excellence.

The provisional telephone questionnaire developed through this process was refined with a larger group of highly effective heads through further telephone interviews. The model interview, developed after the focus group, was piloted and checked for objectivity, reliability, fairness and validity, by listening with care to the responses of other talented headteachers. All the questions were asked in the same words by telephone often by the same interviewer to confirm the validity of the process as a cost-effective way to enable other headteachers or those aspiring to be headteachers to give a detailed account of themselves and to receive feedback on their talents and associated life themes.

Gallup staff are trained to conduct and interpret the interviews consistently measuring inter-rater agreement in many business contexts. The content analysis process needs to produce accurate scoring to standards of over 90 per cent consistency. This needs people who are personable, disciplined and dedicated. Professionally trained analysts produce written evaluations of interviewees including a personal development report. This process ensures the predictive validity of the scoring system. The relationships between life patterns and subsequent job performance has been researched. The highly successful fit between identified performance patterns and job expectations demonstrates that the talent model is coherent and relevant. Training and development activities can start from a personalised appreciation of the strengths of those interviewed following the feedback process.

*In your professional development do you concentrate on overcoming your weaknesses, or developing further your strengths?*

### Ego-driven leadership

In the Gallup Organization model, ego is the chronic desire to define oneself through behaviour, in ways that demonstrate to others that one is valuable and unique. Those with a strong ego need to channel their ego-drive to improve the self-esteem of the staff who work for them. They see themselves as people of significance and believe they have a right to make an impact on others and their environment. Self-confident and self-reliant, they relish independence. A quality associated with high ego is the setting of goals for oneself out of the reach of most people. People with a high ego drive may need more time and support than those developing more through more traditional processes. The development process needs to find the optimum conditions for their success. Their achievements must be recognized if that is what motivates them and they need positive feedback. They may need advocates if colleagues cannot, or refuse to, recognize the potential they have for superlative performance. The associated driving force and risk-taking is about playing for higher stakes. Such people need the opportunity to prove themselves or no one will know what they are capable of achieving. Research shows that there are many unrecognized teachers with such extraordinary talents (Ghali, Holmes and Tomlinson, 1999).

A carefully selected mentor should recognize that ego is a key part of their talent and encourage them to set stretching expectations. The mentor will need to recognize that they have the self-confidence to believe they can achieve something of significance. High self-esteem enables such individuals to pursue challenging goals and achieving these reinforces their high self-esteem. This ego drive needs to be tempered with other qualities such as integrity, social responsibility, fostering relationships and a clear sense of purpose and forward direction.

They may have developed these unique ego strengths because they have had a personal coach, role model or agent who nurtured, channelled and recognized their growth in childhood, adolescence or early in their careers. Peers expected them to perform well in their chosen role and their merits were recognized. Their reputation and their personal attributes developed into life themes. Those seeking to develop talent need to learn to recognize consistencies of thought, feeling and behaviour which underpin the performance of the most gifted. The Gallup model, which might be more fully used in the education service, is based on the development of outstanding strengths.

*Do you have any teachers with outstanding talent in your school?*

## REFERENCES

Bloom, F.E. and Lazerson, A. (1988) *Brain, Mind and Behaviour*, New York, NY: Educational Broadcasting Corporation.

Carter. R., (1998) *Mapping the Mind*, London: Seven Dials.

Erikson, E. (1950) *Childhood and Society*, New York, NY: W.W. Norton.

Ghali, N., Holmes, G. and Tomlinson, H. (1999) *Fast-Track School Leadership*, Leeds: Leeds Metropolitan University.

Hargreaves, A. and Fullan, M. (eds) (1992) *Understanding Teacher Development*, London: Cassell.

Honey, P. (1999) 'A declaration on learning: one year on', presentation at the CIPD National Conference.

McKee, L. (1998) 'Accelerated learning', presentation at CIPD HRD Week.

Sloman, M. (2000) 'Grasping the new opportunities for training', presentation at CIPD HRD Week conference.

# 6

## Neurolinguistic Programming and Professional Development: Improving Communication Skills

### NEUROLINGUISITIC PROGRAMMING

Neurolinguistic programming (NLP) is the study of excellence, a collection of techniques that identify and define how the human mind works, focusing, in particular, on high performers. It is, more technically, a unique synthesis of cybernetics, neurology and linguistics. The particular basis for development is to work out what is the essential difference between people who are outstanding and those who are competent. By developing a practical understanding of how these people succeed, others can learn to apply NLP techniques and achieve the same very high levels of performance. If we learn how the very best performers achieve outstanding results and the associated successful thinking and behaviour patterns, these can then be replicated and transferred in an integrated, appropriate and authentic fashion. The world each person perceives is not *the* 'real' world. Each person constructs a unique model of reality in her or his own mind at an unconscious level and then lives in the model as though it were real. Each of us produces our own map from experience choosing unconsciously to attend to what we judge is relevant. The generalizations based on this map unwittingly modify and distort 'reality' in order that the whole makes sense. In NLP terms most human problems derive from the models in people's heads rather than from the world as it really is.

Neurolinguistic programming skills offer specific and practical ways of making desired changes in your own and others' subjective experience and thus the consequential behaviour, beliefs and values. Neurolinguistic programming therefore offers a sound basis for personal and professional development and can be conceived of:

- as the art and science of human excellence;
- having a highly effective 'technology' for accelerating personal and professional development;
- as an instruction manual for the mind.

Understanding how people do what they do outstandingly well in order to transfer these skills to others is called competency modelling or modelling the structure of human excellence. When a person does something exceptionally well he/she

53

will be conscious of only some, possibly the most obvious, of the thoughts and behaviours that accompany this performance. Effective modelling takes account of three aspects of the subject being modelled:

- behaviour – what the expert does;
- beliefs – the 'mental maps' that are the foundation for the behaviour;
- values – the criteria by which the expert decides on any particular course of action.

Modelling is the ability to discover the expert's map with the intention of helping others learn to reproduce it. Neurolinguistic planning identifies and defines these hidden thought processes and mind patterns as used by top performers in excellent performance. Neurolinguistic programming offers a practical way of achieving a highly generative learning ability with which to produce better results through professional development.

*What are the similarities between this approach and the Gallup Organization model in Chapter 5?*

## CLARIFYING NLP

Sue Knight, whose book *NLP at Work* (1995) provides an easily accessible and useful approach, has been involved in training for many years. Her definition of NLP as presented at the IPD HRD conference in 1998 was: 'Neuro-linguistic programming (NLP) is modelling; the process of observing, analysing and representing the structure of particular abilities (particularly excellence) such that these abilities may be transferred to others, or oneself, in an integrated, appropriate and authentic fashion' (Knight, 1998). Neurolinguistic programming is a set of models about how skills in communication impact and are impacted upon by subjective experience. The techniques used for improving communication are then based on these models. Neurolinguistic programming identifies and defines how our minds work so we can use them more effectively. Building good quality relationships with colleagues and all those associated with the school means that conflict is replaced by co-operation. Developing greater flexibility in responding to the school cultural environment leads to more appropriate responses to the ever-changing demands of school. Managing your mental activities leads to greater self-control and more effective self-management.

*How have you learned from others in your experience?*

Senge (1994) explores this aspect of professional growth and development. The first two of his five learning disciplines are particularly significant:

- *personal mastery* – expanding our personal capacity to create the results we desire;
- *mental models* – reflecting on, continually clarifying and improving our internal pictures of the world, and seeing how they shape our actions and decisions.

Similarly Covey's (1990) book considers the seven habits of highly effective people. The fifth habit is

- *seek first to understand, then to be understood* – using the principles of empathic communication.

Senge and Covey are widely and increasingly used in teacher professional development in programmes which recognize the significance of the relationship between personal and professional development. This focus on personal capacity, clarifying and improving our internal pictures of the world, and using the principles of empathic communication, is directly related to NLP.

Knight shows how NLP training skills help those developing others to:

- match individual learning styles in the presentation of ideas so that each person can understand and develop;
- set compelling goals for training and consistently achieve them;
- recognize patterns in their own and others' language and to challenge these when appropriate to influence change and learning.

Teachers can gain new strategies of learning and motivation to enable them to achieve more highly if NLP techniques are used in the classroom.

Effective leaders seek to augment their own motivation as well as that of others. Negotiation, presentation and influencing skills can all be enhanced through the modelling process, and are aspects of teaching skills insufficiently focused on in initial teacher training and professional development. If we can determine what characterizes excellence in leadership and teaching this can be modelled and learned through NLP techniques.

## THE MEANING OF NLP

The name 'Neurolinguistic programming' comes from the disciplines which influenced its early development. It emerged from an exploration of the relationships between

- neurology – relating to the brain and its functioning, particularly the link between the experience of the senses, physiology and the mind. The neurological processes of seeing, hearing, feeling and tasting form the basic building blocks of our experience. Much of NLP is about increasing our awareness of our neurological system;
- linguistics – verbal and non-verbal aspects of our information processing with the understanding of the link between language and personality, the ways we use language to represent our experience and communicate with and influence others;
- programming – the way we code our experience. Our behaviours and thought patterns, influenced by our beliefs, values and sense of identity, determine our personal programmes. These programmes lead to the results we achieve and the effects we create in ourselves and others.

The relationship between our perceptions, thinking and behaviour is therefore neuro-linguistic in nature. It is the ability to discover and rationalize the programmes we run as manifested in our behaviour, and an awareness of the coding and the modelling process, which provides a basis for effective professional self-development. There are relationships between NLP and an understanding of body language. Eye gaze, facial expressions, gestures, orientation, posture, body contact, dress, odour and territory are all elements linked to body language communication. Rapport is created by matching and mirroring the other person's behaviour – mirroring voice tone/tempo, breathing rate, movement or body posture and other aspects of body language. Learning how to build and maintain rapport is a way of enhancing influence and strengthening relationships. For NLP there needs to be the focus on developing self-belief, confidence and excellent performance, which will be subsequently manifested through body language.

*How could you use an NLP trainer on training days?*

The focus on the positive is crucial, though NLP can also be used remedially to help people uncover, change or transform what is holding them back. Most importantly, however, is how it can be used generatively to enable people to make far-reaching changes to themselves and their lives. To achieve this the power of a well-formed outcome is a central process for self-empowerment. The likelihood of achieving what you really want is enhanced by building compelling goals.


## THE HISTORICAL BACKGROUND

John Grinder, a linguist, and Richard Bandler, an information scientist, developed NLP in the mid-1970s. They were interested in the possibility of being able to duplicate the behaviour, and therefore the power and influence, of highly effective people. They used technology from linguistics and information science, combined with insights from behavioural psychology and general systems theory, to unlock the secrets of highly effective communication, originally by working with some of the world's most effective practising psychotherapists. Virginia Satir, a founder of Family Therapy and Systemic Therapy, Milton Erikson, founder of the American Society of Clinical Hypnosis, and Fritz Perls, the founder of Gestalt Therapy provided the first models whose skills were learned by others. Their methodology, human modelling, was used to build models of how precisely uniquely skilled people perform or accomplish, which demonstrated how all skills are systematic, patterned and rule structured. The process of modelling these skills is learning to take on precisely the skilled behaviour and make it one's own. The highly skilled performer is asked questions about what they do, why they do it, what works and what does not. At the same time observation of the process when carried out particularly effectively leads to new and better questions and, therefore, further refinement. The unconscious competence of very high achievers will mean they may not fully understand what leads to their outstanding distinctiveness.

*Could this be applied to very high-achieving school leaders and teachers?*

Teachers, team leaders and headteachers have learned many of their skills from observation and applying what they have learned. Neurolinguistic programming is about doing this much more systematically and purposefully. Neurolinguistic programming techniques can also reveal what the human model does that he or she, and an unskilled observer, is not aware of. To do this successfully requires the study of the structure of the thought processes and the internal experience of the model, as well as their observed behaviour. The aspects of their internal experience which make them most effective are likely to be associated with a mixture of specific skills and behaviours, combined with the attitudes, beliefs and values that support those behaviours. Bandler and Grinder (1979) developed a unique system of asking questions and gathering information that was based on the fields of transformational grammar and general semantics.

*How does the theory of NLP as presented so far relate to your own learning?*

## THE NINE PRESUPPOSITIONS AND SEVEN PRAGMATIC MODELS

The presuppositions of NLP from the publications of Alder (1994), Andreas and Faulkner (1996), Howie (1997) and Knight (1995; 1998) are:

- *The map is not the territory.* We filter a vast amount of information and give it a unique meaning through our attitudes, perceptions, beliefs and values, and use this filtered information to construct maps or models of reality. Our personal constructs determine our interpretation of reality. Changing a person's map modifies their experience of reality. Personal development is about restructuring these maps for ourselves.
- *People work perfectly. No one is 'wrong' or 'broken'.* Neurolinguistic programming assumes people are intrinsically healthy. The results people have in their lives make sense from the way they process information and organize their thinking. It is possible to change the programme.
- *People make the best choice available to them.* Our personal history is our experience. This structures the choices we can make. The best choice is based on our state, our skills, our resources, our needs, our beliefs, our upbringing, our influences, our sense of self-worth, our feelings about our identity and our known or unknown purpose in life. People can learn from modelling how to make more choices accessible.
- *Choice is better than no choice.* Neurolinguistic programming is about helping people develop more choices that they can access.
- *Everyone has the resources needed to accomplish what they really want.* This includes the capacity to build up the range of skills, thoughts and feelings available and to apply them in different situations. The issue is about developing the resource through enhancing the different skills.
- *There is no failure only feedback.* Every response has value in that we can learn from it more about what adjustments to make in future. The only way to fail is not to learn from experience. We simply need to try something different then we will continue to improve if we use the feedback experience provides.
- *There is a positive intention beneath every behaviour.* It is important to look for the original positive intention in apparently inappropriate behaviour. Unwanted habits are an indication that this activity, at least partially, is attempting to obtain something of value or to accomplish something important. Neurolinguistic programming can help discover what this is and how it can be achieved more effectively.

- *The meaning of your communication is the response you get.* The meaning of a communication is not necessarily what you intended. What the listener experiences is the communication, as interpreted through her/his mental maps of the world. Communicators need to recognize this.
- *You cannot not communicate.* We are always communicating, even if non-verbally. There is body language and posture, but also communication through the face and in particular the eyes. Ninety-three per cent of communication is non-verbal. Thoughts are communication with the self.

Seven of the pragmatic models associated with NLP are built on these presuppositions and are explored below. These provide the opportunities for enhanced understanding and better communication, which are central to improved teaching and leadership skills through professional development.

1) *Sensory acuity and physiology.* Thinking is tied to physiology. People's thought processes change their physiological state. Sufficiently sensitive sensory acuity will help a communicator fine-tune their communication to another person in ways over and above mere linguistics. This skill in developing rapport, the key element of interpersonal effectiveness and influencing through matching processes, can be learned.
2) *The 'meta-model'.* A framework of linguistics for uncovering the 'deep structure' underneath someone's 'surface structure' of what we say to ourselves or others. This includes information not expressed or even known to the communicator and may require skilful questioning by the researcher to gather information to challenge any misinterpretation by the communicator.
3) *Representational systems.* Different people seem to represent knowledge in different sensory modes – seeing, hearing, feeling, smelling and tasting. In NLP these are normally called: visual (V), auditory (A), kinaesthetic (K), olfactory (O) and gustatory (G). The structure of experience may be predominantly interpreted in sounds, pictures or feelings and may be important in influencing learning styles. The apparently same meaning might be expressed in different ways. When participating in a conversation it is important to listen sensitively to recognize which sensory modes are being used by the other person: auditory – 'That sounds good'; visual – 'It's clear now'; feelings – 'That feels right'. When this has been recognized the skill of communicating more effectively can be practised.
4) *The 'Milton-model'.* This is a set of linguistic patterns developed by Milton Erickson, a hypnotist, whose work was another element in the foundation of much of NLP. It is a model for using language persuasively to improve self-communication, to speak to others with influence, to direct another person's mind and to guard against unintentional messages. Erickson developed this skill in his work as a hypnotist. It involves the skilful use of surface structures which can be learned.
5) *Eye accessing cues.* When people access different representational systems, their eyes move in different ways. Bandler and Grinder and their colleagues discovered minimal cues that indicate very specific kinds of thought processes.

These include eye movements, head position, hand/arm positions, legs/feet positions, the face, breathing patterns, voice tone changes and even very subtle clues such as pupil dilation and skin colour changes (Bandler and Grinder, 1979). The voice has tempo, volume, tonality, pitch, clarity and modulation. Developing the skill of interpreting eye movements can support and complement listening skills.

6) *Submodalities.* The structure of internal representation determines the response to the content. Submodalites are subsets and finer distinctions within the three modalities – sounds, pictures, feelings. If you picture someone you admire, it is possible to make the colours more intense. The colour can be turned down until the picture is black and white. For most people high colour intensifies the *structure* of the representation and affects the intensity of feelings about the content, whereas black and white neutralizes it. This process can be practised and managed to change feelings.

7) *Metaprogrammes.* These are aspects of how people process information and make decisions. For example some people are motivated *towards* goals, while others are motivated to move *away from* non-goals. *Towards* or *away from* priorities let you know how people respond to their world. Which of the alternatives a person prefers in a given context will dramatically change how they behave.

*How could you use the nine presuppositions and seven pragmatic models to inform your personal development and professional development in the school?*

## NLP AND HEALTH

There are techniques for diagnosing and intervening with NLP associated techniques which deal with improving health, or managing stress. There are, for example, ways to de-traumatize past traumas and ways to identify and integrate conflicting belief systems that keep people from doing things they want to do. These problems may prevent professional development.

## MODEL NLP EXERCISES

The exercises simplified from Andreas and Faulkner (1996) illustrate the NLP process. Their book has many exercises which cover, in addition to the areas below, discovering your mission, creating rapport and strong relationships, building self-confidence and achieving peak performance. The outlines below illustrate NLP techniques. If you are planning to use them please refer to the original text.

### Circle of excellence

1) Relive confidence – stand up and relive a time when you were very confident.
2) Circle of excellence – imagine a coloured circle around your feet; decide the colour; give it a sound like a soft hum. At the fullest confidence level step out of the circle leaving the confidence inside.

3) Selecting cues – think of a future time when you want to be confident. See and hear the situation just before you want to be confident. Select a cue just before the time occurs.
4) Linking – step back into the circle and feel confident feelings again. Imagine the situation unfolding in the future.
5) Check results – step out again, leaving the confident feelings inside the circle. Outside think again of the upcoming event. Confident feelings are recalled because of pre-programming. You will now feel better about it and will be confident when it arrives.

## Goal achievement process – four distinct exercises

1) Creating a compelling future – set the stage; see yourself in the future in your chosen role; make your goal well formed; make your image compelling; notice the pathway.
2) Developing a plan – visit your goal; see the future; see the past; walk back along the side of the pathway; notice specific steps on the pathway; go back to the present; appreciate the goal.
3) Rapid rehearsal – assume the role; walk the path; 'beam' yourself back.
4) Taking action – assign a realistic completion date; schedule your steps; keep an eye on your mission; do it.

Neurolinguistic programming is useful in four fields: communication, change, mental management and personal development.

## Communication

Neurolinguistic programming teaches us how to get good rapport with another person through the skilful use of body posture and movement, voice tone quality, language content and listening and observational skills; how to interpret meaning; how and what to observe in the behaviours of a person we are communicating with in order to be able to understand her/his inner states; how to prepare and lead conversations; and how to formulate and reach one's own goals (Thompson, 1994). Skilled coaches have unique ways of building deep levels of instant rapport through their ability to match subtleties in behaviour and language that are outside conscious awareness.

## Change

Neurolinguistic programming provides a multitude of interventions that transform personal limitations into resources. Most other approaches in the field of change are content-orientated and explore and relate to the origins of the problem in the past. However, NLP operates more efficiently on the level of the neurolinguistic structures of limitation in the present. The NLP psychotherapist's goal is to understand how the client is proceeding within her or himself to produce the limitations that affect behaviour instead of seeking explanations.

## Mental management

Neurolinguistic programming shows us the cerebral dynamics that enable us to gain control over our minds and our emotions. This is done in a way that enhances the dynamics of spontaneity. Mental management also means:

- being able to learn rapidly;
- being able to control inner states of mind;
- being able to access the degree of motivation that is appropriate to particular circumstances;
- being able to enhance mental and emotional flexibility to face a greater range of situations in a suitable way;
- being able to learn from situations;
- being able to access a neutral inner state at any moment;
- being able to handle fears.

## Personal development

Neurolinguistic programming is unique in the fields of human functioning in that its entire focus is on personal development. It is about how people do things, think, process information and behave. It shows us how to develop dormant resources. We discover how to attain personal and professional goals through creating a compelling life purpose, how to open up to what is within in order to retrieve spontaneously the verbal expressions that are the most adapted to a particular context. It is also about how to be at ease on the functional level, how to face all kinds of difficulties, how to know ourselves better, how to proceed in order to challenge yourself as appropriate and how to uncover your essential value as a human being. Through NLP techniques teachers can learn to change negative beliefs about themselves and the unconscious behaviours and habits that limit success, and better understand their potential to achieve.

*This chapter introduces NLP. You will need to decide if you will take your learning further. Will you?*

Mahony (1999) has written a challenging book using NLP techniques which focuses on headship. This is possibly the only book which concentrates fully on applying NLP in an educational context. The first part explores the known universe, the second life, the universe and everything, and the third what headship is. He suggests that a modelling process that explores four aspects of a role model provides the basis for modelling human excellence as manifested in headteachers, for teasing out the components of success and using them to accelerate the learning of another person. These are:

- the beliefs they hold about their areas of expertise;
- the values they espouse;
- their mental approach or thinking steps;
- their actual behaviour including the physiology they adopt.

If you have had the opportunity of learning something significant for yourself as school leader from another person whose excellence in one aspect of their life you have admired and wanted to emulate,

> cast your mind back and see and hear that person again and recapture how you felt ... when you have seen and heard something that you can now believe is of value to you, hear yourself telling yourself the same thing ... Imagine yourself being like that now and in the future. Because then you can think of a situation that will arise ... and notice how you can take this learning into this situation and realise that you are applying the new understanding from your past experience to increase your choices of action in the present. (Mahony, 1999, p. 12)

Neurolinguistic programming is a manifestation of the Fullan (1993) assertion 'the starting point for what's worth fighting for is not system change, not change in others around us, but change in ourselves'. Mahony suggests you need to not only ask, 'Who am I as leader?' and, 'What do I think as leader?' but to picture yourself fully living the role before you can know the answer. You need to explore whether there are messages inside your head constraining and limiting your success and to put these aside.

The 'Six steps to the heavens' provides the final exercise, in 'Part Three – What is headship?', to integrate all the learning within the book. This is about using the skills, which have been developed through carrying out all the exercises presented in the book. They focus on a heightened awareness, better emotional management, wider analytical and thinking skills, an appreciation of the deeper structure of the language people use, and the development of more flexible behaviour. The responses to the questions are to be placed on six successive flip charts placed on the floor, in order and then in reverse order because the process will have enriched the understanding. Each flip chart represents a space.

1. The environment space – think about the environment where you work – Where do you lead?, When do you lead?
2. The behaviour space – think about your behaviour – What are you good at as a headteacher?, What do you do as a headteacher?
3. The capacity space – think about your skills – How do you want to lead staff?, What can you do as leader?, What are you capable of as leader?
4. The beliefs and values space – think about what you would like to believe is possible – What do you believe about yourself as headteacher?, What does that say about you?, What must be true for you to say that?
5. The identity space – think about the unique person you are – Who are you as headteacher?
6. The community space – create a symbol to represent your linkage to the wider community – What would it be? (Mahony, 1999, pp. 110–11)

Mahoney's book and the exercises are about headship. All the exercises apply equally to any school leader or aspirant school leader. The book refers to the school context. Neurolinguistic programming, advanced psychological skills for the thinking manager, it is suggested, provides useful means for developing educational leaders.

*Does the evidence suggest NLP can help headteachers manage communication, change, mental management and personal development?*

## REFERENCES

NLP in Education Network can be contacted at
*jeff_lewis@noceans.demon.co.uk*

Alder, H. (1994) *NLP: The New Art and Science of Getting What You Want*, London: Piatkus.

Andreas, S. and Faulkner, C. (1996) *NLP: The New Technology of Achievement*, London: Nicholas Brealey.

Bandler, R. and Grinder, J. (1979) *Frogs into Princes: Neuro Linguistic Programming*, Moab, UT: Real People Press.

Covey, S. (1990) *The Seven Habits of Highly Effective People*, London: Simon and Schuster.

Fullan, N. (1993) *Change Forces: Probing the Depths of Educational Reform*, London: Falmer.

Howie, D.D. (1997) *NLP Advanced Psychological Skills for the Thinking Manager*, Leighton Buzzard: Rushmere Wynne.

Knight, S. (1995) *NLP at Work*, London: Nicholas Brealey.

Knight, S. (1998) 'NLP for trainers', paper presented at IPD HRD Week conference.

Mahony, T. (1999) *Principled Headship: A Guide to the Galaxy*, Carmarthen: Crown House.

Senge, P. (1994) *The Fifth Discipline Fieldbook*, London: Nicholas Brealey.

Thompson, P. (1994) *Conversation: The Power of Persuasion* (audio tapes), Nightingale Conant.

# 7

# Developing Creativity, Intuition and Innovation in Schools

## CREATIVITY – THE STARTING POINT

Highly effective school leaders encourage the creativity of staff to find better solutions to school problems. The creative process starts with incubation, which allows alternatives to be considered subconsciously. The creative moment may follow when there is a sudden insight, a mental leap to a new solution. This can occur for both individuals and teams. The arbitrary or accidental is often significant in this process. Serendipity, associated with creativity, is the facility for encountering unexpected good luck as a result of accident, wisdom or exploratory behaviour. The development of professionalism has traditionally concentrated on left-brain skills, with an excessive respect for logic, reason and rationality. Creative staff have a curiosity to consider issues from different perspectives and a capacity to connect concepts from different contexts. Schools are increasingly developing a positive belief in the importance of creative talent and the capacity to identify and develop it. Though some staff may be less creative because of earlier life and professional experience, all can develop and grow. This inner creative resource is however often obscured by fear of the judgements of others.

## SCHOOL CULTURE AND CREATIVITY

Some characteristics of a school culture enhance and others inhibit the development of creativity. When the school is creative, the rules and conventions will inevitably be challenged. A creative individual or team leader changes the school's cultural norms, which otherwise can only provide acceptable or traditional solutions. Creativity always involves a novel response which is adaptive to the current unique reality in the school. This creative process involves a new evaluation of ideas, an elaboration of the original insight, a sustaining and developing of it to the full, and then applying it successfully. Creative ideas are ready for implementation. Innovation is a complementary process, involving planning and implementing, making the creative idea lead to school improvement (Fryer, 1996). Imagination is more important to creativity than knowledge. To find new problems, to search for new possibilities and to reassess old problems from a new perspective requires creative imagination and can mark a real advance in problem-solving capacity.

*What role does creativity play in your school's leadership and management?*

School leaders in this context need to develop and encourage initiative and flex-ibility in teams, and may need to learn this skill working in teams themselves. Flexible multidisciplinary teams are the key to structural change. All staff need to be engaged in decision-making and empowered to make improvements. The key to reaching the highest level of creativity is to integrate creative and judgemental think-ing at the individual, team and school levels. The illusions of art are to serve the pur-pose of a closer and truer relationship with reality. Conceptual creativity is the basis for changing and enhancing the current reality in school. One of the most impres-sive Department for Education and Employment (DfEE) publications (1999) which explores creativity, culture and education, makes profound links across these issues:

> Teaching with creativity and teaching for creativity include all the characteristics of good teaching. These include strong motivation, high expectations, the ability to communicate and listen and the ability to interest and to inspire. Creative teachers need expertise in their particular fields ... but creative teachers need more than this. They need techniques that stimulate curiosity and raise self-esteem and confidence. They must recognise when encouragement is needed and confidence threatened, they must balance structured learning with opportunities for self-direction. (DfEE, 1999, para. 175, p. 95)

Brainstorming (Osborn, 1963), mind-mapping (Buzan, 1993), storyboarding (Disney) and synectics (Gordon, 1961) are different techniques for developing creativity which can be explored.

## MIND MAPS

Mind maps, for example, use images that are often more evocative than words, and more precise and potent in triggering a wide range of associations and think-ing. The techniques used include: emphasis – a clear central image and links with the key concepts, colours, spacing; association – arrows, codes, geometrical shapes; clarity – build on the one key word, make the images clear, the words should be on lines and connected to other lines indicating their relative impor-tance; develop a unique personal style. Taking notes, thinking of new ideas, sum-marizing information is best done using the association of keywords and not in a written linear form. Using mind maps the links between key concepts can be immediately recognized, so recall and review is more effective and rapid. The addition of new information is easy. The more creatively open-ended nature enables the brain to make new connections.

## DEVELOPING A CREATIVE CULTURE

Instant judgement is the opposite of creativity. Creativity and structure are com-plementary as in art. The creative spirit flourishes best in a climate in which ideas and concepts are all-important, a school which is a learning organization where all school leaders publicly develop their own creativity, encourage staff to learn about and improve their own creative processes, and reward those who risk being creative even when they fail. A technique which can be used is imagining life at each extreme of a dilemma, or deliberately creating uncertainty so that complexity is not seen as a challenge to analysis but a signal to engage and trust intuition and emotional awareness. In such techniques it is important to acknowledge and value differences, to allow two conflicting requirements to swirl around and interact. This can transform both and lead to a new way forward.

Eraut (1994) discusses the development of expertise in school management and teaching. The lowest-level skill is *acquiring and interpreting information*. The next, *skilled behaviours* require a combination of tacit knowledge and intuitive decision-making. *Deliberative processes* require propositional knowledge, situational knowledge and professional judgement. The central features of the highest-level skill, *meta-processes*, is about self-knowledge and self-management. This is the level at which creativity is encouraged. Habits are ways of behaving, which, because they are skilled and unthinking, may prevent people from thinking creatively. To challenge habitual thinking is to deliberately ask awkward questions, to revisit ideas and to think in new ways, to practice being creative.

*From the discussion so far, is creativity encouraged in your school outside the curriculum?*


## INNOVATIVE SCHOOLS

If schools are innovative they demonstrate seven characteristics (Higgins, 1995):

1) A stated and working strategy of innovation – staff should question the school's cultural norms. Questioning orthodoxy allows new understandings to emerge. The leader should visibly develop her/his creativity skills.
2) Forming teams – which know they are required to question current assumptions and seek new solutions.
3) Rewarding creativity and innovation – schools traditionally reward responsibility or classroom performance. The achievement of explicit creativity goals for tasks, projects and whole-school issues should be rewarded.
4) Allowing mistakes – the Relative Advantage Principle of Creativity shows that people undertake creative actions if they expect them to confer advantages relative to alternative approaches.
5) Training in creativity – in-service training to develop skills in creative techniques. Those who have limiting beliefs in their creative capability are challenged.
6) Managing the organizational culture – so it is responsive to innovations. Ambiguity provides opportunities for new thinking but may lead to anxiety. Creativity is served by dispelling fears and engendering positive emotions.
7) Creating new opportunities proactively – not simply futures thinking, but creating the future. The school should concentrate their creative acts on the key evaluative domains focusing on the priorities of children and parents.

*Using this definition is your school innovative?*

## CREATIVE ACTION-TAKING IN ORGANIZATIONS

Ford and Gioia (1995) present in detail a number of observations, guidelines, rationales and consequential interventions. The preliminary observations and guidelines are presented here.

1) People create certainty by imposing familiar interpretations on ambiguous or unfamiliar situations. *Guideline*: Doubt what you think you know.
2) Creative actions occur mainly as a response to ambiguity. *Guideline*: Treat ambiguity as opportunity.
3) Creative actions in organizational settings are usually judged according to the standards of multiple social domains. *Guideline*: Tailor creative acts and products to key evaluative domains.
4) Goals for creativity are rarely articulated in organizations. *Guideline*: Establish explicit creativity goals for tasks, projects and programmes.
5) People often have fragile beliefs in their own creative capacity because of inexperience with creative action in organizationally relevant domains. *Guideline*: Enhance creative capability beliefs with a small-wins strategy
6) Confidently held beliefs that the organization (or other domain) is receptive to creative actions are key. Negative beliefs strongly favour familiar actions over creative actions. *Guideline*: Remember the Relative Advantage Principle of Creativity: people undertake creative actions only to the extent that they expect them to confer advantages relative to other behavioural options.
7) Negative emotions favour habitual action; positive emotions favour, and are favoured by, creative action. *Guideline*: Ambiguity leads to anxiety as well as creativity. Creativity is served by dispelling fears and engendering positive emotions.
8) Talent matters, but knowledge and skills can be developed that facilitate creative action. *Guideline*: Creativity is trainable, to the extent that creativity training is domain-relevant.
9) Creative actions produce meaning out of ambiguity. *Guideline*: Don't just sit there thinking ... Do something creative!

*If you are planning creative action-taking follow the guidelines.*

## KIRTON ADAPTION–INVENTION INVENTORY

A psychometric instrument which reliably provides some analysis of creativity is the Kirton Adaption-Innovation (KAI) Inventory which measures the preferred thinking style in respect of problem-solving, creativity and decision-making. Kirton (1991) posits that everyone can be located on a continuum from the highly adaptive to the highly innovative. Adaption is the preference for improving existing practice. Innovation represents a preference for exploring new problems and offering solutions that may challenge accepted practice.

| *Adaptors* | *Innovators* |
|---|---|
| Do it better | Do it differently |
| Work within existing frameworks | Challenge, reframe |
| Fewer, more acceptable solutions | Many solutions |
| Prefer well established situations | Set new policy, structure |
| Essential for ongoing function | Essential in times of change |

The KAI Inventory is a short 32-item inventory designed to assess the adaption–innovation preference. A score of 140 (the maximum) does not make you a better innovator than someone with 110. It means there is a stronger preference for working in the Innovative way as defined by Kirton. The total score is made up to three subscale scores: SO for sufficiency of originality style (number of ideas), E for efficiency (level of attention to details) and R for role and group conformity style (working with, as opposed to challenging, the status quo). The evidence suggests that you are not likely to change your preferred style much over the years, though you may become better at adopting a persona to fit in with an environment. Though there is a large range within each profession you may wish to know that the averages are 80 for civil servants, 95 for teachers and 105 for marketing managers.

Intuition, related to creativity and innovation, is a basis for decision-making, when there is uncertainty or no precedent. When the variables are not scientifically predictable, when the facts do not clearly point the way to solutions, when analytical data is of little use, when several plausible solutions exist and when time is limited, intuitive decisions have to be made. Relaxation and silence allows for an honest reflection and the time to recognise the possibility of self-deception. It is important to be able trust yourself and be open to inner and outer new experiences. The acceptance of non-judgemental attitudes, finding an intrinsic satisfaction from expanded consciousness, and being willing to accept things, all combine to provide a basis for letting intuitive and creative decisions emerge.

*Is developing your creativity a professional priority?*

## CREATIVE STRATEGY

The current and emerging problems and concerns of all stakeholders in the school community provide the raw material for strategic advantage. Strategy is the cyclical iterative process for continuous improvement. There may be breakthroughs and creative loops but the process is continuous. A capability for learning and innovation is integral to school strategy development. The connections between strategy and daily school life stimulate new ideas. Creative schools focus on innovative ways to create unprecedented customer (that is, pupils and parents) educational value not on beating competitors. Creative strategy is achieved through internal innovative new ways of working, but also by seeing competitors as useful sources of learning. Creative swiping is learning from other schools and, more challengingly, other organizations outside education, using benchmarking imaginatively. Innovative thinking can be the key to short-term competitive advantage as well as long-term growth

Creative advantage schools demonstrate a number of characteristics (Williams and Knight, 1994). They welcome the impossible as an opportunity. They make no false promises to achieve the impossible but enjoy attempting to do so, using external influences and opportunities to increase their own learning. Recognizing the power of dilemmas, they improve their internal skills in identifying and working with them. Such schools have an ability to forget, and think afresh about ideas and issues in new teams. They value challenge and support as part of the internal culture, and cannot tolerate complacency. They believe in 'good enough' solutions to avoid perfectionism and detail which slows down strategic commitment. They think strategy development is for the whole school, and strive for strategies where the whole is more than the sum of the parts. A capability for learning and innovation is key. The links between the day-to-day and the strategic provides connections to stimulate new ideas.

*Does your school have a creative strategy? Is it a creative advantage school?*

## DE BONO

De Bono has been concerned with serious creativity for many years (De Bono, 1970). He sees his work as designing software for the brain. Lateral thinking is for changing concepts and perceptions, to provide an escape route from standard patterns of thinking. Premature judgement prevents playfulness and creativity. The right side of the brain represents innocence which plays a role in creativity, particularly in artistic expression. De Bono developed the Six Thinking Hats System, a form of parallel thinking, which is designed to introduce random concepts and provocative ideas:

1) White Hat   Data gathering – facts, figures, information needs and gaps.
2) Red Hat     Intuition and emotions – feelings.
3) Black Hat   Judgement and caution – the logical negative.
4) Yellow Hat  Benefits and why it will work – the logical positive, looking forward to results, but also for value in what has happened.
5) Green Hat   Provocations, alternatives and creativity – proposals, provocations and changes.
6) Blue Hat    Overview and process control – thinking about the subject, meta-cognition.

One team member can her/himself or ask another person, or the whole team, to adopt or take off a particular colour of hat. The hats provide an opportunity to switch thinking. Sometimes it is possible to follow a sequence of hats to structure group thinking. The Six Thinking Hats process can make space and time for creativity.

## CREATIVITY AND THE MANAGEMENT OF CHANGE

Arguably, the book which best presents the range of implications of creativity for those wishing to develop as a leader in the management of change is Rickards (1999). The book concentrates on what creativity can contribute to management.

The challenge Rickards presents offers a broad understanding of management, and the significance of the many contributors to thinking, with chapters on creativity – the slumbering giant of organizational studies – and innovation. However, he also makes clear the links to many other issues dealt with in this book – on marketing and strategy, decision-making, culture and climate issues, leadership and managerialism and the management of change. The penultimate chapter presents postmodernism, a jolt to the system, with a 'bluffer's guide' to postmodern terms. The chapter on creativity provides an outstanding short history of the development of the concept.

## THINKING LIKE A GENIUS

Michalko (1998) examined the thinking strategies of geniuses and sees as central their ability to think productively not reproductively, because they have the capacity not to be skewed by the prism of past experience. Geniuses reconceptualize problems in many different ways, making their thoughts visible, using unique combinations of verbal, visual and spatial abilities. Most importantly they produce constantly. Geniuses generate a rich diversity of novel and unpredictable alternatives, constantly combining and recombining ideas, images and thoughts in their conscious and unconscious minds, forcing relationships out of juxtapositions between dissimilar subjects. The swirling of opposites creates the conditions for a new point of view to bubble freely from the mind. Geniuses tolerate ambivalence in opposites and the apparently incompatible, think metaphorically and prepare themselves for chance serendipitous, occurrences.

*Could you practise the skills of a genius?*

Imaginization (Morgan, 1993) is a managerial skill which aids the development and understanding of individual creative potential and the finding of innovative solutions. The strategic termites, whose nests are products of random self-organizing activity where structures emerge in a haphazard and unplanned way, provide a metaphor and inspiration for developing coherent approaches to strategic management and change. The spider plant provides another metaphor for an organization. Futureblock as conceived here may relate very directly to education, that is: change, change, change with, nevertheless, all kinds of factors in the current situation reinforcing the status quo. The exploration of such metaphors can be particularly useful in breaking free of immobilizing patterns.

*Create a metaphor to describe your school as an organization.*

Visionizing (Parnes, 1992) and VanGrundy (1992) is the breaking of habitual mental associations and the forming of new ones. Visionizing is the deliberate development of creativity. The Creative Problem Solving (CPS) cycle is elaborated fully and is explored as a training and facilitation process. The starting point may be a *conforming person* who relies totally on past experience to programme her/himself to continuously plod ahead in known proven ways. The second stage is the *cre-*

*ative–adaptive person* who is sensitive to problems and challenges, and creatively solves them by modifying or adapting behaviours. The *creative–innovative person*, the Visionizer, deliberately dreams, envisions and uses creative problem-solving techniques to turn these images into the best reality it is possible to achieve. Parnes (1992) provides a rigorous training programme for creative professional development.

## BLOCKS TO CREATIVITY

The blocks to creativity, perceptual, intellectual, emotional in the individual, and cultural and environmental within the school can be challenged.

### Perceptual blocks

- Difficulty in isolating the problem.
- Tendency to delimit the problem area too closely.
- Inability to see the problem from various viewpoints.
- Seeing what you expect to see – stereotyping.
- Saturation.
- Failure to use all sensory inputs.

### Emotional blocks

- Fear to make a mistake, to fail, to risk.
- Inability to tolerate ambiguity; overriding desires for security, order; no appetite for chaos.
- Preference for judging ideas, rather than generating them.
- Inability to relax, incubate, and 'sleep on it'.
- Lack of challenge; problems fail to engage interest.
- Excessive zeal; overmotivation to succeed quickly.
- Lack of access to areas of imagination.
- Lack of imaginative control.
- Inability to distinguish reality from fantasy.

### Intellectual blocks

- Solving problems using an incorrect language (verbal, mathematical, visual) as in trying to solve a problem mathematically when it can more easily be accomplished visually.
- Inflexible or inadequate use of intellectual problem-solving strategies.
- Lack of, or incorrect, information.
- Inadequate language skill to express and record ideas (verbally, musically, visually).

### Cultural blocks

- Fantasy and reflection are a waste of time, lazy even crazy.
- Playfulness is for children only.

- Problem-solving is a serious business and humour is out of place.
- Reason, logic, numbers, utility, practicality are good; feeling, intuition, quali-tative judgements, pleasure are bad.
- Tradition is preferable to change.
- Any problem can be solved by scientific thinking and lots of money.
- Inspiration is taboo.

### Environmental blocks

- Lack of co-operation and trust among colleagues.
- Autocratic manager who values only her/his ideas; does not reward others.
- Distractions – phone, easy intrusions.
- Lack of support to bring ideas into action.

## MEASURING CREATIVITY

There is a diagnostic instrument (unknown source) which allows the measure-ment of creativity using 14 dimensions:

1) A fear of failure results in staff drawing back and not taking risks, settling for less in order to avoid anxiety or the shame of failure.
2) A reluctance to play results in a literal, overserious problem-solving style, and not 'playing around' with ideas. This fear is of seeming foolish or silly by experimenting with the unusual.
3) Resource myopia is the failure to see one's own strengths and appreciate the resources, people and things, in the environment.
4) Overcertainty is a rigidity in problem-solving responses using stereotypical reactions; persisting in behaviour that is no longer functional and not challenging current assumptions.
5) Frustration avoidance is giving up too soon when faced with obstacles, avoiding the pain or discomfort often associated with change or novel solu-tions to problems.
6) Being custom-bound results in an overemphasis on traditional ways of doing things, with too much reverence for the past and a tendency to conform when it is not necessary or useful.
7) An impoverished fantasy life results in the mistrusting, ignoring or demean-ing the inner images and visualizations of the self and others. The over-valuing of the so-called objective world shows a lack of imagination.
8) A fear of the unknown results in avoiding situations which lack clarity or which have uncertain probability of success. This results in the overvaluing of what is known against what is not known, with an excessive need to know the future before moving forward.
9) Those with a need for balance have an inability to tolerate disorder, confu-sion or ambiguity. An excessive need for balance and symmetry results in a dislike of complexity.
10) A reluctance to exert influence may come from a fear of seeming too aggres-

sive or pushy in influencing others. There may be a hesitancy to stand up for what one believes or ineffectiveness in making oneself heard.

11) A reluctance to let go is trying too hard to push through solutions to problems, with insufficient ability to let things incubate or to let things happen naturally. This may be from a lack of trust in human capacities.

12) An impoverished emotional life results in a failure to appreciate the motivational power of emotion. This results in a lack of awareness of the importance of feelings in achieving commitment to individual and group effort.

13) An unintegrated yin–yang is not using sufficient ways of getting at the essence of things, and polarizing things into opposites rather than knowing how to integrate the best of the apparently contradictory. Without integration there is no unified perception of the wholeness of the universe.

14) Sensory dullness is not adequately using one's primary senses as a way of knowing; making only partial contact with self and the environment. The capacity to feel and explore atrophy and there is limited sensitivity.

*Would you seek to overcome blocks to your personal creativity?*

## HOW TO DEVELOP CREATIVITY

1) *Capture spontaneous ideas.* Be ready to capture ideas that flash into your consciousness at the oddest moments. Have a notebook ready day and night to write them down. One word is enough to avoid losing the inspiration – but if possible capture and start to develop the idea there and then.

2) *Develop ideas.* As soon as you can, work at developing your idea – by yourself or bounce it off someone else. Two subconscious brains are better than one. Do not be afraid to look a fool. If the idea is a good one, the kudos from its success is far greater than the embarrassment of suggesting a non-starter.

3) *Make space.* If your conscious brain is full of worries and work there is no room for inspiration. To encourage creativity set aside time and space to welcome ideas. Relax – somewhere warm, comfortable, calm, and quiet – let your mind wander over the length and breadth of your life. Capture the ideas that come to you.

4) *Seek inspiration.* The donkey plodding in steady circles around the well may have time and space for creative thinking but lacks inspiration. If you are tired and drained by your daily work, you will need to make a special effort to move beyond your normal routine into an environment which sparks creativity.

5) *Push out the boundaries.* Seeking inspiration or confronting a problem, think widely around your topic. View it from different angles, from above or below. Take a bird's eye view. Adjust the time – in a month? Next year? Play around with size – if it were smaller? If there were more? Change the colour, texture, structure.

6) *Avoid straight lines.* Write your ideas about how your brain works – in three dimensions. Start in the middle of the page and capture ideas like branches of a tree. Write in a straight line only if a train of thought follows a straight line. When random thoughts occur, jot them anywhere – but jot them all.

7) *Be positive.* Expect to get good ideas. Expect your brain to work for you all the time. Expect to be the person others turn to for inspiration. Encourage them

when they bounce an idea off you. Expect them to encourage you. Create a positive atmosphere in which everyone thrives on creative interaction.

*Will you start on this process now?*

## REFERENCES

Buzan, T. (1993) *The Mind Map Book*, London: Penguin.

De Bono, E. (1970) *Lateral Thinking: Creativity Step by Step*, New York, NY: Harper and Row.

Department for Education and Employment (DfEE) (1999) *All Our Futures: Creativity, Culture and Education*, London: DfEE.

Eraut, M. (1994) *Developing Professional Knowledge and Competence*, London: Falmer.

Ford, C.M. and Gioia, D.A. (eds), (1995) 'Guidelines for creative action taking in organizations', in *Creative Action in Organizations: Ivory Tower Visions & Real World Voices* (pp. 355–67), Thousand Oaks, CA: Sage.

Fryer, M. (1996) *Creative Teaching and Learning*, London: Paul Chapman Publishing.

Gordon, W.J.J. (1961) *Synectics: The Development of Creative Capacity*, New York, NY: Harper and Row.

Higgins, J.A. (1995) 'Innovate or evaporate: seven secrets of innovative corporations', *The Futurist*, September–October pp. 42–8.

Kirton, M.J. (1991) 'Adaptors and innovators', in J. Henry (ed.), *Creative Management*, London: Sage Publications.

Michalko, M. (1998) 'Thinking like a genius', *The Futurist*, May, pp. 21–5.

Morgan, G. (1993) *Imaginization: New Mindsets for Seeing, Organizing and Managing*, London: Sage.

Osborn, A.F. (1963) *Applied Imagination*, New York, NY: Scribner's.

Parnes, S.J. (1992) *Visionizing: State-of-the-Art processes for Encouraging Innovative Intelligence*, Buffalo, NY: Creative Education Foundation.

Rickards, T. (1999) *Creativity and the Management of Change*, Oxford: Blackwell Business.

VanGrundy, A.B. (1992) *Idea Power: Techniques & Resources to Unleash the Creativity in Your Organization*, New York, NY: American Management Association.

Williams, C. and Knight, A. (1994) 'Achieving creative advantage', *Ashridge Journal*, December.

# 8

---

# Managing Stress and Managing Time

This chapter explores the management of stress and time in a broader context to clarify how teaching relates to other work. Within the profession there is a new stronger focus on teacher workload issues but also increasingly there is concern about bullying of teachers. This difficult area is focused on first. An article about teachers in the *Observer* (Pollard, 2000) opens with 'In the average school, nearly one in six (teachers) has been bullied in the last six months'. Cary Cooper, leading researcher on stress asserts:

> There are two types of bully. The psychopathic bully has low self-esteem and may not be particularly good at their job. He or she bullies to enhance their status. It's a personality disjunction and the numbers are relatively small and stable. The other type is the overloaded bully who has too much to do themselves and dumps on others. This sort of bullying is increasing.

A survey by Cooper at the Manchester School of Management found that one in four workers had been bullied in the last five years, but in teaching the proportion was one in three. The significance of this for the number of teachers who intend to leave the profession may be underestimated because victims may be unwilling to talk about bullying.

The bullying barometer used suggests you are being bullied when:

- your presence or opinions are ignored;
- you are denied information about your performance;
- you are given an unmanageable workload;
- you are given unreasonable deadlines;
- you are humiliated or ridiculed;
- your work is excessively monitored;
- gossip and rumour are spread about you;
- faults are continually found with your work.

*Is there bullying in your school? Of pupils? Of staff?*

## EUROPEAN HEALTH AND SAFETY WEEK

The Health and Safety Executive (2002) supported the European Safety and Health Week in October 2002, which had a special focus on stress. The supporting documentation shows that 40 million people throughout Europe experience mental and physical abuse in the workplace on a daily basis, and most suffer in silence. An estimated half million UK workers report they have been made ill by work-related stress. The Fact Sheet (8) shows the following stressful characteristics of work.

### CONTEXT OF WORK

| | |
|---|---|
| Organizational culture | Poor communication, low levels of support for problem solving and personal development, lack of definition of organizational objectives |
| Role in organization | Role ambiguity and role conflict, responsibility for people |
| Career development | Career stagnation and uncertainty, under or over promotion, poor pay, job insecurity, low social value to work |
| Decision latitude/control | Low participation in decision making, lack of control over work (control, particularly in the form of participation, is also a context and wider organizational issue) |
| Interpersonal relationships at work | Social or physical isolation, poor relationships with superiors, interpersonal conflict, lack of social support |
| Home–work interface | Conflicting demands of work and home, low support at home, dualcareer problems |

### CONTENT OF WORK

| | |
|---|---|
| Work environment and work equipment | Problems regarding the reliability, availability, suitability and maintenance or repair of both equipment and facilities |
| Task design | Lack of variety or short work cycles, fragmented or meaningless work, underuse of skills, high uncertainty |
| Workload/ workpace | Work overload or underload, lack of control over pacing, high levels of time pressure |
| Work schedule | Shift working, inflexible work schedules, unpredictable hours, long or unsocial hours. |

For each of the issues explored below, the suggestion (Fact Sheet 22) is that the following three questions are asked. What action is already being taken? Is it enough? What more needs to be done?

| | |
|---|---|
| Culture | Is there good open communication, support and mutual respect? |
| | Are views from workers and their representatives valued? |
| Demands | Are staff overloaded or underloaded, do they have the capabilities and capacities for their tasks? |
| | What about the physical (noise, vibration, ventilation, lighting etc.) and psycho-social (violence, bullying etc.) environments? |
| Control | Do individuals have sufficient say in the way their work is carried out? |
| Relationships | How are relationships between colleagues and colleagues and managers? |
| | What about relationships between managers and senior managers? |
| | Is there evidence of any bullying or harassment? |

| Change | Are workers anxious about their employment status? |
| | Are they confused by workplace changes and what it means for them and their colleagues? Clear communication helps – before, during and after change. |
| Role | Do people suffer role conflict (conflicting demands) or role ambiguity (lack of clarity)? |
| Support, training and | Is there adequate induction for new recruits, and staff whose jobs have changed? |
| individual | Are staff given social support? |
| factors | Is account taken of individual differences? e.g. Some members may thrive on working to tight deadlines; others may like the time to plan. |

These might provide a basis for considering how healthy your school is as a work environment both for staff and pupils who are workers in your school. Throughout this book there is a focus on the wider working and professional environment which recognizes the unique characteristics of teaching but also that there are real benefits to be achieved by considering the similarities of work with others.

*Given this model, how healthy is your school?*

## CONQUER YOUR STRESS

Cooper and Palmer (2000) present a positively supportive short book with this reassuring title. There are practical exercises throughout, and the first author is the leading academic researcher on stress management. All the chapters are intended to support your professional growth directly. The opening chapter defines stress, explains the physical consequences of stress, and provides a self-assessment of stress for you – psychological, behavioural and physiological/physical. There is an assessment of the causes of occupational and organizational stress – relationships, the organizational structure and climate, those intrinsic to the job, from the role in the organization; those associated with careers, and the home–work interface.

The central chapters are about changing thinking to conquer stress, changing behaviour to conquer stress and improving your physical health to help you conquer stress. There are eight helpful activities in the chapter on changing thinking which would provide the framework for a school in-service day with a 'Stress-inducing beliefs indicator', and a 'Thinking errors audit'. Changing your behaviour here is achieved through social support, assertiveness training and time management (see below); and improving your physical health, supported by another self-assessment questionnaire concentrates on exercise, nutrition and relaxation. Cooper and Palmer focus here on the management skills of conquering stress, which can lead to learning greater confidence if you follow through the activities and develop an action plan derived from this process.

*How do you conquer your own stress?*

## MANAGING STRESS AND PREVENTING BURNOUT

Gold and Roth (1993) open their book with a chapter entitled a profession in disillusionment which they characterize as extremely stressful with an incredible dropout rate of teachers early in their careers, with the early stages of burnout already prevalent in initial teacher training. This was ten years ago. Teachers are at risk in an inherently stressful profession, and though the numbers of teachers leaving the profession in the first five years is well recognized, teachers are not prepared to deal with the conditions and are prepared to react to the stressful elements in their personal and professional lives. Gold and Roth conceive of stress and burnout as very different.

Stress, for Gold and Roth, is a condition of disequilibrium within the intellectual, emotional and physical state of an individual; it is generated by the individual's perception of a situation, which results in physical and emotional reactions. It can be either positive or negative depending upon the interpretations of the situation. Burnout is a syndrome which emanates from an individual's perception of unmet needs and unfulfilled expectations. It is characterized by progressive disillusionment, with related psychological and physical symptoms which diminish self-esteem and develop gradually over a period of time. If burnout is so defined it is the responsibility of every teacher to become aware of her/his own needs and expectations. Equally it is the responsibility of those who are responsible for their welfare. Gold and Roth, working with young teachers early in their careers, argue that there are three domains of need:

- *Emotional–physical needs* – security, serenity/harmony, self-acceptance, self-confidence, self-esteem, energy-stamina, calmness, safety, good health, physical fitness.
- *Psycho–social needs* – sense of belonging, self-understanding, psychological comfort, self-control, acceptance, success, confidence, intimacy, compassion, making acquaintances, close relationships, collegiality, emotional support, interactions, friendship/companionship, love, security.
- *Personal–intellectual needs* – discovery, intellectual fulfilment, intellectual excitement, novelty, innovative techniques, encouragement, mental gratification, inquiry, intellectual stimulation, creativity, new ideas, aesthetic experiences, intellectual challenges, critical thinking, positive thinking, self-analysis.

*Does your school attempt to meet these needs? How successfully does it do so?*

Gold and Roth, as in many books dealing with stress, provide a programme for managing stress alongside their analysis. Communication to enhance personal and professional effectiveness is about the power of listening, non-verbal communication skills, questioning skills, paraphrasing, awareness of perceptual style, the individual's model of personality types, and self-insight through communication. Self-disclosure is one way of achieving self-awareness. Self-awareness can lead to the achievement of self-esteem. Self-disclosure is the process of revealing your feelings or emotions to others. The principle behind this is that the expression of feelings to others provides an improved basis for recognizing those feelings and hence for dealing with them. Self-disclosure is letting others know who you are inside. Effective participation in the feedback process as recipient similarly involves good communication skills. This leads into developing communication skills for providing effective feedback and interpersonal support for others. There are a number of strategies which are explored and demonstrated in practice. There are seven key *Individual Insight Strategies* for personal growth (Gold and Roth, 1993, p. 130):

- Identify and clarify (awareness) what your needs are from each of the three domains of need
- Recognize how you are affected by not meeting those needs by listing your feelings and behaviours
- Identify what triggers your old responses
- Understand your old defence system and why the specific trigger produces it
- Realise how you are now dealing with problems and list specific ways you want to change
- Determine new coping skills to meet your individual needs
- Choose motivational rewards to keep you encouraged and progressing.

At the *Interpersonal Support Strategy* level the Model for Change includes the phases of Awareness, Acquiring Understanding, Practising Changing and Gaining Control. This is not a simple analytical process. The process of Acquiring Understanding is learning about what your feelings are communicating to you about your own needs. Sometimes it is relatively straightforward to remember what the emotions are and how one is reacting to them. In order to understand the underlying cause, a more sophisticated skill of analysis is required. It is about trying to reveal why you are feeling and behaving as you do, that is, what unmet needs are causing you to behave as you do.

The *Guided Group Interaction Strategy* requires group cohesiveness, the sharing of information, individual insight learning, commonality, the offering of hope, the development of communication techniques, genuine caring for others, modelling, catharsis and commitment. These build on the earlier factors and are about helping all group members to develop skills at the individual and interpersonal level through group processes.

The conclusion of all this process is developing an individual life plan which includes learning awareness, acquiring understanding, practising changing and gaining control for managing your emotional–physical needs, psycho–social needs and personal–intellectual needs. This is the programme for action. The guided Group Interaction Strategy provides a basis for developing a school programme to provide the professional health solution for school staff.

*Consider the links between this analysis of stress management and emotional intelligence.*

## STRESS REDUCTION

Practical stress reduction can be managed first of all through *the physical approach*. *Breathe* slowly and deeply, lying on your back, and try to breathe through your stomach a few minutes a day. *Posture* when corrected makes your muscles relax, sitting or standing as straight as possible. *Exercise* is the way of burning off emergency energy, particularly after a stressful day at work. Approaching the physical limits releases chemicals – encephalins and noradrenaline – which lead to relaxed feelings. Excessive amounts of inappropriate food – rich meals with red meat and caffeine, nicotine and alcohol – undermine physical health.

*The conceptual approach* is about reducing the number of things to worry about. *Role division* is about sticking to one role at a time. Having career *targets* will clarify what is important. *Planning* avoids the waste of mental energy. If all commitments are written down the brain can then concentrate. *Decisiveness* is important, particularly with the smaller decisions where the wrong decision is relatively insignificant. This approach is about being clear and acting effectively.

*The psychological approach* is about alternative activities to the stress of work. It is about taking part in *games*, particularly competitive games, which provide an alternative form of winning and losing and therefore places a more appropriate value on work. *Mental exercise* through cultural activities which expend mental energy, creates more new forms of tension and energy. It will also clarify the relative significance of work stress. *Creativity, laughter and love* are all beneficial, as is *danger*, as a way of finding inner peace, after dangerous activity and surviving.

There is some ambivalence about *the spiritual approach*. Basic skills in relaxation have been developed to an almost mystical level in eastern philosophy and religion. There are adherents of Buddhist meditation and yoga. From Zen Buddhism and Transcendental Meditation to martial arts like judo and karate there are specific skills which develop the ability to relax. *Meditation* is about emptying the mind of all worldly cares, leaving it free to focus inwards to find true wisdom. The same mind-emptying techniques can be used to leave the mind free to go to sleep. *Mind–body training* is developing because the Western tradition regards the mind and body as separate. Non-violent martial arts such as t'ai chi and postural therapies like the Alexander technique and yoga allow the learning to be in touch with your body and hence improve your capacity to relax. *Self-hypnosis*, auto-suggestion, even at an elementary level develops the ability to relax. Autogenic Training is the best known of such techniques. *Visualization* of a detailed picture can make it difficult for the brain to distinguish between that and actually being in the situation. It is possible, through visualizing a situation when one felt happy, to feel some of the peacefulness associated with that time. This can be practised with different memories to develop the capacity to re-create that feeling. There is a growing acceptance of new approaches allied to the spiritual in non-traditional forms, which can provide means for focusing on the personal as a basis for professional development. Aromatherapy, reflexology and hypnotherapy may be more effective alternatives to complement telephone help lines or counselling sessions.

*How does your school support the management of stress for staff?*

In *Change Forces* (Fullan, 1993, p. 57) Farber summarizes the process of burnout as follows:

(i)   enthusiasm and dedication give way to
(ii)  frustration and anger in response to personal, work-related, and societal stressors, which, in turn, engender

(iii) a sense of inconsequentiality, which leads to

(iv) withdrawal of commitment and then to

(v) increased personal vulnerability with multiple physical (headaches, hypertension, and so on), cognitive ('they're to blame'; 'I need to take care of myself'), and emotional (irritability, sadness) symptoms, which, unless dealt with,

(vi) escalate until a sense of depletion and loss of caring occurs.

You will need courage and skill to recognize any of your colleagues who are moving in this direction using your emotional intelligence. School leaders need to establish systems to recognize and prevent burnout. Wellness programmes need to be at the heart of this.

## MANAGING CONFLICT

There are two types of behaviour associated with managing conflict – co-operativeness, the extent to which one party wishes to satisfy the other, and, assertiveness, the extent to which a party wishes to satisfy her/his own concerns. Conflict is assumed to be problematic but can be both negative and positive.

- *Negative* – diverts energy from the task at hand, destroys morale, polarizes individuals and groups, deepens differences, obstructs co-operative action, produces irresponsible behaviour, creates suspicion and distrust, and decreases productivity.
- *Positive* – which opens up an issue in a confronting manner, develops clarification of an issue, increases involvement, improves problem-solving quality, provides more spontaneity in communication, is needed for growth, and strengthens a relationship when creatively resolved. This is associated with negotiating skills which can be about managing conflict.

The management of conflict in school can be either destructive or productive depending on the skills of those managing the context.

## TIME MANAGEMENT

The Institute of Management Foundation Checklist 016 (*Managing Your Time Effectively*, Institute of Management, 1998) is a distillation of the wisdom of the institute providing a framework for detailed planning only outlined here.

1) Establish how your time is spent.
2) Determine your problem areas.
3) Tackle the enemy without.
4) Set and agree priorities with your boss, your colleagues and your subordinates.
5) Tackle the enemy within.
6) Build in response times to your work.
7) Plan for things to go wrong.
8) Remember the health check.

Time management is an element of personal organization and managing stress because it positively ensures the best use of the limited time available. It is about being efficient in order to create time to be effective. There are many programmes to support more efficient time management but the technical process outlined below is at the heart of many of them. Time Manager International states that the Time Manager itself is a personal tool to relate short- and long-term planning and the daily calendar. Many of the associated techniques relate to other issues in this book. The circular process described here, common to many of these programmes, needs to be carried out with rigour:

- Setting life goals, which leads to prioritizing and focusing the use of time – professional development processes assist in this.
- Keeping a daily time log, which leads to the identification of the present use of time and time-wasters.
- Management of time-wasters, which leads to increased discretionary time.
- Wise use of discretionary time, which leads to the accomplishment of the goals.

The important issue is to carry through an analysis of using time effectively *once* and then do something about it. You should learn how well organized you are and then respond by planning to deal with this.

*How well organized are you?*

1) Do you waste time?
2) Do you know how you use your time?
3) Have you kept a time log for a week to explore how you use your time?
4) Do you write a 'to do' list at the start of each day?
5) Do you know which items you must do during the day?
6) Do you make sure that you finish the urgent, often the important and difficult, items of your 'to do' list before moving on to the other items?
7) Do you use your best work times to tackle major tasks?
8) Do the meetings you are responsible for use time well?
9) Can you quickly find items in your files, and on your computer?
10) Do you meet deadlines with time to spare?
11) Do you ever say 'No' when asked to do something?
12) Are you able to delegate tasks to your colleagues rather than doing them yourself?
13) Do you check with colleagues how they are managing their time?
14) Are you able to handle staff who waste your time?
15) Do you arrange to have some quiet time during which you can work undisturbed every day?
16) Have you been able to match your daily work with your medium- and long-term aims with clear time frames?
17) Do you spend time planning what you will be doing in your career in five years' time?
18) Does your work team meet to set medium- and long-term goals?

19) Do you celebrate when you complete a task?
20) Are you calm and rational in the face of time pressure?
21) Do you let colleagues know how you are feeling about things at work?
22) Can you relax during your leisure time without worrying about school?
23) Do you feel happy about the way you are using your time?
24) When work planning gets difficult does your heart sink?
25) Are you angry when you or your colleagues are unable to complete a project on time?

Meetings, see Chapter 11, can be a major and frustrating waste of time because at a meeting it is difficult to use the time any alternative way. They may be unnecessary, have no unambiguous purpose and no clearly structured time frame. The meeting process can become irrelevant because there are no clear decisions, or the minutes may not communicate those decisions or say who will do what when. The pre-planning should guarantee efficiency with the agenda timed, and only those present who need to be there, and ideally only for the time they need to be there. This is a major issue of time management but your responsibility is to manage effectively the time in meetings you are responsible for and to be sufficiently skilled to advise others on how to use the time of others effectively.

*How well do you manage your time? How well are meetings managed in your school? How well do you manage meetings?*

## POWER

French and Raven (1960) identified five bases of social power in a widely accepted model. The exercise of power by those in leadership positions has implications for stress in the school.

- Reward power – the ability to provide others with something they desire in exchange for compliance.
- Coercive power – is the opposite and is exercised by withholding rewards as sanctions for non-compliance. Coercive change destroys the possibility of renewal – using laws, regulations and policies. The process of mastering the rules smothers energy and destroys all zest, spontaneity or creativity.
- Expert power – is the ability to gain compliance on the basis of knowledge, information or skills. This is often evident in a particular situation.
- Referent power – is available to individuals who are able to command the admiration and respect of others and gain their trust. They have particular characteristics and qualities as role models so others want to identify with their goals.
- Legitimate power – is associated with the formal role in the organization.

How status, responsibility, authority and the associated 'power' are exercised has profound implications for the climate of a school and its implications for a healthy school. McClelland (1975) suggests there are two ways people experience and express power needs. The negative is a personalized power concern: that is, power used to serve oneself, enjoying displaying the trappings of prestige and using others for selfish purposes. The alternative is, socialized power concern:

that is power used in the service of others, by someone who is emotionally and socially mature, who helps others grow and succeed, shares with others a long range vision, and participates in coaching and supporting others.

*How is power used in your school?*

## HEALTHY SCHOOLS, AND HEALTH AND WELL-BEING IN THE WORKPLACE

There have been many initiatives to support the development of healthy schools. This will be a major issue for school leaders in the future. Hoy and Tarter (1997) produced two versions of The Road to Open and Healthy Schools: A Handbook for Change, one for primary schools and one for middle and secondary schools. Within the book there is a climate instrument, the Organizational Climate Description Questionnaire (OCDQ) which explores the openness of the professional interactions, and the Organizational Health Inventory (OHI) which captures the health of interpersonal relationships in the school. All the information that is required to administer and score the scales is provided in the book. The metaphor of health is used to describe the climate of the school and the metaphor of personality to assess the school's degree of openness, that is, how authentic, caring and supportive are the interpersonal relationships.

They provide helpful and fully elaborated analyses of and distinctions between the concepts of culture and climate. One approach suggests that culture consists of shared assumptions and ideologies whereas climate is defined by shared perceptions of behaviour. Culture is developed from the disciplines of anthropology and sociology, is more abstract and provides a rich description. Climate is derived from psychology and social psychology, is more concrete and the basic purpose is to describe and improve. The OCDQ measures three critical aspects of headteacher and teacher behaviour. The OHI explores the health of interpersonal relations among 'students, teachers, administrators and community members'. These measures can provide a basis for tackling stress.

A booklet produced by the Institute of Directors (2002) is about managing health, safety and well-being at work to boost business performance. The Institute of Directors recognizes the significance of many of the issues raised at the start of this chapter as the following quotations illustrate:

With the range of health-related issues widening constantly – from back pain, bullying, sick-building syndrome, corporate manslaughter, alcohol, smoking and drug policies, to HIV/AIDS – it's clear that employers need to take action. (*Ibid.*)

It's no surprise that violence, bullying and harassment are all causes of stress in the workplace. But to what extent are they a problem?
- A recent study on violence at work showed that people working in small businesses were more likely to be threatened or assaulted than those in large organisations
- Working directly with members of the public puts people at a higher risk of violence

- The Chartered Institute of Personnel Development say that violence and bullying often goes unrecognised
- Bullying can take many forms involving the abuse of power, and may include racial and/or sexual harassment. (*Ibid.*)

Those responsible for reducing stress and managing the health, safety and well-being of those in schools are shown how their needs are aligned with those of individual employees.

*Is your school becoming healthier?*

## REFERENCES

Cooper, C.L. and Palmer, S. (2000) *Conquer your Stress*, London: Institute of Personnel and Development.

French, J.R.P. and Raven, B. (1960) 'The bases of social power', in D. Cartwright and A.F. Zander (eds), *Group Dynamics: Research and Theory* (p. 612), Evanston, IL: Row Peterson.

Fullan, M. (1993) *Change Forces*, London: Falmer.

Gold, Y. and Roth, R.A. (1993) *Teachers Managing Stress and Preventing Burnout: The Professional Health Solution*, London: Falmer.

Health and Safety Executive (2002) *Working on Stress* (incorporating Fact Sheets 8 and 22), October, European Agency for Safety and Health at Work.

Hoy, W.K. and Tarter, C.J. (1997) *The Road to Open and Healthy Schools: A Handbook for Change*, Thousand Oaks, CA: Corwin Press.

Institute of Directors (2002) *Health and Wellbeing in the Workplace*, London: Director Publications.

Institute of Management (1998) *Managing Your Time Effectively*, London: Institute of Management.

McClelland, D. (1975) *Power: The Inner Experience*, New York, NY: Irvington.

Pollard, J. (2000) 'Please sir, you're a bully', *Observer*, 2 April.

# 9

## Career Development and Development as a Professional

### THE CHANGING CONTEXT

In the 1980s career planning was apparently straightforward. Organizations recruited those with potential and, through careful selection, ensured they had commitment. They provided training and management development schemes as a result of which the talented and loyal were promoted and prepared to train others, because there was no fear of redundancy. It was possible for employees to plan family lives, to anticipate changes of location and the timing of progress up the hierarchy. All apparently benefited from this long, stable career ladder.

In contrast, now jobs are scarcer and more precarious, with the world changing at an unprecedented rate, all employees need to be resilient, flexible and capable of adjusting their sights at short notice. This does not yet apply to teaching but developments discussed below may have an impact on this. Career ladders are now sustained for as little as three to five years in many organizations, though the more traditional professions in particular have not yet responded to this new career model in the wider world.

Careers have to be planned using new life planning skills with sharper goal-setting feeding into the process. Kanter (1989) encouraged workers to improve their marketability through keeping their professional knowledge and technical skills up to date so they could be applied in many different contexts. However, now even those on fast-track schemes can find themselves plateaued unless they are adept at coping with change because of the very fast track which has kick-started their careers. Employers know they need a committed talented flexible workforce to survive, even when the employment they offer is not permanent and long-term, so they have to explore what they can offer to achieve this. This involves identifying career strategies for all individuals and trying to align these with current corporate needs, whilst conscientiously maintaining and developing individual skills.

### MANAGING YOUR CAREER

Yvonne Sarch was asked by the *Observer* in a short series, The Science of Success (copy undated) in an article 'Future perfect' to explain how truly brilliant careers were achieved. The checklist derived from her book, *How to be Headhunted*, was:

1) Be autonomous – take responsibility. Integrity is about loyalty to personal values. You should look for rewards for performance rather than loyalty payments for long service.

2) Keep your options open – those who change jobs are seen as advancing their careers, though headhunters and others making judgements will check that these moves were progressive. In the career-building years, ages 25–35, career zigzags every three years are considered healthy.

3) Top up your skills – employers will pay handsomely for skills, financially, or in quality of life or with personal development opportunities. Transferable skills include managerial and professional skills, language skills, supervisory skills and an understanding of the application of information technology.

4) Top up your knowledge – use management development or other courses. Specialized knowledge maintains your marketability in the short term but can limit flexibility if it is too narrowly focused.

5) Keep your head over the parapet – you have to tell people about yourself, your capabilities and your work. Your employability will be strengthened by being significant and noticed.

6) Think ahead – you should be thinking about the job after next. Early career choices can be decisive.

7) Service your CV – update this every three months. This forces you to consider what you have done and to consider progress, and to look for gaps. It should be two to three pages long, highlighting achievements which were attributable to you and had a work-wide effect. This might be broader than the school.

8) Network – keep an active network based on work and your interests. This will help you understand what is going on in other organizations you might want to target. Networking helps provide a wider balanced life. It is not about cultivating useful people but learning from mixing with people with similar interests, abilities and preoccupations.

9) Choose the right employers – some corporate or school cultures will suit you better than others. Flatter structures have shorter career ladders. More hierarchical organizations may be less flexible and have more precarious corporate cultures.

10) Enjoy what you do – when you know what you enjoy find it in job satisfaction, challenge and self-fulfilment. You should know what you want then you can attempt to achieve it.

*How seriously do you take your career planning?*

## THE PSYCHOLOGICAL CONTRACT

The new psychological contract requires the employer to agree to provide a breadth and depth of experience through planned career moves, with a clear view of the wider field of activity, and to assist in supporting a network of contacts to identify new opportunities. Robertson and Rousseau (1994, pp. 249–59) defined a psychological contract as 'An individual's belief regarding the terms and conditions of a reciprocal exchange agreement between that focal person and another party ... a belief that some form of promise has been made and that the terms and conditions of the contract have been accepted by both parties'.

Recruitment, retention and reward strategies will need to be more imaginative and open to negotiation. This is developing in schools. You may wish to consider seeking professional advice on career reframing using a professional occupational psychologist. Even if you remain a full-time teacher, the skills of portfolio careerists – scenario planning for career development, rehearsing pathways into the future, expanding your individual vision and developing mental constructs to respond to uncertainty – will be part of the networking world you should learn to access. New tools and technologies will provide you with self-organized learning for transferable skills.

The search for job satisfaction should be central in your career planning. Job satisfaction used to require job security but the changed psychological contract means this is not as certain as it used to be. Even in teaching there can be no long-term guarantee unless the teacher meets the new learning needs of pupils. The wider work culture involves risk-taking, with a requirement for an entrepreneurial commitment, the need for strong professional peer and team loyalties, performance-based awards, the acceptance of the judgements of fair appraisers, parallel career ladders and trial management roles for specialists. For those who develop high-level skills there will be security of employment but not necessarily in the same school, company or role. The associated job satisfaction provides self-respect and personal status and pride in yourself because there is the opportunity for independent thought and action, and personal growth and development. More widely, and more recently in teaching, it is important to have the skills to respond positively to effective assessment and appraisal, which should help you evaluate your strengths and weaknesses with confidence, identify areas for improvement and development, and select appropriate learning experiences for the future.

*Do you have job satisfaction? Do you recognize this context for your career?*


## STRATEGIES FOR CAREER DEVELOPMENT FOR PROFESSIONALS

Watkins and Drury (1994) used a focus group to explore this at a time when companies, which had expected people to develop their own careers, were moving back towards providing support for career development. The four strategies were derived from a focus group with their judgements about them:

1) *Developing a new mindset* – learning to live with doubt and uncertainty; maintaining a positive outlook; aiming for a balanced life. They did not regard work or a high profile career as the sole measure of success, and were more concerned with achieving a balance between work, self-development, career, family and community relationships. They defined success as being able to realize their potential by making contributions in all aspects of their lives and being able to manage the interactions with others effectively to make this happen.

2) *Learning to promote and market one's skills, networking and cultivating relationships.* The idea of self-promotion and marketing one's skills was viewed

with some distaste by many, as it might be by many educational leaders. The mid- and late-career professionals regarded it as vulgar and 'very unBritish' though the more traditional networking was accepted as appropriate. This appears to be important within an ethical framework.

3) *Developing self-insight and taking personal charge.* Very few of the focus group were aware of the availability of a wide range of personality and career tests designed to help individuals work out their strengths and weaknesses and career direction, though they did acknowledge the value of career planning. Though some companies were over-rigid in focusing career planning, most participants judged that the difficulties in developing a career plan were because of the levels of uncertainty in the company and the environment.

4) *Developing a Range of Competencies.* The erosion of professional status in the early 1990s had been a shock, though the realization that the maintenance of technical proficiency was no longer sufficient was slow to dawn after this had occurred. They agreed on the growing importance of skills including marketing, negotiation, client care, project management and cross-functional skills, but they had rarely translated this awareness into action. Learning to trust the judgement of others in a team-based situation after years of working with total individual control was problematic.

*How do you characterize your professionalism?*

Planning a career in education now has greater importance since the teacher's career may not continue to follow the historical trajectory. Though schools are still hierarchical with a focus on upward career progression, here as elsewhere there may need to be greater focus on role adaptation, project teamworking and lateral job movement. Schools need to learn how to retain, motivate and develop the potential of those who have traditionally been expected to look after themselves. Schools and teachers need a shared career development agenda. Moving between schools has traditionally been a way of teachers accessing career progression. Fast-tracking is part of this process now at system level. In business there might arguably be less emphasis on those selected at an early stage and more on the shifting population of high-potential managers to be developed when they show unusual ability. In schools, perhaps there has been insufficient emphasis on both.

## DEVELOPING YOUR CAREER IN EDUCATION MANAGEMENT

Thody (1993) focuses on developing skills by preparing to meets the needs of the market. She recommends career awareness, your determination of a career policy, locating the career markets and ensuring that you achieve career development in your current post. There is further guidance on applying for career opportunities, being aware of what Thody calls non-standard products, being interviewed and negotiating the contract. Teachers and school leaders are learning how to negotiate salary and conditions at appointment. The shifts in ownership of careers in business – the belief that the individual was in the 1980s and early 1990s totally responsible for his/her own development, back to this being a shared commitment, were about who takes responsibility for making development happen.

The school will ideally have systems in place for career counselling and, given the uncertainty about budgets, it is useful for the school to have taken at least some preliminary steps towards preparing for crisis counselling. The implication is that a school needs to determine exactly what its role is and to plan for:

- Career counselling – establishing the future direction of a career in the light of the individual's ambitions, interests and aptitudes.
- Coaching – practical help with CV writing, answering job advertisements, interview techniques and methods of handling job offers, networking and use of contacts
- Advice on the job search – from opening up the search from the advertised to the unadvertised job market, to providing objective information and research on companies or schools to whom applications or 'on spec' letters might be addressed. This is becoming possible in education.
- Crisis counselling – deals with the immediate aftermath of a redundancy announcement, with guidance on how to handle the shock, and how family and friends should be informed. This can be a particular problem with suspensions for teachers.

*Does your school assist you in career development?*


## TEACHING AS A PROFESSION AND TEACHERS AS PROFESSIONALS

The General Teaching Council (GTC) is intended to raise the status of teaching as a profession. This will have profound implications for the newly emerging teaching career and the careers of those who are currently teachers. Teachers are professionals, though the precise meaning and implications of this concept are problematic. Until recently the UK Inter-Professional Group to which representatives of most professions belong would not accept teaching as a profession. This organization defined the principles of a profession (UK Inter-Professional Group, 1995) as:

1. A profession must be controlled by a governing body.
2. The governing body must set adequate standards of education as a condition of entry or achievement of professional status.
3. The governing body must set ethical rules and professional standards which are to be observed by its members.
4. The rules and standards enforced by the governing body must be designed for the benefit of the public, and not for the private advantage of the members.
5. The governing body must take disciplinary action if the rules and standards it lays down are not observed or a member is guilty of bad professional work.
6. Some types of work should be preserved to the profession by statute, not because it is for the advantage of the members, but because for the protection of the public, it should be carried out only by persons with the requisite training, standards and disciplines.
7. The governing body must satisfy itself that there is fair and open competition in the practice of the profession.
8. The members of the profession must be independent in thought and outlook.
9. In its particular field of learning the profession must give leadership to the public it serves.

There is no reason why, according to this definition, teaching should not become a profession though currently the precise definition and limits of teaching are more insecure. Another issue of current concern is the development of para-professionals, support staff and what teaching work does require the 'requisite training, standards and discipline'. It could be argued that teachers' associations are acting to protect their members rather than the public in attempting to control and limit the work of such para-professionals. This may require a clearer definition of precisely what the unique skills of a teacher are, defined not to protect teachers but to protect their clients. There have been significant changes for architects and doctors in redefining these boundaries. Nurses and doctors are equally professional.

## INSTITUTION OF MECHANICAL ENGINEERS

Members of the Institution of Mechanical Engineers might be perceived as a profession as distinct from teaching as any career and profession could be. That is why it is worth considering how you relate to their model of professional development and its relationship to careers. There is a recognition embedded in the statements below, taken from their professional documents (Institute of Mechanical Engineers, 1998) that employment security is no longer guaranteed, and that this is precisely a reason to develop professionally for career development.

PROFESSIONAL DEVELOPMENT
A process of planned personal growth which will enable all professional engineers to reach their full potential. It is the acquisition of knowledge, experience, skills and the development of personal qualities necessary for the execution of professional and technical duties throughout an engineer's working life by which the individual will retain marketability.
WHY CPD?
Your first degree was one stage in a lifetime of learning experience in both your business and non-business life. Before you could practise as an engineer you had to complement your degree with industrial training and experience. That process will continue throughout your career:
YOU ARE RESPONSIBLE FOR YOUR OWN CAREER DEVELOPMENT AND SELF-IMPROVEMENT.

*A PLANNED APPROACH*
- proper career planning and personal development is the key to success
- you should identify aims and set objectives at every stage of your career development, continually reviewing and adapting to any changes whether they are foreseen or not
- the guide and professional development record are vital tools for successful career development

*DEVELOPMENT NEEDS*
- each stage of your career should be evaluated against specific, measurable, attainable, acceptable, and time-bounded objectives
- a necessary step in CPD is to identify realistic career aims and to review them regularly

- in planning your career you should take into account the interface with your employer, profession, your family and society as a whole.

Educational leaders and teachers in the emerging environment may increasingly seek professional advice from an occupational psychologist. Indeed LEAs and schools may wish to move into professionalizing in this area. This might include scenario planning in career development, rehearsing pathways into the future which expand the individual's vision and providing mental constructs to support new ways of responding to uncertainty.

## MANAGING CAREERS INTO THE TWENTY-FIRST CENTURY

Careers are defined in personal terms (Arnold, 1997), have a subjective element, concern sequences of employment-related experiences, are not confined to employment only, can include employment in different occupations, do not necessarily involve high-status occupations and do not necessarily involve promotion.

The changing career model within the education system is emerging because of the need to recruit, manage and develop human resources much more effectively. For the individual teacher this means more than creating situations which provide security, challenges and opportunities for self-development. Core employees, as teachers largely are currently, require broad skills. Supplemental teachers, most obviously supply teachers are just-in-time employees, but the technical and managerial roles, even heads and teachers who are not required full time may increasingly be outsourced. The posts which are outsourced in business are frequently more strategic, though in schools this mainly involves non-teaching staff at present.

*How do you understand any possible changes in the teacher's career model in the next ten years?*

## ONLINE LEARNING

The National College for School Leadership (NCSL) initially with the National Professional Qualification for Headship (NPQH) has been developing leadership skills using online training and development. This is extending to middle management and bursars, and recognizes the change from hierarchy to network and the more team-based models which are emerging. In 2002 the NCSL was piloting a DVD-based team-focused working programme for schools based on research in the health service.

Arnold (1997) argues that competency based training and qualifications may risk the loss of the innovation, risk-taking and excellence which are now recognized as important. Employers supporting self-development need to be supportive rather than deterministic. The offering of development centres which present work simulations, role-playing, group discussions and presentations to establish competencies and development needs are increasing. Associated performance appraisals need to distinguish the evaluation of past performance from developmental needs to be expressed through personal development plans, career exploration and with a sound conceptual structure for thinking about people and work environments.

## ADULT LIFETIME DEVELOPMENT

Four authors, Erikson, Super, Levinson and Schein, presented by Arnold, explore adult lifetime development. Here we will briefly consider Erikson and Super.

Erikson (1980) built on Freud's psychoanalytical psychology but argued that the conscious rational self was more dominant. More importantly for careers he argued that there are four phases of psycho–social development during adulthood which are, like those in childhood, about resolving tensions between opposing forces.

1) *Identity v. role confusion* is the adolescent identity crisis. There is a strong need to identify who one is to resolve this tension. Success in establishing a secure identity leads to greater control of the future and the development of self-esteem and self-confidence. There is the danger of being unable to establish a secure identity but equally important of ending with a rigid and inflexible self-identity which cannot be sustained. Young teachers may not yet have resolved this tension.

2) *Intimacy v. isolation* is an issue during the 20s and early 30s. If a person has successfully established an authentic identity, she/he should next learn to reach out to others and value them through establishing relationships not only with people, but also organizations or causes, without losing a sense of self. The two opposing dangers are of immersing oneself in a relationship so deeply that the sense of self is lost, or of self-absorption and isolation through the fear of loss of identity.

3) *Generativity v. stagnation* occupies much of adulthood. It is about bringing on the next generation, and handing on one's knowledge, experience and accomplishments to young people. Erikson emphasized that this can be about altruism through parenthood for example, but it is also about teaching. Failure to achieve generativity means stagnation and a self-centredness.

4) *Ego integrity v. despair* is about the acceptance of life and one's place in the universe, though this will normally be after retirement. Failure to achieve ego integrity can lead to despair which may show itself as disgust and a turning outward of the hostility one feels inside. This may apply to older staff.

The implications for career management may involve seeking new opportunities in the early stages of teaching and exploring different activities, interests and experiences. These should be connected and focused whilst allowing an opportunity to develop important aspects of potential. Arnold suggests that Erikson underplays the importance of achievement in the focus on identity/role confusion and intimacy/isolation but asserts that these life stages recognize the sometimes underestimated importance of identity and relationships at work. The generativity/stagnation phase for people in mid-career is for those who have a deep understanding of the world of work to act as mentors or coaches and to offer opportunities for individuals to express the achievements, characteristics or creations that represent their achievement.

Super (1990) applied ideas from developmental and humanistic psychology to careers for 50 years. A model of the adult career concerns emerges from this work, which has similarities with the Erikson model.

*Exploration (15–24)*

Crystallization          Developing ideas about the general field of work you
                         would like to be in.

Specification            Turning the general preference into a specific choice of
                         occupation.

Implementation           Making plans to enter the occupation and carrying them
                         out.

*Establishing (25–44)*

Stabilizing              Setting into an occupation, including supporting and
                         developing the self, and adopting a lifestyle consistent
                         with it.

Consolidating            Making the self secure in the occupation, and demon-
                         strating one's value in it.

Advancing                Increasing earning and level of responsibility.

*Maintenance (45–64)*

Holding                  Retaining one's position in the face of changing technol-
                         ogy, competition from younger employees, and other
                         pressures.

Updating                 A more proactive version of holding – keeping abreast
                         of changes in one's work demands and personal goals.

Innovation               Finding new perspectives on familiar tasks, and new
                         ways of doing them.

*Disengagement (65+)*

Decelerating             Reducing load and pace of work, perhaps by delegation
                         if work circumstances permit.

Retirement planning      In terms of finance and lifestyle.

Retirement living        Learning to live without work.

*How do you evaluate these models of adult development as they relate to you and
to friends and colleagues?*

## THE CAREER STRATEGIST

In conclusion we will look at an approach to the future of careers from the USA
published in the journal, *The Futurist*. This model has useful checklists for teachers and school leaders planning for the future. The title is significant – 'The new
career strategist: career management for the year 2000 and beyond'.

  Barner (1994) suggested that the career strategist needs to:

1) Carefully track the broader trends – seeking growth opportunities or potential
   career roadblocks.
2) Develop a clear picture – of your career and lifestyle needs, to track the internal changes that reflect fundamental shifts in personal needs and values.
3) Accurately benchmark your skills – against the best. Use professional networks, attend professional meetings.
4) Form contingency plans – to cover the widest range of potential career

changes, best case and worst case, maintaining professional networks, tracking emerging job opportunities and keeping résumé updated.

5) Develop your portable skills – rather than solely the contextual knowledge of the workings of your own organization.

There are four associated key survival skills

1) Environmental scanning – tap into computer and personal networks, to continually benchmark your skills, prevent their technological obsolescence, gauge the current market value of your skills, identify potential employers and fast-breaking employment opportunities.
2) Portable skills – be able to use standard financial software, project management, total quality improvement tools. These may be particularly important in teacher development.
3) Self-management – manage your own work alone, or be management-coached or work in a self-directed work team.
4) Communication skills – face-to-face and written communication tools, increasingly essential in geographically dispersed and culturally diverse jobs, and in high-stress time-limited situations.

| Today's career planners | Tomorrow's career strategists |
| --- | --- |
| Assume stable, fixed career paths | View career paths as fragmented and subject to change |
| Equate career success with trophy collecting | Equate career success with personal satisfaction |
| Focus on fixed long-term goals | Focus on multiple short-term objectives |
| Create a plan that is linear | Develop a plan multidimensionally, clustered around several objectives that fulfil career needs at a particular point in one's life |
| Believe that goals are age-dependent | Believe that goals are independent of age |
| Develop a plan that is rigid, with goals developed early and never re-examined | Create a plan that is flexible, with goals that are developed early and continually reassessed and contingency planning regarded as essential |
| Track progress through external career | Track progress by the degree to which career decisions markers satisfy personal needs |
| Assume that the organization that they work for will chart their career direction | Assume they will have to chart their own career direction, because they cannot rely on the organization they work for to do it for them. |

*Are you a career planner or a career strategist?*

## REFERENCES

Arnold, J. (1997) *Managing Careers into the 21st Century*, London: Paul Chapman Publishing.

Barner, R. (1994) 'The new career strategist: career management for the year 2000 and beyond', *The Futurist*, September–October, pp. 8–14.

Erikson, E.H. (1980) *Identity and the Life Cycle: A Reissue*, New York, NY: W.W. Norton.

Institution of Mechanical Engineers (1998) documentation about CPD.

Kanter, R.M. (1989), *When Giants Learn to Dance*, New York, NY: Simon and Schuster.

Robertson, S.L. and Rousseau, D.M. (1994) 'Violating the psychological contract: not the exception but the norm', *Journal of Organizational Behavior*, 15, pp. 245–59.

Sarch, Y. (1992) *How to be Headhunted*, Random House Business Books.

Sarch, Y. (1998) 'Future perfect', in a series: The Science of Success, *Observer* (undated).

Super, D.E. (1990) 'Career and life development', in D. Brown and L. Brooks (eds), *Career Choice and Development*, 2nd edition, San Francisco, CA: Jossey-Bass.

Thody, A. (1993) *Developing Your Career in Education Management*, London: Longman.

UK Inter-Professional Group (1995) *Annual Report, 1995*, UK Inter-Professional Group.

Watkins, J. and Drury, L. (1994) *Positioning for the Unknown*, Bristol: University of Bristol.

# 10

## Training, Coaching and Mentoring

### THE NEW TRAINING CONTEXT

People learn and develop through training, coaching and mentoring. Sloman (2000), Director of Management, Education and Training at Ernst & Young, asserts that it is time for 'Grasping the new opportunities for training'. This reappraisal of training requires the identification of training needs, the design and delivery of training activity and post-training evaluation and reinforcement. Training in schools, only part of continuing professional development (CPD), should be fully integrated into the management processes. The preparation and promotion of the training strategy and its expression as a plan is a key task. The training culture, linked to performance management must be identified, articulated, managed and monitored by the CPD manager, who needs the ability to influence, strategic awareness, the consultancy skill of effective diagnosis, and technical expertise about online learning.

- Learning need – should drive the whole process but new business models drive a new agenda and create new training needs. Identifying training needs becomes more critical.
- Platform – the new technology (Internet/intranet/web) offers an exciting platform, particularly when used in conjunction with course-based training and experiential learning.
- Learning support – must be supplied appropriately. It will be affected by both learning needs and technology. New technology will drive needs. Appropriate provision of learning support is the responsibility of the learning and development professional.

*Is training planned rigorously in your school?*

Simmons (2000) defined benchmarking, as the practice of being humble enough to admit others are better, and being wise enough to learn from them. This will include benchmarking any high-performance tool, technique or process which helps you achieve business objectives by solving problems, creating opportunities or improving business results. This can be achieved by what appears to be a simple process of:

1) Learning about your own practices.

2) Learning from the best practice of others.
3) Making changes to meet or beat the best in the world.

## COACHING AND MENTORING

Coaching is impacting profoundly on the education service. Coaching is performance focused and performer centred. Executive coaching for school leaders could be based on the models of excellence developed by Hay McBer, located on the website of the NCSL (www.ncsl.org.uk). Coaching is a potent system for enhancing personal development Your personal coach will ask searching questions that others may be unwilling or unable to ask. Life coaching takes a broader perspective in that it focuses on losing what you no longer need, focusing on what you do want, and successfully achieving these in a broader context than the school. Coaches carry out for individuals a similar role to management consultants for the whole business. They provide solutions to problems and act as agents of change, but only the individual can make things happen. Coaches also benefit from having help in clarifying what they want from life and how to set and achieve realistic goals. Having a life coach is like having a personal management consultant. Executive coaching might be defined as helping professional people to reflect upon their work in rigorous ways and to establish new patterns of behaviours.

*Do you formally use a coach in any part of your life?*

## COACHING, COUNSELLING AND MENTORING

Coaching may start with the coach demonstrating the task, the trainee practising the task, and the coach giving feedback and reviewing progress. Coaches may be less competent at performance than the people they are coaching. A competency is defined as knowledge, skills and attitudes, all manifested in behaviour. Coaching is different from counselling which is problem based. Coaching is preparing for future opportunities. Training and mentoring are also different from coaching. You may well be in a coaching role part of the time, and therefore need the skills of a coach – understanding the use of body language, active listening, questioning skills, building rapport, building trust, being non-judgemental, being candid and challenging, being able to work from other people's agendas and giving encouragement and support.

The distinctions between coaching and mentoring allow for a range of interpretation. Coaching is about improving skills and knowledge for people who want to improve their game; mentoring is about the preparation for future change. Counselling is very different and an area which is not easily directly aligned to work; it is about social context, removing barriers and looking backwards to childhood traumas to get to the negative aspects of personality. Psychotherapy is about trying to solve existing problems. Coaching assumes you are well but could be even better. In their brochure, *The School of Coaching*, The Industrial Society definition of coaching is 'The art of facilitating the performance, learning and development of another'. Mentoring has associations with the older and wiser supporting the development of the younger and less experienced. A new role for mentors is inducting new staff more quickly, improving the recruitment and retention of key people, identifying high-potential managers more effectively and identifying their key competencies. Encouraging diversity, improving communications, leadership development and succession planning are all elements of this. The mentor brings experience, perspective and distance, has a long-term relationship and bridges the gap between individual learning and corporate learning.

*How are coaching and mentoring understood in your school? How are you involved in coaching and/or mentoring?*

## COACHING

Executive coaching is helping professional people reflect upon their work in a frank and rigorous way to establish new patterns of behaviour as a consequence (Caplan, 2003). The qualities of a coach as consultant require her/him to be a good listener; capable of handling sensitively and neutrally both personal and professional issues; experience; the capacity to see the world through another's eyes; the ability to change without threat. Coaching supports the authorship of self-development since the purpose of coaching is to help precipitate and support changes in practice that benefit the individual and the organization. The ideal outcome is for an individual to become a reflective, evidence-based practitioner who will continuously evaluate and develop his or her working practices. Kinlaw (1999) provides another definition: 'Coaching is a mutual conversation between manager and employee that follows a predictable process and leads to a superior performance, commitment to sustained improvement, and positive relationships.'

A leader as coach enables a person to perform at their best and brings out the best of their ideas and achievements. Leaders as coaches develop and articulate what the organization is trying to do, create environments where employees believe in themselves, determine what needs doing, then do it. They know they cannot solve all problems so delegate real strategic power, authority and responsibility. The role is to unleash initiative by 'controlling' conceptually not procedurally. Coaching can be of teams in an environment where people work in self-managed teams that identify and solve problems on their own.

## LIFE COACHING

Life coaching is the psychological equivalent of a personal fitness trainer. Coaching is the facilitation and development of personal qualities. One-to-one life coaching allows focus on synergistic and complementary intra-personal issues at a far deeper level.

Life coaching for executives is about how to:

- achieve more in less time, become more focused and effective;
- possess greater self-confidence and self-esteem;
- become more energized, committed, motivated and better team players;
- stay on track with their vision, objectives and goals;
- become inspired communicators and develop better relationships;

- solve problems quickly, think more creatively and get breakthrough results;
- have a greater sense of personal control and therefore be less stressed, more aware;
- adopt a more positive attitude and outlook, making permanent shifts and changes;
- achieve more balance and fulfilment in their life.

### Ten commandments of coaching

Holt (2000), on the other hand, concentrates on coaching for managers:

1) Stop just managing – coaching is the key to success in today's organizations.
2) Coaching means helping others to help themselves.
3) Confidentiality is the key – lose their trust and 'the game is over'.
4) Establishing rapport is an absolutely essential coaching skill.
5) There is no right way to coach – different people and different situations require different approaches.
6) Coaching can also be very effective upwards and sideways in an organization.
7) In times of personal or organizational turbulence, coaching can be an absolute godsend.
8) To become a real leader and to bring out the best in your people, learn the art of coaching.
9) Remember: you need to coach the whole person, not just the employee.
10) Coaching is for (almost) everybody – managers, parents, teachers, you and me.

*Would you consider using a life coach?*

## COACHING FOR ATHLETES AND SCHOOL STAFF

The skills of athletics coaches, who have made the move to business coaches, can be transferred to education. For coaches, winners are made not born and the coach's role is to deliver customer-built performance development so that athletes perform better. If teachers can develop the skills of outstanding coaches with their pupils the learning in the classroom will be greatly enhanced. This applies when we are talking about those developing skills and the culture within education. The coach improves performance both in terms of results and development, the double vision of the dream and the milestone. For coaches the role is to plan back from the dream, 'to provide wings to fly and roots to grow'. In this context it is worth considering the role of team leader in the new performance management model and, though this person may not always carry out a wider coaching role, the roles of goal-setting and objective-setting need to be aligned.

The key behaviours for the coach include accepting personal ownership for seeking the opportunity to make the winning difference, taking responsible risks in deciding what to do with the behaviours, acting effectively and efficiently and learning from experience and share it (Kalinauckas and King, 1994). Success is a combination of talent and motivation. In this context motivation is defined as consisting of two dimensions. Intensity is about how activated, how energized the performer is and how much effort is being put in. Direction is about focus. Extrinsic motivation loses its power of reinforcement. The more rewards a person has the less need there is for the same type of reward. Those who are intrinsically motivated have an inner striving to be competent and self-determining and to master the task and be successful. They are driven by inner pride.

McNab (2000), Scottish triple jump record holder for six years, for 11 years Scottish National Athletics coach, and script consultant and technical adviser for the film *Chariots of Fire*, asserts that coaching admits no limit to human performance. He identified good coaches as follows:

- They are success driven.
- They are highly orderly, organized men and women who prefer to plan ahead.
- They tend to be warm and outgoing.
- They have finely developed consciences and are in tune with appropriate values in their culture.
- They are open, trusting men and women.
- They score high on leadership qualities.
- They are dominant take-charge types.
- They are prone to blame themselves and to accept blame.
- They exhibit high levels of psychological endurance.
- They are usually mature emotionally and face reality in a direct manner.
- They feel free to express natural aggressive tendencies in a manner appropriate to their role.

McNab suggests that the media emphasis on the aggressive coach is unbalanced. There are four styles he recognizes:

- Director – who tells performers what to do, which is most appropriate in the early stages of learning.
- Coach – who sets the priorities but uses a flexible approach which takes account of the performer's input based on experience.
- Counsellor – for a performer with considerable experience and the coach sets the general outline, but the performer has considerable flexibility in implementation.
- Facilitator – for a performer who has considerable self-knowledge and takes more and more responsibility for deciding priorities.

A good coach may well have one of these as a preferred style but can sustain working in all four as long as required, and can encourage those they are training to move back into an earlier phase when it is necessary in new circumstances. An effective coach will say what needs to be heard not what she/he needs to say. Coaching bridges the gap between aspiration and achievement. In business it helps employees to progress through induction and inclusion to performance, by identifying knowledge and skill needs. Coaching makes the difference because it pulls answers from people rather than pushing information into them. It helps people to articulate and to realize their personal visions. Given the situation in education, if coaching leaves people feeling positive about an organization that has invested in them and helps them improve their personal organization, it should also help reduce the loss of teachers from the profession. Since coaching is about change it facilitates performers through the process of change.

*How do you respond to these definitions of coaching? Are you developing your skills as a coach?*

## THE CHARACTERISTICS OF COACHING

There are various fallacies about coaching according to Cunningham (1998):

- Coaching is carried out only by special people called coaches – the implication is that coaching skills need to be developed in all.
- Coaching only applies to one-to-one work – effective team coaches are able to assist teams to become teams.
- Coaching is all one thing – coaches now focus on the particular needs of individuals, on real performance improvement.
- Coaching is about adding new knowledge and skills to someone – time management is an example where people often have the training but habits which undermine their commitment to change. Coaching can be about ingraining a new habit.
- If the coach strays outside simple instruction in knowledge and skills, they are in danger of getting into psychotherapy – listening and understanding what is really concerning a person and offering support is not straying into psychotherapy. Good managers give encouragement, and skilled coaches enable people to learn how to learn despite bad managers.
- Coaches need to be expert in something in order to coach – coaching is about helping people set sensible learning goals and in assisting them in finding resources to meet them.
- Excellent coaches are born not made – coaching is about developing a new mindset, particularly for those who already have the skills. Any development programme for coaches must be carried out in a coaching style and by allowing the participants to drive the process.
- Coaching is vertical – vertical coaching is less practicable in de-layered organizations. Horizontal peer coaching and upwards coaching in new skill areas may be complemented by learning groups where co-workers have an objective to coach each other in relevant skills.
- Coaching has to be face-to-face – face-to face coaching is the obvious way. Phone and e-mail can provide additional means which may be necessary in view of new communication technologies particularly within virtual teams.
- Coaching is about fixing immediate performance problems – this appears to imply coaching is remedial and for those who are failing. Modern sports players of exceptional ability still use their coaches who are employed to help them take a strategic approach to learning, which can, in the short term, result in a lowering of performance.

Coaches require the integrity which comes from asking for feedback on performance in the coaching role and responding to it, and a willingness to share their own successes and failures. All managers learn by introspection but for coaches it is a central part of the role (Kalinauckas and King, 1994). There is a need for flexibility, since any coach has a limited range of options in their portfolio of skills, and needs a certain humility about their own limitations. The core skills of coaches are mental (the capacity for rigorous observation and analysis of performance, and the skills to structure the coaching process) and interpersonal (questioning, listening, giving and receiving feedback, communication and motivating). A coach is an enabler rather than someone who has answers and has the capacity to develop the learner beyond the limits of a coach's personal knowledge and experience. This, arguably, is central to the motivation of the coach who is frequently working with people whose skills in the area they are being coached in have already outstripped the actual performance of the coach, but who need the coach's expertise to achieve even higher levels of performance. There is now a British Coaching Academy, which might be a source of recommendations should you require a coach, though personal recommendation is normally the best way to find your coach. However, these skills are not yet widely recognized and available within the education service though coaching is widely used.

*Is coaching given sufficient priority in the education service?*

## PEER COACHING

Peer coaching which is more collegial is, in principle, more professional. It is a potent way of collaborative working to ensure co-operative professional development. The fundamental purpose of peer coaching for teachers is to improve teaching and learning by encouraging teachers to work together as colleagues. Many problems encountered by the teacher in the classroom can be resolved if the teacher changes his or her behaviour in positive ways. A firm bond of trust must be established between peer coaches if meaningful improvement is to take place. Those engaged in peer coaching need to be knowledgeable about the cognitive aspects of teaching and to recognize the distinct nature of peer coaching in relationship to appraisal and performance management. Sufficient resources, including time, need to be made available. Peer coaching may not be an appropriate tool for use with all teachers, and it can be effective for headteachers.

## BEING COACHED

Coaching for higher performance requires the commitment of those being coached. The skills needed include:

- assertiveness – a need to have clear views about what it is you want to learn;
- taking initiatives – a willingness to actively seek out the coach;
- openness and honesty – telling the coach the reasons for not completing a task successfully;

- asking for feedback and suggestions – positively seeking feedback;
- networking – developing supportive relationships;
- clarifying objectives – as the focus changes;
- taking responsibility – for your own learning.

*How effectively are you able to learn from being coached?*

## MENTORING

Mentoring relates to guiding, counselling, coaching and sponsorship based on experience, perspective and distance. It is a relationship rather than an activity. The advantage of a mentor has been the greater breadth of vision, specific knowledge and wisdom that they can often bring to support teachers at the start of their careers. There has not always been high-quality training in mentoring because there has been the assumption that the highly skilled, who may well have been trained on techniques such as questioning styles, time management and working together on teaching techniques, may not have had as much focus on the emotional side and may not be aware of the true potential of the task. The enormous loss of teachers from the profession in the first three years may be a result of inadequate emotional mentoring support. Where mentors have the dual role of providing professional advice and emotional support, mentoring and coaching may need to be handled by different people. Team leaders may not make the best mentors. Such relationships might be better handled by someone who would not normally directly influence the mentee. If the objective of the mentoring programme in school is about changing the mentee's behaviours as part of a culture change programme, this will be different from if the focus is to improve the performance, develop their skills or improve their long-term career development. If the focus is on developing the skills of existing high performers or technical specialists, external mentors may be more appropriate. The mentor, almost by definition, has greater knowledge and experience, is a better performer within the areas being developed and has the ability to transfer those skills.

British Aerospace has mentors in senior positions, often on different sites, who have no direct managerial responsibility for graduate trainees, but have a strategic overview of careers in the company and the company's development. The 400 graduates recruited each year are mentored by one of the top 1,500 managers in the business. At each of the three one-week training modules for graduates in their two-year induction period mentoring is integrated into each module. The first shows the graduates what they can expect from their mentors but underlines their personal responsibility for driving the relationship. The second reviews progress and relates mentoring to personal development, while the final module focuses on career management and the role mentoring could play in the future. This level of strategic planning does not occur in the education service. The individual teacher needs to make coherent the relationships between any mentor they may have, the team leader and coach. The mentor will take a long-term strategic perspective of the needs of the individual within the service.

The emergent role for mentoring might be:

- inducting new staff more quickly;
- improving recruitment and retention of key people;
- identifying high-potential managers more effectively;
- identifying key competencies;
- encouraging diversity;
- improving communications;
- cost-effective development.

## COACHING WOMEN

There is a particular argument for the increased use of mentoring in women's development. Mentoring accelerates women's career progression, and in the USA has led to greater job success and satisfaction. Women do face different problems from men in such relationships. There can be accusations of tokenism, stereotyping and lack of access to information and influencing networks. Mentors are often crucial in introducing women to the power structures of organizations. Mentors and female mentees may have to handle gossip and jealousies. The skill and quality of the mentor are more important for women than the gender of the mentor, though some women prefer a woman mentor. It is important that the mentor believes in the potential of the female mentee to contribute and makes the commitment to invest the necessary time to develop her, and has the skills, experience and knowledge to develop her potential. This requires self- awareness – and awareness of how her or his style and behaviours have an impact – as well as insight into the style and behaviour of the mentee.

Mentoring has focused on the early part of a teacher's career and has been about ensuring satisfactory classroom performance, and learning how to improve classroom performance. This part is a prerequisite for a career. These mentors need:

- knowledge and understanding required to facilitate someone learning to become a teacher;
- understanding classrooms, learning and the role of the teacher;
- understanding how teachers learn about classrooms;
- understanding how one adult may help another learn;
- understanding the non-classroom aspects of a teacher's role;
- understanding the concerns and experiences of beginner teachers.

If the process is carried out within a school, it is better carried through by senior management. It is about creating new model leaders. The model above suggests that there is a clear rationale for the use of skilful mentors who have been identified provided the aims of mentoring are clear. However this is carried out it is important to make the mechanisms and structure clear and to gain top management commitment. Mentoring does not create a learning organization but it does contribute to it. It creates relationships which are often demanding and challenging, but it may provide the essential support for people who may find themselves more isolated in organizations than before.

*How effective are mentoring processes in your school?*

## FEEDBACK

Feedback on performance to reinforce success and correct mistakes is central to all these processes. The skills of feedback are required of team leaders, coaches and mentors. The basic guidance below applies to all these roles though there will be particular emphases. It might be argued that it also applies in all contexts from informal daily contacts to the formal performance appraisal interview.

- Be specific – provide evidence of any general conclusions by referring to actual events.
- Be constructive – if faults need to be discussed, concentrate on the lessons to be learned and on ways of improving.
- Avoid abstract comments about personality or attitude – concentrate on behaviour and the specific effects of good or poor performance, and on practical objectives for improvement or development.
- In the annual appraisal – do not attempt too much, too quickly. Highlight the key points. If there are many issues to discuss, consider having more than one meeting. Much of this should have been dealt with during the previous year.
- Encourage the teacher to examine and assess her/his own performance – feedback is more than simply telling.
- Avoid being drawn into an argument – discuss the reason for any difference in opinion rather than just disputing the teacher's views.
- Do not play the amateur psychologist – avoid the temptation to offer 'helpful' suggestions about underlying psychological reasons for certain behaviour.
- If change is needed – explain why. Help the teacher to work out an action plan.
- Be prepared to change your own approach and views – learn from the teacher's perception of your performance in whichever role you are playing.
- Remain available for further advice – encourage the teacher to seek feedback rather than fear possible criticism.

*How effectively do you give feedback? How effectively is feedback given to you?*

## REFERENCES

Caplan, J. (2003) *Coaching for the Future*, London: CIPD.

Cunningham, I. (1998) 'Coaching skills: a practical workshop', IPD HRD conference presentation.

Holt, P. (2000) *Coaching for Growth*, Dublin: Oak Tree Press.

Kalinauckas, P. and King, H. (1994) *Coaching: Realising the Potential*, London: IPD.

Kinlaw, D.C. (1989) *Coaching for Commitment*, San francisco, CA: Pfeiffer.

McNab, T. (2000) 'Coaching skills', IPD HRD conference presentation.

Simmons, C. (2000) 'What's best in training', IPD HRD conference presentation.

Sloman, M. (2000) 'Grasping the new opportunities for training', IPD HRD conference presentation.

# 11

## Interpersonal Skills, Decision-Making and Team Learning

### TEAMWORKING

Teamworking involves a fundamental change in the way people work. The use of team leaders for the new performance management model in schools may actually inhibit the development of teams because it concentrates on team leaders working with individuals, not as leaders of teams. Team-based organizations with the associated de-layering would require only three levels for all staff in a large secondary school. Teamworking is proving effective in some change situations when the new team leader role is very different from that of a manager, or even the traditional head of department. The team leader has a specific task to do and is then encouraged to work with an autonomous team. This is the philosophy behind the DVD, which the National College for School Leadership (NCSL) planned to make available to 1,000 headteachers in 2002 and which recognizes teams as understood in the wider organizational world.

There are five elements of interpersonal competence in interpersonal relationships between individuals and within teams. These include the following capacities:

- to receive and send information and feelings correctly;
- to evoke the expression of feeling;
- to process information and feelings reliably and creatively;
- to implement a course of action;
- to learn in each of the above areas.

All these capacities can be learned and they are more complex to apply in a team with many relationships.

West-Burnham (1992) confirms that teams need to be understood in this wider context.

- A team is a quality group and quality programmes depend on effective teamwork.
- Teams in schools are often teams in name only.
- Effective teams display nine key characteristics (see below).
- Clear values, pride and appropriate leadership are prerequisites to effective team working.

107

- Teams cannot operate without a clear task, regular feedback and review, and openness and candour.
- Team processes involve lateral communication, collaborative decision-making and outcomes in terms of action.
- Effective teams balance task and process.
- Team-building requires awareness of the stages of team development and the factors influencing individual behaviour.
- Team development involves seeing learning as a crucial component of team activity.
- Teamwork requires a range of generic skills.
- Quality circles are not an alternative to teams but provide an alternative perspective.
- Effective teams may well mature into self-managing teams with significant implications for roles and school structures.

The key characteristics West-Burnham presents are:

1) Explicit and shared values.
2) Situational leadership.
3) Pride in the team.
4) Clear task.
5) Feedback and review.
6) Openness and candour.
7) Lateral communication.
8) Collaborative decision-making.
9) Emphasis on action.

*Given the definition above, does your school work through teams? What is the role of team leader in your school?*

## MANAGEMENT TEAMS: WHY THEY SUCCEED OR FAIL

There is the complementary argument (Belbin, 1981) that in successful teams the individuals need to fulfil nine defined roles, and that a successful team comes from building roles around the group members' primary and secondary roles. The Belbin model has been widely used in schools to explore the characteristics of individuals and teams. What there has been rather less of is the strategic planning to build on the characteristic strengths and to plan their complementary use. The caricature below, a development of an approach used in business, assumes that the people are simply manifestations of the role, but contains sufficient challenge to deserve consideration.

*You could consider how you respond to the description of these roles. Is it helpful or destructive?*

1) Plant – creative, imaginative, unorthodox. Solves difficult problems. Also impa-

tient, hopeless at communicating and should be allowed nowhere near people management. We have all met one. Right now he or she is probably your boss.

2) Resource instigator – extrovert, enthusiastic, communicative. Inspires every-one, spreads the word, develops contacts. Then, once the project is under way, quickly loses interest. Better known as the office 'bullshitter'.

3) Co-ordinator – mature, confident, trusting. Perhaps not the cleverest or most creative member of the team, but good at clarifying goals and promoting deci-sion-making. Probably the most natural chairperson, even if they are currently making the tea.

4) Shaper – dynamic, outgoing, highly-strung. Challenges, pressurizes and finds ways round obstacles, but is also prone to bursts of temper. The one who flings their computer out of the window after failing to access e-mails.

5) Monitor evaluator – sober, strategic, discerning. Lacking drive and the ability to inspire, currently more likely than not dismissed as the office carpet – there simply to be trodden on.

6) Teamworker – mild and accommodating but indecisive in crunch situations. Every team needs its drones, as vital as getting the task done as the high-flyers and creative brains. Just do not go out for a drink after work with one.

7) Implementer – disciplined, reliable, conservative. Turns ideas into practical action. But watch out – has a tendency to be inflexible and needs persuading of an idea's validity before proceeding. Has been sitting in the corner opposite bringing the same sandwiches for the past century or so.

8) Completer – painstaking worrier, who searches out errors and omissions. Can be breathtakingly pedantic, but someone has to scour the small print. Think nerd, think clerk, think the last person in the office you can imagine ever having achieved anything. But as they say, God is in the detail.

9) Specialist – the equivalent of the goal-kicker in American football, brought in on a short-term basis to provide specific skills in rare supply. So single-minded and narrow in outlook they can only be tolerated in short bursts. So there is a point to the office bore who tells you exactly what route to take home every day.

*The Belbin questionnaire is widely available including in the book referenced. It may be helpful to use it with your team to explore strengths and roles.*

In Chapter 2 there was a discussion of FIRO-B as it applies to individuals. It can also be applied to teams. There are a number of models of group development. In FIRO-B the inclusion phase includes the selection of team members, team size and defining the boundaries. The control phase is about sharing out the work, expert-ise, leadership and participation. The affection phase is about personal feedback and support, building trust so that criticism is not threatening. On successful com-pletion of the three stages, individuals move from being a group to becoming a team. Peak performance occurs when inclusion and control issues are fully resolved.

## TEAM-BASED REWARDS

Team-based rewards are payments or non-financial incentives provided to members of established teams and linked to the performance of the group. This is one element of reward strategy or performance-related pay which has not been explored in the education service, partly because teams in schools are not teams as defined above. Ministers are now (2003) starting to explore team rewards. Rewards are shared among members according to formula, or an ad hoc basis for exceptional achievements. If individual performance pay is considered inappropriate for teachers because teaching is team-based, then team-based might be a useful addition. Financial rewards for individuals are partially determined by assessments of their contribution to the team. School Performance Awards, payments to schools to be shared between staff, may be conceived of as focusing on the staff as a team.

The link into team pay works best if teams

- stand alone as a performing unit for which clear targets and standards can be agreed;
- have a considerable degree of autonomy – team pay is likely to be most effective in teams that are, to a large degree, self-managed operations;
- are composed of people whose work is interdependent and where it is acknowledged by members that the team will only deliver if they work well together and share the responsibility for success;
- are stable, where members are used to working with one another, know what is expected of them to be fellow team members and know where they stand in the regard of their colleagues;
- are mature, where teams are well established, used to working flexibly to meet targets and capable of making good use of the complementary skills of their members;
- are composed of individuals who are flexible, multi-skilled and good team players, while still being capable of expressing a different point of view and carrying that point if it is for the good of the team.

This may be why they are inappropriate for schools.

*Given the extended definition above do you work in a team?*

Butcher and Bailey (2000) suggest that what they perceive as the current overemphasis on the importance of teams is being reduced because teams are underperforming, because they are seen as ends not means. The assumption that all are fully committed, are present when decisions are taken, and are all open and working closely together is naive. Teamwork in the business world, they suggest, is too often simply about team meetings.

The solutions of the managers they surveyed to make teams genuinely work was:

- give 'real teams' that nurture change and innovation the space and resources to grow;
- challenge the way teams are talked about, deployed and developed;
- ensure that teams have clear purposes;
- create and develop teams with their outputs and operating circumstances in mind;
- track, review, measure and reward team and individual performance, not activity;

- create a culture to facilitate the high performance of different teams;
- communicate strategic priorities, encourage individual accountability and promote human resource (HR) policies that reflect a selective approach to teams and teamwork;
- become a role model of 'performance focused teamworking'.

*How important are teams in achieving school improvement in your school?*

## DECISION-MAKING

All those in leadership roles and all in schools need to make formal decisions as well as the many professional practice decisions that are made daily. In order to achieve this:

- both headteachers and subject leaders need to be able to collect and weigh evidence, make judgements and take decisions;
- they need to be able to analyse, understand and interpret relevant information and data;
- they need to think creatively and imaginatively to anticipate and solve problems and identify opportunities for development;
- they need to demonstrate good judgement, knowing when to make decisions personally, when to consult with others and, for those in middle management positions, what are the limits of their responsibility.

Decisions need to be made in different ways appropriate to the circumstances:

- by the headteacher/subject leader alone;
- through a consultative process;
- through a team or group process;
- by staff with delegated responsibility.

The problem or situation should clarify which method is most appropriate. There is no one way which is always suitable. Decision-making through a team or group process is arguably more complex than other means. Decisions do need to be made and it should be clear who will implement them. The requirement for acceptance of, and gaining high-quality commitment to, the decision from those who may not be involved in decision-making is central to determining which process is appropriate. The best way will depend on the importance of the quality of the decision and the extent to which the headteacher/subject leader has the information or expertise to make it on her/his own. More important it will depend on the extent to which others, collectively, have the necessary information to generate a better quality solution, the extent to which the problem is structured and the extent to which their acceptance and commitment is critical to effective implementation. Decisions about the curriculum in a school or subject area may clearly require a whole-staff decision or support for a decision, though the quality of support from a large teaching and support staff, will be difficult to judge.

For other decisions it will depend how likely it is that the headteacher/subject leader's decision will be accepted positively because it is efficient to make it this way. With more complex issues it will depend on the extent to which others are committed to the school goals as represented in the objectives and how explicitly the problem is stated. This might apply to equal opportunities policy development. Equally important, the extent to which staff are likely to be in disagreement over alternative solution needs to be known.

For major decisions it is important to understand the school culture, and to recognize that the decision-making process must be appropriate for the particular school. In primary schools there can more frequently be whole-staff decision making. In secondary schools the process is often more complex.

*How are different decisions made in your school? Are the processes acceptable to the staff?*

## AUTOCRATIC, CONSULTATIVE, GROUP OR DELEGATED DECISIONS

- When an *individual autocratic decision* is appropriate the headteacher/subject leader will solve the problem or make the decision her or himself using information already available, or obtained from others. The language of autocracy seems inappropriate in schools but headteachers/subject leaders have to make decisions firmly and quickly when appropriate.
- After *consultation* the decision will be made after sharing the problem with individuals and getting ideas or suggestions, or obtaining collective ideas or suggestions within a group. The headteacher/subject leader still makes a decision after the consultative process.
- For *team or group decisions*, the group generates and evaluates alternative solutions and searches for consensus. The headteacher/subject leader as chair should not influence the group to accept her/his solution. Any solution implemented will have the support of the group.
- *Negotiated decisions* require different skills because the power relationship is different and usually two groups, or their representatives, attempt to reach an agreement. Within schools this normally occurs if the headteacher negotiates with staff representatives. The negotiation/consultation distinction needs to be recognized.

If the problem or decision is delegated, the headteacher/subject leader will provide the framework, but the person to whom the decision is delegated is responsible. The headteacher/subject leader may ask to be informed of the solution or process. It is important to clarify whether a decision-making responsibility has been fully delegated. It will be important for the headteacher/subject leader to know how the decision is to be made.

*Are decisions made by the right people in the right way in your school?*

## POWER, AUTHORITY AND INFLUENCE

School staffs may not respond positively to the language of power, authority and influence, but in the decision-making process it is important to distinguish these, and to understand them in the context of the culture of school leadership. In the process of policy formulation and decision-making in schools, power is a resource, authority is legitimate and recognized power, and influencing is a personal skill and part of the leadership process. These may be mutually supportive.

Since headteachers/subject leaders exercise power, it is helpful to distinguish between four forms of power:

- resource power (the power to insist that things happen, coercive);
- position power (power from the role);
- expert power (power from knowledge, expertise and wisdom);
- personal power (power from personality or charisma).

You need to understand how you are using power or authority when influencing teams. New sources of power and legitimacy are continually emerging in schools, most obviously through the use of information and communications technology, both in planning work and taking decisions about its purpose. As a leader you need to be aware of these.

*How effective are you at decision-making? Evaluate your own power and authority*

## MEETINGS, COMMITTEES AND GROUP DECISION-MAKING

Hardingham (1999) suggests that meetings frequently fail because of inadequate preparation. It is essential to articulate and agree the purpose of the meeting, which is frequently assumed to be of value, particularly in meetings built in as routine. This may lead to confusion and conflict because of the waste of time. The process of the meeting must be designed to achieve the purpose of the meeting. During the meeting it is important to continue to clarify this purpose and how effectively the process and practice is achieving that purpose.

Committees, working parties and planning teams are used particularly in secondary schools because of the size of the staff. The language is important and needs to be agreed within the school, for example committees are often more permanent, working parties have a shorter lifespan with a specific job to do, planning teams are of equals. The reasons for group deliberation and judgement include:

- a fear of too much authority in a single person;
- the representation of interested groups;
- the need for the co-ordination of departments, plans and policies;
- the transmission and sharing of information;
- the consolidation of authority and motivation through participation.

In primary schools it is apparently simpler because all staff can be involved in all decisions more easily. However, this may mean that all staff become involved in all decision-making and this may be an inefficient use of time. The misuse or abuse of meetings and their impact on the scarce commodity of time appears to cause enormous frustration for school staffs.

The disadvantages of group decision-making are

- the high cost in time and money;

- the danger of compromise at the level of the least common denominator;
- indecision;
- a tendency to be self-destructive;
- the splitting of responsibility so nothing gets decided;
- the tyranny of the minority.

In schools, committees, teams or groups are misused if they:

- replace a manager;
- are used for research or study;
- deal with unimportant decisions;
- make decisions beyond the participants' authority;
- are used to consolidate divided authority.

*How effectively does your governing body add value?*

The successful operation of committees requires clear and appropriate authority, size, membership, subject matter, an effective chairperson, minutes which are about action, and cost-effectiveness.

It may be your responsibility to ensure that decisions are taken and implemented. There is a discussion below about the particular skills and characteristics needed for chairing meetings. The failure to take decisions in any circumstances leads to immense frustration. Decisions need to be taken because of the need to improve performance and to ensure higher-quality learning. You will need to recognize that this will possibly involve conflict, the risk of being wrong, being called to account and, at times, a requirement to cope with a bewildering range of facts and alternatives. Managers need to enjoy this responsibility since, possibly because of the culture within the profession, there has tended to be blame for apparently wrong decisions, rather than for inertia. You need to have the courage of your convictions.

A rational decision-making process may be appropriate which involves in outline the process presented below. Clarity is important particularly where the process will be open to question.

- Define the situation.
- Establish criteria.
- Generate alternatives.
- Evaluate and test.
- Select.

This logical process applies to any decision which can be made rationally and needs to be followed rigorously. Attempting to short-circuit the process will lead to unsatisfactory decisions. However this does not mean it need take a long time.

*How effective are meetings, planning teams and committees in your school? How could this be improved?*

## CHAIRING MEETINGS

Headteachers and senior staff, including team leaders, will normally chair meetings though others may be more skilled in this role. The chair needs to recognize the strengths and weaknesses of those attending the meeting, to try and use their strengths and prevent their weaknesses frustrating the purpose. This purpose needs to be clear, the attendance appropriate, the participants prepared, and the use of time carefully planned. The chair needs to generate a high commitment to achieving the purpose, and to the quality of outcome. There needs to be clear responsibility for all actions to be taken afterwards and a mechanism for review. Action points and responsibilities for action need to be recorded.

Four stumbling blocks to successful chairing are:

- The chair should seek ideas rather than give information.
- She/he may be genuinely seeking to solve problems but prevent creativity by the way she/he chairs.
- She/he may use power unwisely. The role outside the meeting, which is the reason they are chairing, may inhibit open proposals.
- She/he may have a high level of antagonism towards ideas different to her/his own.

Holding meetings to make decisions is associated with collegiality and professionalism. It is therefore essential to develop the skill of chairing meetings. Not all chairs are able to recognize what are intended to be helpful responses. The chair may recognize that meetings can be sabotaged by boredom, impatience, hostility, or rivalry, but may not be prepared to deal with these. You should learn to face up to these problems. However, a chair who is exercising all the skills discussed above and is focusing on the processes which enhance the quality and range of contributions according to the skills of those present will reduce the likelihood that these problems will be destructive.

The chair is ideally a servant to the meeting, helping the group to use its intelligence. Rotating the role may prevent an individual becoming too powerful. The chair should avoid competing with group members, listen to all, not permit anyone to be put on the defensive, use every member of the group, keep the energy level high, keep the members understanding what is expected of them, keep her/his eye on the expert, remember that the chair is not permanent and not manipulate the group. This involves working hard at the techniques of chairing.

*How effectively do you chair meetings? How effectively chaired are other meetings that you attend?*

## JUDGEMENT

School leaders need to make judgements about values, about the nature of reality, the environment in which they are operating, and about actions. The first two are more fundamental and important. The higher the level of judgement required the less possible it is to find objective tests to assist. Judgement is a fundamental continuous process, integral to thinking. School leaders need to clarify the rationale for judgements they are making. These may be based on rational decision-making processes or on intuition. For the intuitive creative decisions there is no predictability of the decision; it is unique. The variables are not scientifically predictable. The 'facts' may be limited and not point the way to a solution.

Analytical data may be of little use. There may be several plausible alternatives supported by good arguments. Time may be limited and there is pressure to come up with the right decision. This is the time when you need to be secure in your capacity to exercise judgement. It is also essential that you have created a culture or climate where your colleagues will accept your rationale when this happens.

*How well do you make decisions?*

## PROBLEM-SOLVING AND CREATIVITY

The decision-making process may be rational. Problem-solving often requires different skills. Problems may be less well structured, so the goal is clear but the actions which will lead to solutions less clear. The novelty, complexity and ambiguity of a problem will make decision-making less well structured. Creative problem-solving, which is discussed more fully in Chapter 7, requires high motivation and persistence. The phases of creative problem-solving have similarities to the rational decision-making process:

- preparation – understanding and identifying the problem;
- production – development of different solutions;
- judgement – making the highest quality decision;
- facilitating conditions – exploring the problem situation in different ways, turning a choice situation into a problem situation, separating idea generation and idea evaluation, encouraging conflictual thinking, exploring a wide range of alternatives.

The inhibiting conditions, presented in a different context in the chapter on creativity are:

- perceptual blocks – failure to use all sensory inputs, and a tendency to delimit the problem area too closely;
- cultural blocks – assuming that problem-solving is serious, that reason, numbers and logic are good, and that feeling and intuition are bad;
- environmental blocks – lack of co-operation/trust, an autocratic leader who values only her/his own ideas;
- emotional blocks – fear to make mistakes, inability to tolerate ambiguity, overriding desire for security, lack of access to areas of imagination, lack of challenge;
- intellectual blocks – solving problem using incorrect language – mathematical instead of visual for example – inflexible use of intellectual problem-solving strategies

*How successfully do you solve complex problems? Individually? In meetings/teams?*

## DECISION TRAPS

Russo and Schoemaker (1989) present the ten dangerous decision traps to illustrate what needs to be a possible evaluatory framework to monitor your processes, which applies to both rational decision-making and creative problem-solving approaches:

- plunging in – not thinking through scope and nature of problem;
- frame blindness – solving the wrong problem;
- poor frame control – accepting others' limited or wrong definitions of a problem;
- overconfidence – too sure of one's own judgement and opinions;
- taking shortcuts – failing to research the issues fully;
- being unsystematic – failure to follow a systematic procedure by thinking one 'has' all the information;
- poor group process – failing to manage the group decision-making process, or attending only to the view of certain group members;
- ignoring negative feedback – underestimating evidence that runs counter to prevailing wisdom; failing to acknowledge past mistakes or learn from failures;
- not keeping records – which would track the success or failure of decisions; this, too, impedes learning from past mistakes;
- not auditing decision-making so that all flaws in thinking are avoided.

The first to third of these decision traps are thinking and planning activities, the fourth to sixth personal qualities and the seventh to tenth processing skills. All these need to be incorporated.

*Do you avoid all of these?*

## REFERENCES

Belbin, M. (1981) *Management Teams: Why They Succeed or Fail*, London: Heinemann.

Butcher, D. and Bailey, C. (2000) 'Crewed awakening', *People Management*, 3 August, pp. 35–7.

Hardingham, A. (1999) 'The "Crafted Meeting"', presentation at IPD HRD conference.

Russo J.E. and Schoemaker P.J. (1989) *Decision Traps: The Ten Barriers to Brilliant Decision Making and How to Overcome Them*, London: Doubleday.

West-Burnham, J. (1992) *Managing Quality in Schools*, London: Longman.

# 12

## Leadership Development

There have been too many books and articles written on leadership for those who wish to learn to be leaders. This chapter focuses on how you might characterize and develop your leadership by building on your strengths, and explores some models judged to be of value. The National College for School Leadership (NCSL) is now developing many programmes for leaders with a supporting website at which much information about educational leadership can be accessed (www.ncsl.org.uk). In this chapter the approach is to explore alternatives and different approaches to what might become an NCSL orthodoxy.

The four leadership *myths* presented by two members of the London Business School (Goffee and Jones, 2002) can be considered in the education context. Their argument has been adapted for schools.

1) *Everyone can be a leader*. Not true. Many senior staff do not have the self-knowledge or authenticity for leadership. Many highly talented people are not interested in being leaders. There is more to life than work and more to work than being a leader.
2) *Leaders deliver business results*. Not always. Some well-led schools do not necessarily produce short-term results. Some schools with successful results are not necessarily well led. If results were always a matter of good leadership the best strategy would be to seek people from schools with the best results. Things are not that easy.
3) *People who get to the top are leaders*. Not necessarily. A persistent misconception is that those in leadership positions are leaders. They may have made it to the top because of political acumen. Real leaders are found throughout the school.
4) *Leaders are great coaches*. Rarely. There appears to be an assumption that good leaders ought to be good coaches. This relies on the assumption that a person can both inspire and impart technical skills. It is possible that great leaders may be great coaches but this is only occasionally the case.

Effective leadership is about inspiring and winning commitment. Leadership is more about personal authenticity and at times recognizing personal fundamental flaws which limit leadership capacity. Leaders need energy, a strong sense of direction and clear vision, but there are four more unexpected characteristics.

1) *Leaders reveal their weaknesses.* Leaders reveal their personal weakness showing their humanity, confirming that they are people not simply their roles. This shows how others can help them and builds good teamwork. The reality of these weaknesses is often exposed at work if not revealed first. Large organizations, such as the whole education service, can be regarded as machines for the production of conformity. The current fashion for strong cultures may reinforce the pressure to conform. Rigid performance targets encourage rule-following rather than a willingness to think creatively.

2) *Good leaders rely extensively on their ability to read situations.* They pick up and sense soft data, know when team morale is shaky, when complacency needs challenging. They learn about the motives, attributes and skills of important individuals, knowing where to pick up such knowledge. They read teams, analyse the balance between members, the tensions between tasks and processes and how the team builds its capabilities. They decode the cultural characteristics of schools and the subtle shifts in organizational climate. Those who are not great at organizational sensing will find others to do it. Some have a natural ability but others have improved through systematic training in interpersonal skills. Leaders must continually test their situation-sensing instincts against reality.

3) *Leaders care for their people.* Nothing is more likely to cause cynicism than someone with *apparent* concern for others. Effective leaders do not need training to convince staff that they care. They empathize with the people they lead and care intensely about their work. Genuine care involves personal risk – showing some part of yourself and your most strongly held values about work and how it should be carried out. When people care strongly they are more likely to reveal their true selves, communicating authenticity showing they are doing more than playing a role. Genuine care balances the respect for individuals with the organizational task. Caring may take some detachment, to see the whole picture and take tough decisions.

4) *Stress the differences.* Effective leaders use their differences, personal qualities such as sincerity, creativity, expertise, resilience or loyalty. They can use distinctive and powerful skills they have acquired, technical or social, as leadership assets. Passions differentiate leaders – their compelling missions and deeply held beliefs. Leaders learn which of their attributes are most powerful by interacting with others, but seeking new experiences may not be of value given the limitations of time for reflection. This is a particular issue for women and minority groups. The stereotypical differences attributes may not be those they would choose, and strategies to cope are not always easy. There are costs to both avoiding stereotyping and turning stereotypes to personal advantage. Using differences is a critical leadership skill.

*How do you evaluate your effectiveness as a leader? How do you respond to the models presented above?*

## THE GALLUP ORGANIZATION AND SCHOOL LEADERSHIP

The Gallup Organization has researched 'talented' school leaders and teachers over many years, as part of their consideration of the 'talents' that characterize those who are outstanding leaders and performers in many different contexts (See Chapter 5). Their distinctive development and research process was applied to primary school leadership in England in 1999. The NCSL may have too much invested in the Hay McBer research to use alternatives. The Hay McBer model tends to focus on areas for development, assuming these will be the areas of relative weakness which need to be overcome. The Gallup approach, historically based more substantially on work with leaders and teachers in schools, which concentrates on developing strengths rather than overcoming weaknesses, may represent a healthier approach to leadership growth.

The ideographic results for each headteacher and aspirant headteacher were recorded on the profile illustrated in Figure 12.1. The research process demonstrated that the teachers judged to have very high potential demonstrated skills at the same level, on average, as highly effective headteachers in the themes defined below which were those which characterized the highly effective headteachers. This research would appear to demonstrate that when teachers have had at least five years of teaching experience it is possible to further accelerate their career development to move them into headship, and not to do so may damage their professional growth. You may be one of these teachers.

*As you consider the talents below evaluate for each one the evidence to demonstrate your strengths in these themes.*

The technology has been developed so that it is possible, with a telephone interview of about an hour, to provide those seeking to understand talents that are significant for primary school leadership. A coaching interview to provide feedback on the talents defined below provides a strong basis for leadership development.

| | |
|---|---|
| Mission | A clear belief in the purpose and value of education. At the same time a clear 'lifelong' commitment to education and the teaching profession. These are the headteachers who regularly communicate their particular values and sense of worth. They focus all the school's activities and processes on learning and children. Selecting staff who share a similar commitment is for them one of their primary functions. |
| Responsibility | Headteachers who take psychological ownership for their actions. These are not people who 'pass the buck' but instead take personal responsibility and follow through on commitments and obligations. The responsibility theme enables headteachers to live their own values. With their teachers they convey responsibility by delegating ownership and accountability. They understand that their authority stems from the responsibility they show to other people. |
| Focus | Headteachers with focus possess a long-term plan for their school as well as their career and personal life. They have a natural tendency to plan ahead, frequently anticipating events and developing contingencies in preparation. They are goal-oriented – setting themselves and others clear objectives which they work towards in a consistent and direct fashion. Should they be 'blown off course' they rapidly re-orientate themselves. Generally they are people who are in control of their future. |
| Ideation/Concept | High Concept headteachers are constantly feeding their minds with new ideas. They spend time thinking about new ways of doing things and different possibilities. They like to build linkages and connections between events, ideas and opportunities. At the same time they are likely to stimulate others to think. |

When concept is high and there is insufficient activation, a degree of inertia can be created in a school. Conversely without Concept the Activator may fail to think things through.

| | |
|---|---|
| School awareness | The headteacher's ability to help keep a finger on the pulse of their school through listening to people, teachers and parents. They sense what is going on through their interactions and involvement. At the same time they are supportive of their teachers and though they listen and understand will 'hold the line' over key issues of policy and principle. |
| Communication | Headteachers with the Communication theme have an intrinsic ability to put their thoughts into words. They are great storytellers, able to 'connect' and stimulate a range of audiences from pupils to teachers, parents and governors. At the same time they are effective listeners, understanding the ideas, concerns and points of view of others. |
| Credibility | Such headteachers have a healthy level of self-belief. They are generally proud of their professionalism and success. Similarly they want and need the recognition that goes with that success. However, they also understand that respect and standing in the school community has to be earned and to that extent will lead through example. |
| Achiever | Headteachers with the Achiever theme tend to be busy and active. They have a big personal agenda with some stretching goals which apply both to their personal and professional lives. They measure themselves by the amount of work they get done. Bad days are when things are left incomplete or unattended to. Frequently they will measure their productivity against others. Achievers need focus to gain direction and purpose. |
| Activator | The Activators make things happen. They like to see progress and will move issues and ideas forward to satisfactory conclusions. Naturally competitive, they also like to win and occasionally when faced with problems they will work around them and drive through them. They possess a 'let's do it' attitude. |
| Command | Headteachers with the command theme are naturally assertive people. They experience little difficulty in exerting their influence. When faced with resistance and challenge they can bring extra reserves of determination and energy to bear. In combination with Responsibility the Command theme enables the headteachers to enact their values and principles. They see themselves as leaders not followers. |
| Relator | Headteachers with a natural drive to want to get close to people – both pupils and parents alike. As heads they take people with them due to the quality of individual relationships they create. They understand that youngsters learn easily from teachers they trust and like. Overall they are open, supportive and positive about people. At a personal level they frequently act as coaches and mentors to colleagues and at the same time have people who invest directly in them. |
| Empathy | The ability to read the feelings of another human being – to put themselves in the other person's shoes and to see the world from their perspective. Empathy, not to be confused with sympathy, is found in all great teachers and leaders, enabling them to understand the needs, feelings and ambitions of people, tailoring the response or solution accordingly. |
| Individualized Perception | The rare gift of being able to understand and appreciate the differences between people. In teachers and headteachers the theme manifests itself in an appreciation of the strengths of individuals thereby enabling the headteacher to 'set people up for success'. In teaching situations the individualized learning needs of pupils are focused on and appropriate teaching given. Headteachers strong in this theme attempt to build positive relationships with all children and adults, focusing on their positive qualities and strengths. Individualised Perception and Arranger are highly complementary themes. |
| Developer | A clear sense of satisfaction and pleasure from helping others learn and achieve success. Headteachers with the Developer theme believe they make a difference |

|            | to people's lives. They are free in their praise and encouragement of young people, invest in others and can readily see the connection between teaching and learning. |
|------------|-------------|
| Stimulator | An ability to raise the morale within a school community frequently through humour and personality. The great stimulators know when to inject humour. They can also excite others through their ideas and plans for the future. |
| Discipline | Disciplined headteachers have high levels of personal organization. They present as efficient, thorough and well-ordered people who plan in detail and follow things through to completion. Invariably they will complete tasks ahead of schedules or deadlines. Though they may not like paperwork and administration, they deal with it smoothly and quickly, clearing things so that they can focus on more significant elements of their work. |
| Arranger   | An ability to arrange and orchestrate complex and often conflicting demands – in primary school frequently balancing the needs and demands of pupils, teachers and parents. Key to the Arranger theme is the capacity to juggle resources (people, money, teams) in order to create the optimum conditions for learning to take place. An essential element is the headteacher's ability to play to the strengths of their individual teachers. |

*How do you respond to this profile and theme definitions for a primary school headteacher?*

The Gallup Organization also has a web-based StrengthsFinder™, which again uses the model which builds on strengths. For an individual there will normally be five stronger themes. As can be seen in the example below, where the introductory comments only are presented, this gives some indication of the value of the approach concentrating on the positive. A full report would normally be approximately six times the length. The claims that are made are not excessive 'applying the themes may increase your satisfaction and your productivity'. The idea of signature themes to explore strengths clearly relates to the themes considered above for headteachers. Senior leaders in the education service use the Gallup approach.

From your responses to the StrengthsFinder™ certain patterns have emerged. Out of the 34 themes there are five themes that may be your signature themes. Signature themes are those spontaneous, recurring patterns of behaviours as well as feelings and thoughts that people resonate in expressing and mark their strengths as individuals. Read the listed signature themes and study them to see how they fit your own behaviours. Applying these themes to your life may well increase both your satisfaction and your productivity.

| *Strategic Thinking* | Your Strategic Thinking theme enables you to sort through the clutter and find the best route forward. It is not a skill that can be taught. It is a distinct way of thinking, a special perspective on the world at large. This perspective allows you to see patterns where others simply see complexity. |
|----------------------|-------------|
| *Self Efficacy*      | Self-Efficacy is similar to self-confidence. In the deepest part of you, you have faith in your strengths. You know that you are able – able to take risks, able to meet new challenges, able to stake claims and, most importantly, able to deliver. |
| *Ideation*           | You are fascinated by ideas. What is an idea? An idea is a |

The GALLUP® Profile PRIMARY HEADTEACHER INTERVIEW

| Name | | Town/County | |
|------|--|-------------|--|
| Company | | Date | |
| Interviewer | | ID No | |
| Analyst | | | |

| AN IDEOGRAPHIC STUDY | | | | | |
|----------------------|--------|-------------|---------|----------|--|
| | Themes | Low Evidence | Evident | Strength | |
| PURPOSE | MISSION | | | | |
| | RESPONSIBILITY | | | | |
| DIRECTION | FOCUS | | | | |
| | CONCEPT | | | | |
| | SCHOOL AWARENESS | | | | |
| | COMMUNICATION | | | | |
| MOTIVATION AND AUTHORITY | CREDIBILITY | | | | |
| | ACHIEVER | | | | |
| | ACTIVATOR | | | | |
| | COMMAND | | | | |
| RELATIONSHIPS | RELATOR | | | | |
| | EMPATHY | | | | |
| | INDIVIDUALIZED PERCEPTION | | | | |
| | DEVELOPER | | | | |
| | STIMULATOR | | | | |
| WORKSTYLE | DISCIPLINE | | | | |
| | ARRANGER | | | | |

**Figure 12.1** The Gallup profile and theme definitions

concept, the best explanation of the most events. You are delighted when you discover, beneath the complex surface, an elegantly simple concept to explain why things are the way they are.

| | |
|---|---|
| *Desire* | You want to be seen as very significant in the eyes of other people. In the truest sense of the world you want to be 'recognized'. You want to be heard. You want to stand out. You want to be known. |
| *Activator* | 'When can we start?' This is a recurring question in your life. You are impatient for action. You may concede that analysis has its uses or that debate and discussion can occasionally yield some valuable insights, but deep down you know that only action is real. |

## LEADERSHIP – A HISTORICAL FOCUS

There is a danger in concentrating excessively on the present. Grace (1995) presents a historical focus which puts current leadership orthodoxy in context.

1) *Leadership, class and hierarchy* covers from Victorian values through to the 1940s. School leadership was moral leadership. The cultural, patriarchal and hierarchical features of English society all assisted the rise of the 'headmaster' as school leader, with the role a cultural attribute of his class position. He was characterized by moral energy and a sense of purpose. His secular authority arose from an explicit connection with class hierarchy. The sacred authority was legitimated since all hierarchies were ordained by God. Management was about social control.

2) *School leadership and social democracy* is the theme from the 1940s to the 1970s. This was the time of the near hegemony of professionalism in social, political and cultural life. The professionally expert was an example of meritocratic success, committed to innovation, a modernizer and consultative in operation, a team leader. The 'good' school of the social democratic era was one characterized by harmonious staff relations and humane teacher–pupil relations achieved by the application of sensitive personnel management, the introduction of pastoral care systems and a pedagogic regime which place 'the needs of the child (or young person)' at the centre of the educational or organizational culture. This headmaster (Musgrove, 1971) has a different stereotype.

> He has earned promotion through his reputation as a super-teacher and even because he is famous for a 'system'. He may have written books and addressed professional conferences. He will probably have gained a reputation as a 'progressive and an innovator'. There has been a post-war imperative for aspiring teachers not to uphold traditions but to subvert them. This means in brief that the new head will have opposed streaming, corporal punishment, eleven-plus selection, single-sex education, insulation from parents, the prefect system (unless elective), traditional examinations, didactic or even expository class teaching – and above all, he will have paid special attention to 'group work'. In recent years he will have espoused the teacher-group as well as the pupil-group; he will have been a champion of team-teaching.

3) *Leadership, accountability and the marketplace* covers the 1980s and 1990s, a period of greater state control, decentralization and institutional autonomy. There are traditional academic standards, enterprise education and the development of a competitive market culture. There is a new executive freedom, a new form of management empowerment, allied to the image of managing director. However the market is unprincipled, it allows no moral priorities in its patterns of distribution. Chubb and Moe (1990) state approvingly from the USA: 'Britain has already broken with tradition and moved boldly towards a choice-based system of public education. The whole world is being swept by a realisation that markets have tremendous advantages over central control and bureaucracy.'

For Grace (1995) there are alternative approaches:

> Religious-educational ... traditions give pre-eminence to the spiritual and moral responsibilities of leadership, to notions of vocation in education and to ideas of commitment relatively independent of reward or status. (*Ibid.*, p. 66)

> a feminist reconstruction of the concept of an educational leader is necessary. Such leadership would involve a move away from notions of power and control over others towards a leadership defined as the ability to act with others. Leadership would involve being at the centre of a group rather than at a hierarchical distance from it. (*Ibid.*, p. 61)

## FLAWED LEADERSHIP

Given all this there is a need to come to terms to understand the cynicism about some leaders and leadership. Bogue (1994) strongly expressed the reasons for this:

> There are academic cheerleaders, looking for the parade so they can get in front. They are status fondlers worrying only about the appearance of their calling card. They are information wizards with computer records and electronic mail addresses. There are educational firemen occupied with crises of their own making. They are trivia worshippers checking forms in stock and occupying their time and energy with the minutiae of their unit or campus, enamoured of technique but devoid of vision. They are academic mannequins veneered in status but empty of passion and caring. And there are leadership amateurs attempting to guide a precious enterprise with fluffy and empty notions about the content of their work.

| | |
|---|---|
| a flawed sense of role | a condition of empty vision |
| a contempt for ideas | a condition of empty mind |
| a neglect of constructive values | a condition of empty heart |
| a retreat from servant ideals | a condition of empty spirit |
| a violation of cultural norms | a condition of empty sensitivity |
| a sacrifice of honour | a condition of empty character |

*Reflect on the flawed leaders you know to avoid their weaknesses.*

## THREE EDUCATIONAL LEADERSHIP MODELS

There are three models of educational leadership you could consider.

### Five leadership forces necessary for the creation of effectiveness and excellence (Sergiovanni, 1994)

1) *Technical* – sound management techniques – planning and time management, contingency leadership theories and organizational structures.
2) *Human* – harnessing available social and human resources – improve morale, develop loyalty in subordinates, provide support and improve others' skills.
3) *Educational* – expert professional knowledge and understanding as they relate to 'teaching effectiveness, educational program development and clinical supervision' – these three for competent schooling.
4) *Symbolic* – focusing the attention of others on matters of importance to the school's 'sentiments, expectations, commitments and faith itself', express their vision through words, symbols, and examples ... rising above the daily managerial and structural activities and recognize the importance and significance of what the schools truly value.
5) *Cultural* – articulate school mission and purpose by defining, identifying and supporting the values and beliefs of the school. 'cultural life in the schools is a constructed reality and school principals can play a key role in building that reality'. This constructed reality or culture consists of norms, a shared past, common expectations, meanings and a drive towards a future.

### Strategic leadership (Guthrie, 1990)

For Guthrie, successful modern leaders repeatedly exhibit important characteristics and engage in common activities. These are:

1) *Vision* – possess a vision of what the organization with which they are connected should be like.
2) *Inspiration* – know how to motivate and inspire those with whom they work.
3) *Strategic orientation* – understand the major operational levers which can be employed to control or change an organization's course.
4) *Integrity* – are intensely sensitive to and continually reflect upon the interaction of external environmental conditions and internal organizational dynamics.
5) *Organizational sophistication* – understand the fundamental components of strategic thinking that can be used to guide or alter an organization.

### Four competences of a true leader (Bennis, 1992)

1) *Management of attention*: the communication of an extraordinary focus of commitment which attracts people to the leader.
2) *Management of meaning*: the communication of the leader's vision, making his/her dreams apparent to others and aligning people with them.

3) *Management of trust*: the main determinant of which is reliability and con-stancy.
4) *Management of self*: knowing one's skills and deploying them effectively – without which leaders can do more harm than good.

*How helpful are these different models of leadership for assisting you in defining leadership for yourself for your professional development?*

Cleveland (2002), in a different context, explores leadership as a profession with eight attitudes indispensable to the management of complexity:

1) A lively intellectual curiosity – everything is related to everything else.
2) A genuine interest in what other people think – and why they think that way – which means you have to be at peace with yourself.
3) A feeling of special responsibility for envisioning a future – different from a straight line projection of the present.
4) A hunch that most risks – are there not to be avoided but taken.
5) A mindset that crises are normal – tensions promising, complexity fun.
6) A realization that paranoia – and self-pity – are reserved for those who do not want to be leaders.
7) A sense of personal responsibility – for general outcomes of your effort.
8) A quality I call 'unwarranted optimism' – some more upbeat outcome than from adding up expert advice.

*Do you have these eight attitudes – and how can you develop them further?*

In conclusion I refer to four books created in North America and one from the UK which may be of interest for those seeking a different forms of evidence. Leithwood and Hallinger (2002) have brought together, in the *Second International Handbook of Educational Leadership and Management*, evidence from many of the leading international academics and researchers in the field. Jenlink (2000) edited the yearbook of the National Council of Professors of Educational Administration (NCPEA) entitled *Marching into a New Millennium: Challenges to Educational Leadership*. Kowalski (2001) edited the following yearbook entitled *21st Century Challenges for School Administrators*. These pro-fessors provide a helpful breadth of focus with over 40 papers which are based on evidence from different contexts. Alternately another distinctive USA approach is the use of the created biographical as a means of communicating more effectively the developmental experience. Bolman and Deal (2002) present a successful *Reframing the Path to School Leadership*, following through the first year in post of a school principal and newly appointed teacher. *Handbook of Educational Leadership and Management* (Davies and West-Burnham, 2003) provides a UK-based more academic consideration of leadership. It is important to challenge received wisdom about leadership development.

## REFERENCES

Bennis, W. (1992) *On Becoming a Leader*, London: Addison-Wesley.

Bogue, E.G. (1994) *Leadership by Design*, San Francisco, CA: Jossey-Bass.

Bolman, L.G. and Deal, T.E. (2002) *Reframing the Path to School Leadership*, London: Sage.

Chubb, J. and Moe, T. (1990) *Politics, Markets and America's Schools*, Washington, DC: Brookings Institution.

Cleveland, H. (2002) 'Leadership: the get-it-all-together profession', *The Futurist*, September–October, pp. 42–7.

Davies, B. and West-Burnham, J. (2003) *Handbook of Educational Leadership and Management*, London: Pearson.

Goffee, R. and Jones, G. (2002) 'Mantle of authority, mastering leadership', *Financial Times*, 1 November p. 5–6.

Grace, G. (1995), *School Leadership: Beyond Education Management: An Essay in Policy Scholarship*, London: Falmer.

Guthrie, J.W. (1990) 'Effective educational executives', paper presented to IIP, Manchester.

Jenlink, P.M. (2000) *Marching into a New Millennium: Challenges to Educational Leadership*, Folkestone: Scarecrow Press.

Kowalski, T.J. (ed.) (2001) *21st Century Challenges for School Administrators*, Folkestone: Scarecrow Press.

Leithwood, K. and Hallinger, P (2002) *Second International Handbook of Educational Leadership and Administration*, Dordrecht: Kluwer Academic.

Musgrove, F. (1971) *Patterns of Power and Authority in English Education*, London: Methuen.

Sergiovanni, T. (1994) *Moral Leadership: Getting to the Heart of School Improvement*, San Francisco.CA: Jossey-Bass.

# 13

## Performance Management

### POLICY DEVELOPMENT

Performance management is a strategic and integrated approach to delivering success to organizations by improving the performance of the people who work in them through developing the capabilities of teams and individuals. Performance management can be aligned with the culture and professionalism of teachers since the appraisal process developed in the early 1990s had been a partial response to demands from teachers for professional appraisal. It was clear, however, that that model was excessively bureaucratic and failed to involve the delivery of professional development. It was excessively cluttered up with personnel-speak rather than being focused on real breakthroughs in performance improvement. The new policy for performance management was developed in the late 1990s. In 1999 the DfEE contracted Regional Performance Management Consortia initially to deliver one day's training to all headteachers in 2000, and then to provide performance management consultants to support all schools in establishing performance management policies and in setting objectives for every teacher by the end of February 2001. These contracts were terminated in 2002. Performance management for teachers has frequently been extended to all staff, with training in skills such as setting objectives, monitoring and evaluating performance, providing feedback and linking the objectives to personal development and school strategic planning.

In business where structures have been flattened and processes reengineered horizontally, less hierarchical management systems remain. Schools have not moved significantly in this direction. They do not build performance improvement for competitive advantage. Leadership requires highly visible demonstrations of senior managers using and benefiting from performance management. Performance management must demonstrably provide clear access to high quality development opportunities. In view of the history of appraisal, the emphasis has been on the distinctive new emphasis of performance management.

Performance in business is partially delivered by teams and arguably the DfES model concentrates insufficiently on this. There is a need for an enormous commitment to communication of the rationale for performance management to ensure commitment at all levels. Effective performance appraisal is the cornerstone for performance management and personal development. The key principles for individual performance review at Great Ormond Street Hospital presented by the training and development manager (Bonham, 1999) are relationships, communication, objective-setting, planning, feedback, personal development plans, and training. There is no association with disciplinary processes. This is a different approach from the objectives only model in teaching.

*How effectively does performance management work in your school? And for you?*

## ELABORATING THE DEFINITION

Performance management is about planning for performance, developing to improve performance, measuring performance and rewarding performance. It involves a strategic and integrated approach to delivering sustained success to schools by improving the performance of all staff and by developing the capabilities of teams and individuals. The team–individual relationship needs clarification. Performance management is concerned primarily with the achievement of results and hence success for pupils. The process required to achieve these results develops the knowledge, skills and competencies of teams and individuals. The enormous differences in performance need to be recognized, measured and understood. Those who have high potential for example need to be fast-tracked through the profession. We cannot afford to underuse, frustrate and therefore lose the highly talented through a levelling down process.

*Does your school know who are the outstanding teachers?*

## PROVIDING THE REWARDS

The commitment is to achieving a school vision through planning for improvement, coaching to fulfil the plans, reviewing progress continuously and rewarding achievement. This will involve training, career development, personal and team recognition and pay, which at least takes account of performance. There is not a professional consensus as to how effectively the current (2002) salary structure achieves this. However, some schools are breaking free of the bureaucratic and emotional restrictions associated with performance appraisal to create strategic levers for improving performance. Performance management can achieve strategic change, build new cultures and make quality improvement happen. If schools are genuinely collegial, the salary structure should at least acknowledge those who contribute particularly effectively to the teams.

There are four critical factors for effective performance management:

- Behaviours – the most important, so people are clear what behaviours are expected of them.
- Environment – creating a culture where people can take risks, innovate and develop.
- Clarity – about what is expected, with team processes to communicate understanding in larger schools.
- Knowledge and skills – with development needs regularly reviewed and opportunities to meet knowledge and skill needs.

*Are these critical factors part of your school's performance management process?*

Excellence in teaching and leadership requires comparable capabilities and, therefore, rewards. Twenty-five per cent of headteachers received what might be called performance-related pay between 1993 and 1999. There is apparently no evidence that these were the most effective headteachers. Less than 1 per cent of teachers were so paid. There are three significant differences between excellent and average teachers and excellent and average school leaders. We need to recognize what can be enormous differences in performance. The excellent have:

- the knowledge and skills necessary to perform teaching and leadership tasks extremely effectively. They obtain great personal satisfaction from their work. For others it is possible to identify the critical behaviours which will help them overcome their limitations in knowledge and skills;
- motivation that comes from high inner drives and needs which are met by performance of the work itself. They set themselves high standards. Highly effective teachers and leaders ensure that pupils and teachers receive reinforcing individual rewards and motivation, not generalized approval;
- unique intellectual, emotional and physical talents that give them a decided advantage over others. There is a unique match between the abilities required by the work and the natural ability of the excellent performer including in teamwork. Their outstanding talents need recognition.

*How do you evaluate yourself against these knowledge, motivation and talent dimensions?*

## CREATING THE PERFORMANCE CULTURE

For a school this will involve:

- defining and communicating values and strategies;
- creating a school that will implement values and strategies;
- measuring performance;
- creating an effective performance feedback system;
- providing social consequences for performance;
- relating compensation to performance;
- involving staff in a continuous effort to improve performance.

To implement maximum performance management (Boyett and Conn, 1995) heads and team leaders must be willing to accept responsibility for the performance of staff and hold them accountable for their performance. They must have confidence in staff as well as high expectations. Significant performance problems can be solved through working for changes in the behaviour of and developing the potential of teachers. There is a genuine need to improve school performance, as international comparisons show, but also as the level of performance of many of those leaving schools show more directly.

*How effectively does 'performance' improvement add value in your school?*

## PERFORMANCE-RELATED PAY AND PERFORMANCE MANAGEMENT

Performance-related pay has not been clearly defined in the debate about paying teachers. A highly successful model for paying teachers, with teacher agreement, in the USA (Douglas County, Colorado), includes individual performance-related pay, team-based pay, school-performance pay, and pay for knowledge and for skills as well as experience. The current (2002) UK salary structure, with the uncertainty about whether the post-threshold payments and those to the leader-ship team are technically 'performance-related pay', is problematic for profes-sional teachers. If there is to be team-based pay, this may result in some team members receiving more pay for their greater contribution to the achievement of the whole team. The rationale for the salary structure, and the relative contribu-tions of qualifications, experience, competencies, potential and performance, seem likely to remain problematic

We know that not every teacher performs professionally and that their motivation is not entirely intrinsic. There are tens of thousands of astonishingly good teachers. There are tens of thousands of very good teachers. There are others who are not per-forming well enough who could do much better, and some who should not be in teaching. However, it is important to work to improve the performance of all teach-ers who can all perform better and to reward them appropriately when they have done so. It is important for the motivation for the highly effective teachers not to reward equally those who are contributing significantly less. The psychological rewards, more important than pay, are about encouragement, regular balanced feed-back on performance and increased opportunities for professional development.

## PERFORMANCE MANAGEMENT AND ACCOUNTABILITY

Performance management is about communication through continuous dialogue to define expectations and to share in enhancing the organisation's mission, values and objectives. There is mutual understanding about what is to be achieved and a framework for managing and developing people to ensure it will be achieved. This must satisfy all the stakeholders including the wider community, and particularly pupils and parents who can recognize differences in perform-ance. This is particularly the case in primary schools where a full year with a teacher makes an enormous difference in children's learning, which should be readily acknowledged.

The Office for Standards in Education and Hay McBer for the DfEE have researched and developed models for judging good teaching in different ways. A sophisticated analysis of the data now available in schools can make the evalua-tion of performance soundly based. Performance in SATs and GCSEs is the cen-tral measure of how successfully pupils have been educated and schools can set challenging added-value improvement targets which take account of variations in intake ability. What undermines motivation is the imposition of targets to which the schools are not committed. If there is a concern about an excessive emphasis on tests and examinations, other complementary performance indicators can be selected to present what schools have achieved.

*How well does your school use pupil performance data?*

## MEASURING THE IMPORTANT

A set of twelve 'ethos indicators' was suggested as a framework for collecting and analysing data. These were offered not as holy writ but as examples of indicators that a school might use in examining its ethos and relationships, and a way of systematising its self-evaluation and development planning.

Pupil morale; teacher morale; teachers' job satisfaction; the physical environment; the learning context; teacher-pupil relationships; discipline; equality and justice; extra-curricular activities; school leadership; information to parents; parent–teacher consultation. (Riley and Nuttall, 1994)

Such measurement needs to be used in a positive and constructive manner, so teachers will welcome supportive and challenging measurement. Teacher contribution to enhanced pupil performance can be the basis for a more legitimate form of financial reward than payment for time-serving or being promoted to a responsibility post in which the quality of the performance is not evaluated comparatively. The issue of fairness is central.

The focus in business, and possibly in education, is increasingly on team-oriented accomplishment-based measures when possible, with a level of precision sufficient for the purpose. Ideally, a family of measures is preferable rather than trying to force one measure to serve as the ultimate indicator of performance. These measures should be reviewed, and changed when appropriate. Individual performance can be measured in a business-focused way, an activity-focused way, the process- and customer-focused way or a person-focused way. We need to consider the implications of these alternatives for education.

Teachers might be paid for their performance and contribution as individuals, members of teams and as members of a school, for what they have achieved, and for their potential to contribute, the skills and competencies they have developed and will be able to use to help the school improve its performance. Most schemes, which include individual or collective performance awards are designed to recognize and reward outputs. Skill- or competency-based pay focuses on inputs, the capabilities that the individual brings to the job. The logic is that if the individual has appropriate characteristics, improved performance results, so the skills to be developed and rewarded need to be specified precisely. The sophistication of the new skills developed for literacy and numeracy teaching or ICT may need to be evaluated. Competency-based schemes take this further by linking reward to demonstration of required behaviours in practice.

*How do you measure more complex performance indicators in your school?*

## GOAL-SETTING, TARGET-SETTING, OBJECTIVE-SETTING

The process of setting goals and the commitment to achieving goals has a significant relationship to improvement in the performance of individuals and groups. Specific goals result in a higher level of performance than general goals. Difficult goals will result in higher performance than easy goals provided the difficult goal is accepted as worthwhile and perceived to be attainable. Staff participation in school goal-setting does not necessarily result in higher performance and improvement in goal attainment, but it does increase acceptance of and commitment to difficult goals. The level of difficulty for a particular goal should correspond to its relative importance in meeting central school performance targets. Teachers for the same reason need to set their own targets.

The impact of achieving goals is either positive reinforcement or negative punishment. Positive reinforcement works much better. Arguably it has not been used sufficiently in education, because it is thought to be either too soft, or associated with bribery or manipulation. Positive reinforcement should be provided after performance and should be contingent on performance. Creating positive reinforcement requires considerable skill. Pay for performance can support this, though other psychological forms of reward are much more important. Feedback will need to be communicated strongly so the rewards, including the financial, provide positive reinforcement. Performance appraisal is about making reward decisions, improving performance, motivating staff, succession planning, identifying and developing potential, promoting dialogue and, very indirectly, the formal assessment of unsatisfactory performance. Options for development activities include improving performance, working towards future changes in the current role, enriching the current job, moving up or down and across the organization, moving out of the organization and exploring future positions.

*What are the strengths and weaknesses of the current pay strategy? In principle how should teachers' pay be determined nationally and within the school?*

## THE WAY FORWARD

David Miliband, the Schools Standards Minister, at the Performance Management Conference in January 2003 made a presentation, 'School improvement and performance management', in which he insisted that performance management was about improving the quality of the teacher's teaching, the space in which teachers learn from other teachers after professional needs have been identified, honest adult relationships with feedback which recognizes the difference between good practice and excellent performance, and showing that the education service is idealistic and hardheaded and professional to reassure parents and others about higher standards. This speech set the government's performance management agenda for the next five years. The variation in performance between similar schools and the variation in performance between teachers in the same school with similar pupils was unacceptable.

The initial performance management process was to establish a basic sense of accountability and to introduce the performance culture. This involved devising ways of cascading school objectives. This has moved on to a need to demonstrate that development is being taken seriously. It is now important to carry through the more challenging part, exploring behaviours and values. Organizations are becoming less conventional and performance is recognized as more multifaceted.

Teachers are more assertive about their performance goals and on their development. Schools are impatient with a process they do not yet own and which does not add sufficient value. There needs to be a clearer framework for performance, feedback from many sources, profiling for similar jobs and the application of competencies which provides a systematic approach to personal and professional development. High performance behaviours for leaders (Boyett and Conn, 1995) include effective influencing, driving for results, inspiring others; achieving results through people requires teamworking, developing your people, developing yourself; and, thinking the business requires analytical thinking, conceptual thinking, business judgement and understanding the business context.

The *leadership and management styles* have to be aligned with the strategy, purpose and values. This will include questioning whether a more transformational style of leadership is appropriate and with it a greater shift towards greater empowerment. At the level of specific skills this will involve coaching, influencing, motivating, self-development and goal-setting. Innovation can only be stimulated by the appropriate leadership styles which help others find their way through the uncertainty and ambiguity of organizational life. Performance management helps define the appropriate styles and communicates this clearly throughout the organization through actions as well as words.

*Are these styles more in evidence in your school?*

Performance management has to provide a clear understanding of *individual requirements and expectations*. Continuous changes including reorganizations, and a move towards a fluid and flexible structure means that confusion and ambiguity have replaced stability and security. New structures can cause role overload with several reporting lines and different team activities. Schools have had these for some time but not always clarified the connections. People need clear roles and goals to achieve their full potential, and to ensure they are not demotivated and involved in power struggles within the complexities of school life. Defining inputs requires establishing the competencies, behaviours and skills required as essential prerequisites for achieving outputs defined in terms of accountabilities, goals and measures. This requires clarity in objective setting, performance reviews, development plans and the career development process.

*Has performance management achieved this in your school?*

*Team development and success* are means of harnessing the skills and capabilities of the staff to drive through business goals and meet customer expectations. They need to have the necessary mix of skills and abilities, and to be mutually accountable to provide a sense of direction and a way of measuring success. Performance management is to help define what is expected of the team, through coaching, training, facilitation and developing the necessary process skills. Team-based rewards, appraisal systems and objectives all help to shift the culture from individualism to collectivism, to help teams emerge as a powerful force.

*Climate and systems* are linked through communication as the means for translating the vision, mission and strategy into objectives at individual and team levels. Reward strategies, performance review and assessment mechanisms, career progression and training and development activities are aspects of systems that ensure performance is managed. The hard systems require the soft systems for the climate to be healthy. This climate is affected by the style of communication, and is partially determined by the leadership. Climate can be measured and monitored and a positive climate is essential in creating a motivated and high performing workforce.

Schools which are implementing performance management need to be clear about their answers to the fundamental question raised by David Miliband (2003). Staff need to know why performance management is being implemented, and that it is aligned with the school's purpose, values, culture and strategy. There needs to be clarity to reduce the potential for confused messages and contradiction. In team environments this will require a major shift in attitudes and the beliefs of all staff. Team leaders need to lead teams, and be committed to that role – as coach, facilitator and motivator. Assessment, development, recognition and reward need to be based on core competencies and role rather than job descriptions.

*Has this approach anything to contribute to performance management in your school?*

## EVIDENCE FROM THE BUSINESS WORLD

Armstrong (1998) reported the key findings of IPD research at the IPD National Conference. Seventy-four per cent of managers judged that performance management improved employee performance. The focus is more on development than on pay, and on inputs rather than outputs. Flexibility and simplicity are important and context and culture matter. It is vital to evaluate. People believe in it if it is well done. Line managers' views about performance management were that it helps manage the team better (85 per cent), motivates the team (83 per cent) and they thought they gave fair and consistent ratings (83 per cent). The complementary staff views were almost equally positive. They thought they received useful feedback (67 per cent), that the assessments were fair and unbiased (70 per cent) and they felt motivated after the meeting (58 per cent). More businesses were planning to implement performance management. For practical guidance on getting the best out of performance management, Hartle, Everall and Baker (2001) is helpful. Exploring the relationship between the UK context and international developments is possible in West-Burnham, Bradbury and O'Neill (2001) and deliberately more comparatively in Middlewood and Cardno (2001).

*As a leader in school how do you use performance management? How will you improve this?*

## PERFORMANCE-RELATED PAY IN THE USA

This section, focusing fully on performance-related pay for teachers, is based on quotations from four papers from the USA where research appears to be evidence-based. The four papers from different parts of the USA are used to illuminate the issues.

1) 'Teachers' compensation and school improvement; a review of the literature and a proposal to build capacity' – Susan Moore Johnson and Carl H. Pforzheimer Jr.
2) 'New and better forms of teacher compensation are possible' – Odden, Allan (January 2000) *Phi Delta Kappa*, pp. 31–6 (February 2000). Paper prepared for the National Education Association.
3) 'Paying mindworkers: what is the incentive to teach?' (16 May 2000), paper based on presentation to the Council for Greater Philadelphia, Teacher Accountability Conference in Horsham, Pennsylvania.
4) 'Pay for performance: key questions and lessons from five current models' (June 2001) Education Commission of the States.

> First, all schools and classrooms must be staffed with knowledgeable, skilled, and committed teachers. Second, schools must set high performance standards for students and support teachers in providing a rich and challenging curriculum. Third, individual schools must develop strong site-based professional cultures that maintain commitment and promote continuous improvement, and they must have the resources and autonomy needed in order for their programs to work well. (1)

> Compensation can play a unique and constructive role by providing incentives, signalling priorities and structuring work relationships. (2)

> A compensation system is a strategic tool for organizational change in that it defines roles, relationship, and rewards. An effective pay system must be out in front of organizational change, not lagging behind it. (3)

> There are significant differences in the amount of learning taking place in different schools and in different classrooms within the same school, even among inner city schools, even after taking into account the skills and backgrounds that children bring to school. (4)

New teachers now are familiar with workplaces where pay levels are differentiated by skills, responsibilities, experience and performance, and are less interested in trading loyalty for job security than in demanding better working conditions and expecting some form of performance-related pay. However the single salary scale does protect from arbitrary treatment in institutions still marked by favoritism, racism and sexism.

The Tennessee Value-Added Assessment System (TVASS) demonstrates from assessments that teachers' instructional skills, inferred from the performance of students based on state-administered norm-referenced tests, make a great difference and that these are cumulative. It would seem that high-quality teachers are the most likely to leave teaching: 'there is evidence that workplace conditions, including salary, discourage potential teachers from preparing to teach, dissuade certified teachers from entering the classroom, and drive novice teachers to different lines of work'.

New teachers are more ready to consider performance-based pay through new strategies for assessment – peer and administrative observations, documented contribution to school improvement, advanced certification, and students' test scores. Teachers are now expected to greatly expand their knowledge and skills and to work more collaboratively and to participate in school improvement initiatives. The new reform goals for learner- and performance-oriented schools rely on teachers learning new technical skills, reconceptualizing approaches to teaching and learning which requires continuous inquiry, experimentation and reflection.

Schools need:

> a scaffolded system of apprenticeship and mentoring through which teachers can acquire the skills they need in an orderly and sustained way. They need to understand the subject matter in deep and complex ways, to develop new strategies for teaching that content and to use assessment about student performance as they plan subsequent instruction.

Isolation and privacy among teachers still prevail in many schools, thus suggesting that standardized pay does little or nothing to encourage collaboration. Differentiated pay, which enables schools to identify accomplished teachers who can exercise leadership in school reform efforts has the promise of increasingly meaningful staff collaboration. The potential of the pay system to promote and sustain excellence has received little serious attention by educational reformers. The single salary scale is designed to attract those who seek stability and safety in employment, rather than those in search of varied opportunity, uncertainty or risk. It serves to retain those teachers who do not seek to distinguish themselves with external recognition or to be paid or promoted on the basis of their expertise or performance.

Odden suggested that a pay system which responds to all the evidence should involve:

- a staged professional career that includes five levels, deliberately configured in a scaffolded system to support improvement of classroom instruction and school effectiveness;
- an annual salary increase for all teachers who remain in good standing;
- targeted wage increases front loaded and distributed across the board for teachers in early career stages, and awarded more selectively to teachers in later career stages;
- a professional development fund that is investment centred and focuses on school site needs;
- salary incentives at both the district and school site to attract and retain teachers in high-poverty schools or hard-to-staff teaching fields.

The argument can be explored more fully in *Paying Teachers for What They Know and Do: New and Smarter Compensation Strategies*, (Odden and Kelley, 2002).

*What part should pay play in motivating staff to work more effectively?*

# REFERENCES

Armstrong, M. (1998) 'Managing performance', seminar IPD National Conference.

Bonham, S. (1999) 'Great Ormond Street Hospital', seminar IPD National Conference.

Boyett, J.H. and Conn, H.P. (1995) *Maximum Performance Management*, Oxford: Glenbridge.

Hartle, F., Everall, K. and Baker. C (2001) *Getting the Best out of Performance Management in your School*, London: Kogan Page.

Middlewood, D. and Cardno, C. (Eds.) (2001) *Managing Teacher Appraisal and Performance*, London: Routledge.

Miliband, D. (2003) 'School improvement and performance management', presentation at the Performance Management Conference, January.

Odden, A. and Kelley, C. (2002) *Paying Teachers for What They Know and Do: New and Smarter Compensation Strategies*, Thousand Oaks, CA: Corwin Press.

Riley, K.A. and Nuttall, D.L. (eds) (1994) *Measuring Quality: Education Indicators: United Kingdom and International Perspectives*, London: Falmer.

West-Burnham, J., Bradbury, I. and O'Neill, J. (eds) (2001) *Performance Management in Schools: How to Lead and Manage Staff for School Improvement*, Pearson Education. Monitoring School Performance: A Guide for Educators: J Douglas Willms.

# 14

## Ethics, Values, Vision, Mission and Gender

### UNIVERSAL HUMAN VALUES

The Institute for Global Ethics carried out interviews with two dozen 'men and women of conscience' to reveal eight shared values that can guide a troubled world through the tumultuous future. Throughout these interviews with men and women of conscience there was a recognition of an underlying moral presence shared by humanity and a search for a global code of ethics (Kidder, 1994).

1) *Love* – moral behaviour is based on solidarity, love and mutual assistance. Love should come of its own will spontaneously. Meaningful guidance without love is not possible. In the words of a Nebraskan tribal chief, 'We have to be compassionate with one another and help one another, to hold each other up, support one another down the road of life'.

2) *Truthfulness* – we all have a responsibility to keep our promises and not be afraid to say our opinions. People should not obtain their ends through deceitfulness. Technology increasingly forces people to reveal themselves. There is nevertheless a fear that trust, central to honesty and truthfulness, is falling into abeyance.

3) *Fairness* – there is a danger of being overcomplicated about social justice. It is better to concentrate on treating others as one would want to be treated. The pursuit of equality focusing particularly on race and gender is basic. It is suggested that equity, the most important value, has collapsed. Justice is about fair play.

4) *Freedom* – the desire for liberty is central. The concept of degrees of freedom of action, as against excessive constraints on action by political leaders, provides a sense of individuality and the right of an individual to express ideas freely. The principle of individual conscience is central. The effect one upright individual can have is incalculable. Democracy is freedom of expression plus accountability plus equal opportunity.

5) *Unity* – the value that embraces the individual's role in the larger collective concerns co-operation and solidarity. It is a simple *cri de coeur* in a world that is falling apart. Unity embraces a global vision capable of moving humanity from unbridled competition to co-operation. Carried to the extreme individualism is destructive of social life, destructive of communal sharing and destructive of participation. Unity is about putting the community, meaning

the earth and all living things, first.

6) *Tolerance* – is showing respect for the dignity of each of us. There are limits to which others can impose their values. We need to recognize that others have the right to think differently from us. Tolerance is an obligation, or at least a strong desire, to listen to different points of view and attempt to understand why they are held. A native American saw tolerance as 'The spirit that makes you stand up and walk and talk and see and hear and think is the same spirit that exists in me – there is no difference'. The environmentalist's urgency about the depletion of the species comes from tolerance.

7) *Responsibility* – is a sense of self-respect in the present. We are responsible for our grandchildren. You must take care of yourself. To rely on others is a great shame. The talk is of rights, demands and desires, an unquestionable and critical priority for political societies and a lever for genuine development. The important thing is not just to assert rights but to ensure they are protected. Achieving this protection rests wholly on the principle of responsibility. When rights become more important than responsibility, individuals become more important than the community and nobody has responsibility. Rights, demands and desires are nevertheless an unquestionable and critical priority for political societies and an indispensable lever for political development.

8) *Respect for life* – the first element of the Buddhist 'daily prayer' is 'I shall not kill'. It is also central to the Ten Commandments. Thou shalt not kill is an inflexible principle. Even if ordered in wartime to defend his homeland by killing, a Japanese Buddhist monk said 'I would refuse. I would say, "I cannot do this"'. The Prime Minister of Lebanon said, 'I can't imagine myself signing a death penalty for anyone in the world. I think it is completely illegitimate'.

In addition to knowing the difference between right and wrong, it is necessary to have the courage to stand for what is right. Wisdom is 'attaining detachment, getting away from being too attached to things'. Hospitality, obedience, peace (well-managed conflict), stability, racial harmony ('respect for the cultures of other communities, respect for the need to begin to integrate our collective memory contributions and traditions of those who are different' Kidder, p. 12), and a concern about woman's place and the increasing exploitation of women around the world are central. There is a right to a healthy environment. These are perhaps the values we should be expressing through educational leadership.

*Are these universal values? What are your personal values?*

## STATEMENT OF VALUES FROM THE NATIONAL FORUM FOR VALUES IN EDUCATION AND THE COMMUNITY

This more mainstream definition focuses on values in education:

- The self – we value each person as a unique being of intrinsic worth, with potential for spiritual, moral, intellectual and physical development and change.
- Relationships – we value others for themselves, not for what they have or what they can do for us, and we value these relationships as fundamental to

our development and the good of the community.

• Society – we value truth, human rights, the law, justice and collective endeav-
  our for the common good of society. In particular we value families as sources
  of love and support for all their members, and as the basis of a society in
  which people care for others.

• The environment – we value the natural world as a source of wonder and
  inspiration, and accept our duty to maintain a sustainable environment for the
  future.

*How do these relate to the values in your school?*

## BUSINESS ETHICS FOR MANAGEMENT DEVELOPMENT

MacLagan (1995) carried out a literature inspection of managerial ethics programmes to enhance understanding of the implications for management education of current thinking about ethics. The literature inspection suggests that
managerial ethics programmes have the following aims:

1) Raising awareness and stimulating the moral imagination – this should pro-
   voke an emotional as well as an intellectual response.
2) Helping managers create organizations which support ethical conduct –
   enhancing the systems or correcting deficiencies.
3) Enhancing personal and interpersonal skills of a non-cognitive nature – the
   cognitive component is a necessary but insufficient condition for individual
   moral development which it is suggested includes courage, strength of will,
   tolerance and assertiveness.
4) Providing concepts, theories and analytical skills for ethical reasoning and
   decision-making.

It is not clear how fully educational management and leadership programmes
present such a theoretical contextualization of learning about ethics, though
values are more obviously central to education.

Mahony (1997) considered why business should be ethical. If it is about keeping awkward customers and irritating pressure groups off the back, and because
it pays to be ethical, this is an unethical motive. Treating people with honesty,
fairness and respect is a moral principle, not about expediency. Ethics is about
achieving the right balance between two basic human feelings, concern for oneself and concern for others. The focus on 'social responsibility' in the 1970s led
to the Milton Friedman assertion that 'the social responsibility of business is to
increase its profits'. Diverting business from this responsibility with the expectation that the role is to apply resources to tackle society's ills and ethics becomes
judgemental and moralizing. Social responsibility is, however, now fashionable.
Running an ethical business means giving a fair deal to all stakeholders, with the
workforce, customers, suppliers and surrounding community all regarded as
investing in the business like stockholders. More participants in the ethical land-
scape create more scope for competing interests. The wide gap between manage-

ment and ownership demonstrates the need for more imaginative ways for the multitude of owners to acknowledge and discharge more responsibilities. Business schools now provide case studies to present the expanding portfolio of ethical challenges with which managers are confronted. Headteachers and governors face similar challenges. These can include:

- internal workings – the ways in which people are treated – discrimination, confidentiality, teleworking, loyalty;
- customer relations and marketing – pricing and advertising of goods and services;
- relations with other companies – payment of suppliers, working with suppliers who may mistreat workforces, ethical aspects of mergers;
- related to the locality – self-regulation, cultural diversity, bribery, physical environment, working with the community;
- ethical wrongdoing – personal or corporate pressure for excessive results or inadequate supervision. People prefer moral certainties to the discomfort of the partial truth which may be all that is available. Business ethics is the ethics of power, and because power is growing the question is how these forms of power can be used to add ethical value. Ethical business is an activity seeking to find a way between moral defeatism and moral utopianism. Imaginative moral realism is continuously seeking constructive ways forward for business while keeping a wary eye open for ethical dead ends. School leaders operate within such an ethical context.

*What are the implications of this consideration of ethics for your school? Have you had appropriate professional development in ethics?*

## LEADERSHIP, VISION AND VALUES

Leaders are transformative when they are able to shape and elevate the motives and goals of others who need to be challenging and actively attempting to make personal sense out of as much of their world as a possible. Leaders will be able to locate, sort and organize and assimilate large bodies of information for the purpose of solving problems whilst simultaneously aligning this with the clarification of core values and acting in a manner consistent with such values, reinforcing moral and ethical standards. Our professional and social culture persists in creating expectations that great leaders will emerge and become our salvation. This may not be unhealthy since our future welfare depends on our hopes, aspirations and dreams of what might be possible with great leadership. This is the vision, the journey from the known to the unknown creating this future from a combination of facts, hopes, dreams and opportunities. The process often starts in a fumbling, groping way, the leader, team or school reaching forward towards some shadowy dream that cannot initially easily be verbalized or defined. This vision can become the interpretation of the direction in which the organization is going which inspires and illuminates and permeates the school. Crucially the vision articulates and defines the values of the school, the hopes and aspirations of the school for children, community and staff making them real and attainable. The vision is expressed in images, metaphors and models to organize a meaningful view of a realistic, credible, attractive future for the organization for those involved in working in the school and sharing the articulation of the destination, The right vision, frequently expressed by the leader, attracts commitment and energizes people, creates meaning in their lives, establishes a standard of excellence, bridges the present and future, and has an extraordinary power to shape the future by calling forth the skills, talents and resources to make it happen.

*How is the vision in your school articulated?*

## THE VISION OF THE LEADER

In practice then, for the school leader, the vision is a relatively clear, comprehensive picture of your school in the future, the goals you aspire to accomplish for your pupils. You start with inspiring a shared vision and negotiate with others to build a stronger vision collaboratively, modelling the way, and encouraging hearts and minds to get extraordinary things done. Your values are springs of human action, enduring beliefs which when internalized become standards or criteria for guiding your own actions and thoughts, for influencing the actions and thought of others and for morally judging yourself and others. Values are pervasive in the problem-solving of school leaders through their direct stimulation of actions and their roles as perceptual screens and moral codes or substitutes for knowledge in response to ill-structured problems. Values are expressed not only through action but also through one's judgement of the actions of others, and determine a judgement of right or good. Values shape an ongoing, persistent standard or code for action which exists over time. Leadership involves managing the tensions which arise from conflicting values, the different ideals towards which people strive, in the process of which individuals and organizations may be shaped and influenced. Excellent schools are driven by coherent value systems because they are able to aspire to high-performance and worthwhile action. Values can be a lure and a peril; a religious fervour and exaltation can bring out the best and encourage staff to exceed themselves; an unthinking commitment may blind them to their own humanity.

*How secure are you in your values as a leader?*

## LEADERSHIP AND MANAGEMENT

Bennis and Nanus (1995) present an accepted distinction between leadership and management:

> We have here one of the clearest distinctions between the leader and the manager. By focusing attention on a vision, the leader operates on the emotional and spiritual resources of the organization, on its values, commitment, and aspirations. The manager, by contrast, operates on the physical resources of the organization to earn a living. An excellent manager can see to it that work is done productively and efficiently, on schedule, and with a high level of quality. It remains for the effective leader, however, to help people in the organization know pride and satisfaction in their work.

Great leaders often inspire their followers to high levels of achievement by showing them how their work contributes to worthwhile ends. It is an emotional appeal to some of the most fundamental of human needs – the need to be important, to make a difference, to feel useful, to be part of a successful and worthwhile enterprise.


## MISSION

The school's mission statement is derived from and subordinate to the vision and values and linked directly to strategy. It is a concise statement of the purposes and key features of the school, setting out the principles and values that will guide its development. The mission is about implementing the school's long-term vision of the future, and may be supported by a longer statement of its general aims (the things it will try to achieve) and core values (the principles which will guide its development). The clarification of mission is an important part of strategic analysis, and where strategic management is practised effectively within a school, it can be expected that the mission will become influential in guiding action through the process of strategy implementation. As an educational leader you will need to clarify and live coherently the leadership/vision/values/mission/strategy continuum.

The mission development may be viewed as a process which promotes planning, aids decision-making and communication, and facilitates marketing and evaluation strategies. It can be a powerful method of promoting school change. If the school's mission is conceived and written by senior management and ineffectively communicated to the staff and community, it will not be implemented. Similarly, if the ideas and practices enshrined in a mission statement are not evidenced in the actions of management, it will have little influence on decision-making processes. If the statement is so bland as to be applicable to almost any organization, it is not likely to assist your school very effectively in its marketing strategy. The vision and values, often articulated by the leader but incorporating successfully the strong commitment of staff, parents and community, should impact profoundly on policy and practice through the mission and strategic planning processes.

*In your school is the link between vision, values and mission clear? Have you a formal statement articulating this?*


### Challenge Plus: Diversity, Inclusivity and Equal Opportunities

Managing Diversity is a comprehensive management process for developing an environment that succeeds for all employees. Stated as simply as possible, the philosophy of managing diversity asserts that organizations make whatever changes are necessary in their systems, structures and management practices to eliminate any subtle barriers that might keep people from reaching their full potential. The literature on diversity tends to concentrate on race. For educational leaders there is much more exploratory work even in the USA on gender than on race, whereas for pupils and learning the emphasis appears to be on race. As the focus changes from equality to diversity the emphasis changes as shown below:

| Equality focus | Diversity focus |
|---|---|
| Triggered by legislation | Triggered by business imperative |
| Focusing on improving numbers | Focus on improving workplace environment |
| Concern of 'Human Resources' | Concern of everyone |
| Focus on positive action for | Focus on creating opportunities for all |
| minority groups | individuals |
| Removing barriers | Nurturing potential |
| Complying with the law | Developing best practice |
| Bare minimum | Opportunities to improve |
| Piecemeal initiatives | Holistic strategy linked to organisational imperative |
| Have to ... | Want to ... |
| Punishment culture | Reward culture – recognizing benefits |
| Reactive approach | Proactive approach |

Diversity is about valuing individual differences for enhancing individual, team and organizational performance. *Inclusive Schools, Inclusive Society*, which explores the nature of inclusiveness, (Richardson and Wood, 2000) and is produced by Race on the Agenda in partnership with Association of London Government and Save the Children, has a foreword by Doreen Lawrence mother of murdered Stephen Lawrence. Diversity is about inclusivity.

Blair and Bourne (1998) present the features of inclusive schools:

- Leadership – strong and determined on equal opportunities given by head-teacher.
- Listening – listen to and learn from pupils and parents and try to see things from their point of view.
- Parents and community – create and maintain careful links.
- Persons as individuals – try to understand and work with the 'whole child' – concerned with personal, emotional and social development as well as the academic.
- Curriculum – show recognition and respect for pupils' cultural, ethnic, religious and linguistic identities.
- Combating bullying – clear procedures for racist bullying and racist harassment.
- Preventing exclusion – stress on preventative strategies.
- Expectations – high expectations of teachers and pupils, clear systems for targeting, tracking and monitoring progress of individual pupils.
- Monitoring – monitor by ethnicity to see whether all groups are achieving equally, to identify unexpected shortcomings in provision and target specific areas for attention.

Challenge Plus, prepared for the National College for School Leadership (McKenley and Gordon, 2002) is a report on the experience of black and ethnic minority school leaders. This research and the associated references illustrate how relatively little work there has been on this topic, in comparison with women school leaders. This presents all school leaders with the opportunity to understand the challenges facing black and ethnic minority school leaders, but also to develop an awareness of the strategies they adopted to confront negative stereotypes and the low expectations that racism perpetuates for black and ethnic minority staff.

*How is inclusiveness managed in your school?*

## WOMEN AS LEADERS AND MANAGERS

Rosener (1990) demonstrates how women are disproportionately not in senior management positions. Equal pay legislation has not resulted in equal pay though there are more women in higher education and their education performance continues to outstrip that of men. Women are challenging assumptions, seeking the abandonment of the model of a career as an uninterrupted sequence of promotions, demanding the acceptance of taking time out for career or family reasons and drawing on the skills and attitudes naturally developed from their shared experience as women. There are clear differences between the ways men and women describe their leadership performance and how they usually influence people they work with. Men tend to view job performance as series of transactions with subordinates – exchanging rewards for services rendered or punishment for inadequate performance. The men are also more likely to use power that comes from their organizational position and formal authority. The women actively work to make their interactions with subordinates positive for everyone involved. More specifically, the women encourage participation, share power and information, enhance other people's self-worth and get others excited about their work. This evidence suggests that women have more of the skills that align with those of the transformational leader.

*What is the significance of such evidence for your school?*

Sharma (1990) considered the psychology of women in management and the complementary distinct feminine leadership. Management encompasses the full range of women's natural talents and abilities but there are powerful forces resistant to feminine leadership. The masculine corporate culture has high control, competitiveness, an emphasis on strategy, lack of emotion, analysis for rational problem-solving, managerial effectiveness gauged in terms of financial gain rather than employee satisfaction, so that women have to change by adapting and camouflaging their femininity. Men at the top are reluctant to accept women as true colleagues. There is also indifference towards feminine leadership among women. Some women deny its existence and fear that acknowledging it will demonstrate their ineffectiveness. They have learned to accommodate to masculine culture, hence they are not anxious to encourage feminine leadership in subordinates. The reasons for the effectiveness of a feminine leadership style include a strong desire to succeed in men's domain, the capacity for endurance of stress and a higher level of general health in working women, the ability to manage a wide range and number of tasks simultaneously leading to good organizational abilities, intuition and problem-solving, and a willingness to be part of a team. With all these strengths Sharma argues that women will inevitably rise to senior leadership positions, but there is a need to avoid women being marginalized into people-oriented management roles – public relations, human resource management, consumer affairs and corporate social responsibility, staff functions that are peripheral to the more powerful functions. There may also need to be a more sophisticated strategy required as men become entrenched in using the more traditional leadership styles to protect their positions.

Reay and Ball (2000) explore the essentials of female management and women's ways of working in the education marketplace, complementing some of Sharma's arguments. More women are working and more are working full time, accessing higher education though not yet proportionately MBAs. In education the traditional career structure and attitudes are intact, and here also there remains the need to abandon the model of career as an uninterrupted sequence of promotions to positions of greater responsibility. Time out for living with children, and indeed for supporting parents, is interpreted as evidence of lack of career commitment. The second wave of women, it is argued, are not following the traditional command and control style of leadership, but drawing on skills and attitudes developed from their shared experience as women. They know the strength of the informal culture is one of the greatest barriers so assert different definitions of commitment, and seek more challenging assignments. Women use impression management techniques which fit comfortably with informal cultures. Women are more transformational so their subordinates transform their self-interest into group interest. Their power comes from personal characteristics such as charisma, interpersonal skills, hard work, personal contacts rather than the structure, and have the interpersonal skills to make these interactions positive. Men are consistently higher on the transactional element of management and succeed through ingratiation, window dressing, exaggerating credit, using keen, ready and attentive body language, having the appropriate demeanour for next management level, adopting organizational citizenship behaviour, acting to repair image damage and volunteering for extra tasks. The message is that women need executive MBAs not just assertiveness training, and schools and organizations need more effective women leaders.

Alimo-Metcalfe (1998) designed a psychometric instrument for 360-degree appraisal which showed how women were significantly better as transformational leaders because of the quality of their relationship with subordinates on the key factors for transformational leadership. These were: having a genuine concern for others, having political sensitivity, being decisive determined and self-confident, having integrity, delegating and empowering others, networking, promoting and communicating, being accessible, clarifying boundaries and involving others, and fostering critical and strategic thinking. Businesses under pressure and schools, given the percentage of women teachers, are clearly failing to appoint those with the highest leadership skills.

## THE FEMALE ADVANTAGE

Helgeson (1990) explored the distinctiveness of women's ways of leadership:

In mythologies all over the world, female deities are depicted at the loom, knitting together the fabric of human life, spinning out the threads that link the events of the past with the potentialities – the unborn people and events – of the future.

In a web structure, where talent is nurtured and encouraged rather than commanded, and a variety of interconnections exist, influence and persuasion take the place of giving orders. The lines of authority are less defined, more dependent on a moral centre. Compassion, empathy, inspiration and direction – all aspects of nurturance – are connective values, better communicated by voice, by tone, than by vision.

Women typically approach adulthood with the understanding that the care and empowerment of others is central to their life's work. Through listening and responding, they draw out the voices and minds of those they help to raise up. In the process, they often come to hear, value, and strengthen their own voices and minds as well.

The old Warrior virtues – fearlessness, a thirst for combat, single-minded devotion to an ideal, aggression, the ability to conceptualize the other as the enemy, the fierce need to prove oneself in all contests – all these once served the evolutionary human purpose of mobilizing the strongest adult males to preserve and protect other members of the immediate tribe. But advanced technology has turned these virtues into liabilities: aggressive heroics threaten the survival of the larger tribe, the human race.

*What are the implications of this section if you are a woman? If you are a man?*

## REFERENCES

Alimo-Metcalfe, B. (1998) 'Leadership skills', seminar IPD CPD Conference.

Bennis, W. and Nanus, B. (1995) *Leaders: The Strategies for Taking Charge*, Reading, MA: Addison-Wesley.

Blair, M. and Bourne, J. (1998) *Making the Difference: Teaching and Learning Strategies in Successful Multi-ethnic schools*, London: DfEE.

Helgeson, S. (1990) *The Female Advantage: Women's Ways of Leadership*, New York, NY: Bantam Doubleday.

Kidder, R.M. (1994) 'Shared values for a troubled world: conversations with men and women of conscience', *The Futurist*, July–August. pp. 8–13.

MacLagan, P. (1995) 'Ethical thinking in organizations, implications for management education', *Management Learning*, 26(2) pp. 159–77.

Mahony, J. (1997) 'Business ethics: what's in it for you?', *Financial Times Mastering Management, The Reader*, 2, pp. 14–18.

McKenley, J. and Gordon, G. (2002) *Challenge Plus: The Experience of Black and Minority Ethnic School Leaders*. www.ncsl.org.uk/archive, National College for School Leadership.

Reay, D. and Ball, S.J. (2000) 'Essentials of female management, women's ways of working in the education market place?', *Education Management and Administration*, 28(2), pp. 145–59.

Richardson, R. and Wood, A. (2000) *Inclusive Schools, Inclusive Society: Race and Identity on the Agenda*, Stoke-on-Trent: Trentham Books.

Rosener, J.B. (1990)'Ways women lead', *Harvard Business Review*, November–December.

Sharma, S. (1990) 'Psychology of women in management: a distinct feminine leadership', *Equal Opportunities International*, 9(4).

# 15

## Culture, Change and Organizational Health

### CULTURE AND CLIMATE

The culture of a school is more permanent and built into the organization than the climate. It is more difficult to change. The healthy schools initiative is one of several new initiatives, including developments associated with teacher workload, which recognize the importance of schools having a 'healthy' culture. How managers understand the culture of their organization is of crucial importance to developing strategy. Culture is about capability, integrating the cluster of resources and binding the organization together through its network of relationships. It incorporates the basic values, ideologies and assumptions that guide and fashion individual and organizational behaviour. Its effects are seen in the symbols and behaviours. The corporate culture reflects the values and interpretations of senior managers; the organizational culture, on the other hand, embraces many subcultures. There is a possibility that compliance with the corporate culture may lead to an assumption of the existence of a homogenous organizational culture.

School leaders may have problems in growing and changing the existing culture and beliefs and values, and sustaining the commitment and retaining the experience of staff, when they are trying to be more responsive to the demands of the state and parents and the community. However, over time, impartial and open-minded behaviour will lead to trust and then to commitment, and the consequential committed effort which will be co-operative and innovative. Core values are beliefs about how the world should be and how we should behave, with such beliefs guiding actions. Those beliefs, if validated, become assumptions about how the world is. The same holds true for schools, and their values provide the basis for strategy-making, strategy formulation and strategy implementation discussed in the next chapter. School cultures are heterogeneous – there are subcultures around different functions, roles, skills or levels in a school. These create a broader sense of identity but can be counterproductive if they limit co-operation, exacerbate conflict or reinforce entrenched views and positions. This explains some of the difficulties in attempted culture change and in trying to create a more homogenous culture.

*How do you understand the culture(s) in your school?*

### CHANGING THE CULTURE

Changing the cultures of organizations is the central aim of strategic human resource initiatives. The purpose is that employees can be persuaded to align themselves more fully with the goals and priorities of the organization which means they will value their work, value the objectives and purposes of their work, and work hard to achieve these objectives because they are committed to them. Culture management is the process of developing or reinforcing an appropriate culture. It is concerned with the commitment of members to its mission, strategies and values. The outcome is a transformed organization in which leaders trust and inspire their staff so they develop a concern for quality and a commitment to the leader's articulation of organizational goals. Organizational success can be traced directly back to a strong culture founded on a set of beliefs and values. This chapter focuses on the corporate culture approach – the theories and practices of those who advocate that cultures can and should be changed. There are two ways of describing this approach. One is concerned with harnessing and directing employees' commitment to corporate goals and values. The alternative view is that it is describing the prevalent perspective of the senior management only. The culture affects performance because it directs or leads people to shape and fashion conduct in desired directions through the management of meaning. There is an issue about whether planning cultural change is about effective leadership or manipulation.

*Is the 'corporate' culture in your school being managed to achieve success?*

## MANAGING THE CULTURE

Current programmes of change such as business process re-engineering and performance management place an emphasis on new forms of organization. Current programmes are attempting to redefine the meaning of work. The corporate culture approach implies:

- organizations have culture;s
- organizations become more effective when they develop an appropriate strong culture;
- cultures create consensus and unity and motivate staff;
- cultures have an effect on corporate performance when necessary;
- cultures can – and should – be changed with an impact on how employees think about and value their work and their employers' priorities;
- it is the responsibility of the senior managers to shape culture (Open Business School, 1999).

Cultures impact on how people think and feel, and not just how they behave. Senior managers in excellent companies may seek to instrumentalize people's behaviour in order to achieve prescribed ends. If a weak unfocused culture results in poor performance, the corporate culture approach will be a solution to organizational problems that have arisen from the company not addressing its cultural dynamics issues. If staff are successfully encouraged to want what the senior managers want them to want, to value what senior managers want them to value and to be committed to the activities and purposes of the senior management, it appears to eliminate the need for management (see Morgan, 1986, below). Books such as *In Search of*

*Excellence* (Peters and Waterman, 1982) define the nature and importance of dealing in symbols for senior management, and for them the direction and management
of cultures and symbols becomes the primary task for managers.

*How is the culture in your school changing, or being changed? Is it a strong*
*culture?*

## THE LEADER, LEADERSHIP AND CORPORATE CULTURE

This focus on the headteacher as leader is complemented by a renewed focus on
distributed leadership. Distributing the leadership may be about enhancing and
refining the corporate culture, or embedding it more effectively. Corporate culture
is ideological because it is concerned with power and interests – reflecting the managers' values, though not necessarily organizational realities; management power,
including the power to manipulate symbols and meanings; the managers' preferred
view of the organization; and defining away aspects of the organizational process
which contradict the consensual focus of corporate culture. The deeper layers of
these cultures and the cultural context of the organization may remain unchal-
lenged. There is a discrepancy between the emphasis on shared values and purpose
and the enormous differentials in power and influence. The emphases on efficiency,
rationalization, productivity, advances in technology, control, hierarchy, the dominance of typical male values, and glorification of leadership may need to be challenged. There is a potential contradiction in the high responsibility of senior
management for initiating school culture and change projects, which are about
achieving consensus and commitment. It is useful to consider the forms or features
of the school culture that are currently regarded by management as rational and
desirable, and where these came from since change will result in reformed structures, processes and culture. Culture, subcultures and counter-cultures characterize organizational life through social norms and customs. Modern organizations
are sustained by a myth of rationality though these socially constructed realities
suggest every aspect of organization is rich in symbolic meaning.

## CHANGING THE CULTURE

What is important for the education service, particularly for less successful
schools, and presumably for subgroups within schools, is the belief that the culture can be changed and managed in the context of the concerns above. The
implication for the process would be:

- the senior management team are explicit about the desired corporate values,
  and communicate and stress them constantly;
- the values are broken down and operationalized through competencies and
  training. Staff know what the values mean in practice and are trained in the
  constituent elements;
- staff are encouraged by a whole range of processes and mechanisms to adopt
  and display the new values;

- staff are trained and rewarded, recruited and appraised on their capacity and willingness to demonstrate these values in their behaviours;
- the cultural values make sense and their appeal to customers makes sense. The values relate to what the school and staff believe they should be doing;
- the values supply the basis for a coherent architecture, an integrating theme around which the different ways the school works are built. The corporate culture is presented as a reflection of the underlying reality.

*How fully and genuinely is leadership and changing the school culture distributed in your school? How does senior management understand their relationship to the rest of the staff?*

Change is about schools adapting to new pressures and requirements from outside the school. The changes driven from outside are part of the institutionalizing process rather than the result of fresh organizational learning. The limitations of senior management cultural beliefs and values may mean they do not have the capacity for recognizing the need for change. Within the school the cognitive structures, schemata or scripts, may result in shared mindsets or paradigms that are so taken for granted that they are not even recognized. The organizational frame of reference or culture of the staff may be different from that of senior management. The power of the designers and the powerlessness of those on whom change is being imposed is itself a form of communication. The method of change selected reflects cultural values. Any cultural change may be a reflection on the values of the senior managers previously responsible or those who were associated with it. In change situations key leaders must not only articulate the message but also represent it and model it in their own behaviours, at both symbolic and real levels.

*How is the management of change achieved in your school? How do you contribute to this?*

## UK CULTURE IN AN INTERNATIONAL CONTEXT

There is some analysis of the specific features of national cultures largely initiated by Hofstede, (1980) which has led to consideration that the British might learn from the commitment, loyalty, deference, obedience and shared values which made Japan so successful. Hofstede's factor analysis led to four underlying dimensions of culture in international contexts which may be of particular value to those working in multicultural schools, but also to put current cultural issues in schools in a new context using this model.

- Power distance (PDI): an indication of the extent to which a society accepts the unequal distribution of power in organizations.
- Uncertainty avoidance (UAI): an indication of the degree to which the members of a culture/society tolerate uncertainty or ambiguity.
- Individualism (IDV): an indication of the degree to which the culture/society emphasizes personal initiative and achievement rather than collective group centred concerns.

- Masculinity (MAS): an indication of the extent to which the dominant values in a society reflect the so-called 'masculine' tendencies of assertiveness, the acquisition of money and property and not caring for others.

Hofstede related PDI and UAI to the structure of organisations with PDI being about the concentration of authority (centralization) and UAI with the structuring of activities. These are dimensions for interpreting national cultures but may have implications for schools in their cultural context.

## IMAGES OF ORGANIZATION

Morgan (1986) suggests that metaphors are sets of linguistic processes whereby aspects of one object are carried over to another object. That is, meaning is created by understanding one phenomenon through another. Morgan has suggested that metaphors are a basic structural form of experience through which human beings engage, organize and understand their world. Morgan's (1986) ten images of organization clarify distinctive models, with associated 'cultures', which require different forms of re-engineering for planning change. One of these is of the organization as culture, but the others relate to other 'cultures'.

*Consider organizations you know that particularly exhibit each of these images.*

1) *Mechanization takes command: organizations as machines.* This image is based on scientific management and bureaucracy. The focus is on setting goals and objectives and going for them; organizing rationally, efficiently and clearly; specifying every detail so that everyone will be sure of the jobs that they have to perform; and planning, organizing, controlling. Controlling, is seen to limit human capabilities, moulding humans to fit the mechanical organization, rather than building it round their strengths. In some schools there are pressures in this direction.

2) *Nature intervenes: organizations as organisms.* Organizational needs and environmental relationships are born, grow, develop and die. There are parallels to molecules, cells, complex organisms, species and ecology in the individuals, groups, organizations, population (species) of organizations, and their social ecology. Open systems theory makes the links from goals, structures, interrelated subsystems, efficiency to survive, organization–environmental relations and organizational effectiveness. Organizations as organisms can satisfy needs at the physiological, security, social, ego and self-actualizing levels (Maslow). The biological model suggests that these complex needs must be satisfied if humans are to lead full and healthy lives in healthy organizations.

3) *Towards self-organization: organizations as brains.* This organization is conceptualized as an information processing system capable of learning to learn, or as a hologram, capable of self-organization. The concern is to improve the capacities for organizational intelligence, to disperse brain-like capacities throughout the organization, and with the brain conceptualized as an information processing system. This does not have the full focus of a learning

organization. This model takes account of modern brain research. Cybernetics is the study of information, communication and control processes, associated with the process of negative feedback, in which deviations are reduced at each and every stage of the process. The four principles of the cybernetics theory of communication and learning for systems are that they must:

(a) have the capacity to sense, monitor and scan significant aspects of environment;
(b) be able to relate this information to the operating norms that guide system behaviour;
(c) be able to detect significant deviation from these norms;
(d) be able to initiate corrective action when there are discrepancies.

This raises the issue as to whether organizations, understood as brains, can learn to learn as learning organizations. The brain has the capacity to organize and reorganize so perhaps its holographic character can be used to create organizations which are able to learn and self-organize.

4) *Creating social reality: organizations as cultures.* The ideas, values, norms, rituals, beliefs, the culture of industrial society are reflected in organizations such as schools. In Japan the cultural values of the rice field are shown in the intensive teamwork in back-breaking bursts of planning, transplanting and harvesting, which combine with the spirit of service of the samurai in the managerial clans, which is elitist and highly meritocratic. Shared meaning, shared understanding and shared sense making are all different ways of describing culture. Culture is a process or reality construction that allows people to see and understand particular events, actions, objects, utterances, or situations in distinctive ways.

5) *Interests, conflict and power: organizations as political systems.* Organizations, like governments, employ some system of 'rule'. The most common varieties of political rule in organizations are autocracy, bureaucracy, technocracy, codetermination, representative democracy and direct democracy. Conflict, which arises whenever interests collide, can be personal, interpersonal or between rival groups and coalitions, and will be present in all organizations. Different sources of power provide organizational members with a variety of means for enhancing their interests and resolving or perpetuating organizational conflict.

6) *Exploring Plato's cave: organizations as psychic prisons.* These organizations have excessively strong cultures. Organization members are trapped in thoughts, ideas and beliefs which are possible in that extreme context, prisoners of organizational ideologies, ensnared by conscious and unconscious processes, with repressed psychodynamic and ideological forces masquerading as rational. This metaphor may be too dramatic for most schools, but staff can be trapped by unconscious concerns and strivings associated with Freudian psychology manifested at school level. Rationality is often the irrational in disguise in extreme forms of compulsiveness. This may be an extension of other models discussed above.

7) *Unfolding logics of change: organizations as flux and its transformation.* There are three logics of change:

(a) the self-producing systems that create themselves in their own image (autopoiesis) through internally generated change. We may be able to change the nature of change by replacing egocentric images with ones that recognize our interdependence with others;

(b) related cybernetic ideas that suggest that the logic of change is enfolded in the strains and tensions found in circular relations. The mutual causality encourages us to give particular attention to the nature of relationships and interconnections and to manage and reshape these to influence patterns of stability and change;

(c) change as a product of dialectical relations between opposites. This encourages us to understand the generative opposites and to manage change by reframing these oppositions.

8) *The ugly face: organizations as instruments of domination.* These are exploitative and dominating with the powerful imposing their will on others. This may be class based and may ignore work hazards leading to occupational diseases and industrial accidents to meet the demands of the organization. The rational and efficient may provide the basis for actions that are profoundly irrational or even catastrophic for others. These organizations may manifest dysfunctional or unintended consequences of the excesses of the otherwise rational. Domination may be intrinsic in the organizational design.

*Consider how fully all of these images of organization apply to your school. How would you manage the process of change if required?*

## METAPHORS

Metaphors provide the unwritten rules by which people know how to behave and react. People quickly learn how to follow these rules to the extent that certain patterns of behaviour become ubiquitous to the organization, and mark it out from other organizations, giving a distinct identity and distinct flavour or feel. That is why culture change is difficult and time-consuming, and it may not be possible to change it in any predictable and controlled way. Since Peters and Waterman (1982), the culture metaphor seems to have provided a vehicle for changing organizations to make them more responsive to altered conditions and hence improving organizational effectiveness. There remain questions about the process of changing the culture and the indeterminate link between culture and organizational performance, though this may be due to the difficulty of measuring both culture and performance. There is a danger that the publication of mission statements redefining the culture, or training and exhortation to change, impact negatively. Where reasonably rapid changes have occurred this is usually the result of changing the people. Changing the culture means changing the behaviour of people for ever. If culture is a manifestation of the attitudes and behaviour of the people, there is a mutual interaction between culture determining behaviour and behaviour determining culture.

The promises, explicit or implicit, between the organization and the individual are the psychological contract. Organizational change processes may break or severely strain this organizational relationship. When this occurs the resulting loss of trust will impact on all staff. If staff leave as a consequence of change there is an inevitable requirement for greater commitment and effort from those remaining. The changed culture will have an impact on career expectations (see Chapter 9). It is important to understand what has been changed and how these changes are perceived by those affected since it is the latter that will influence future attitudes and behaviour. A central issue is the perceived fairness or equity of the changes. If the inequity and imbalance is caused by the employer reneging on the psychological contract, this will lead to less effort and lower commitment.

*How would you characterize the psycholological contract in your school?*

## CHANGE, JUSTICE AND THE ORGANIZATIONAL HIERARCHY

Managing change is not so much about distributive justice as procedural justice, which can be enhanced by participation in decisions about decisions. The reasons behind the actions need to be perceived to be legitimate. Distributive justice is associated with individual outcomes whereas procedural justice is associated with organizational outcomes such as organizational commitment. Modern cultures of empowerment, if genuine, require all members to take responsibility for themselves and to work closely with each other, if necessary taking over responsibility from each other. Any attempt to enforce a more participative mode will result in counter-dependence, that is, rebellion and possibly total non-compliance, because the management has unilaterally violated the psychological contract. This process involves a gradual transfer of control through negotiation so the psychological contract is maintained. The process of the rebuilding of trust will inevitably be gradual. It is much more effective to concentrate on changing behaviour rather than attitudes as a means of changing the culture. There is a danger that managers may not be able to recognize this distinction. It is, for example, difficult to rate performance in leadership or initiative through behaviours when people do not know what they have to do to improve performance. These behaviours must be specified in terms that are observable and measurable.

A research project carried out for the Chartered Institute of Management Accountants (CIMA) by the Manchester School of Management at UMIST, found that it was the senior managers who came out most positively in favour of the new wave, as defined below, even though they had the greatest difficulty in coming to terms with it. Though middle managers might be expected to oppose because they have most to lose in terms of status and career opportunities in the new culture, this was not the case. There were tendencies in both to enjoy the control over their own destiny and their day-to-day roles and responsibilities, but a keener desire to maintain control over the destiny, roles and responsibilities of others. Some organizations had used the language of the new culture – networking, empowerment – which they applied to conventional programmes of change. If structural change is to be effective, a number of other issues have to be dealt with, but it is difficult to deal with them without changing the culture. It may be difficult to make the changes without destroying the commitment which is necessary to carry them through. The new wave does require a recognition that the consequences of implementation could be incoherence, demoralization and confusion. Not carrying them through, however, could result in a failure to survive.

## THE DIRECTION OF THE NEW WAVE

The past – characterized by reliance on:

- universal laws (e.g. span of control);
- hierarchical control/chain of command;
- discipline imposed by management;
- fragmented, mechanistic, directive approach to problem-solving;
- single-function specialisms;
- individualism;
- job description setting out tasks and responsibilities.

The future – characterized by an emphasis on:

- appreciation of contingency and ambiguity;
- commitment/effective use of human resources;
- self-discipline accepted by employees, facilitated by management;
- holistic, recursive, participative approach to problem-solving;
- multi-functional teams;
- mutual dependence;
- continuously reviewed and renegotiated assignments.

If these characterizations are accurate, then it might be argued that the education service has not yet moved on to the future, though arguably the past culture was not as intense as in other organizations.

## MAPPING AN EFFECTIVE CHANGE PROGRAMME

The Institute of Management (1996) recommended the following sequential process.

1) Map the current structures and culture – identify and recognize the values, behaviours, beliefs and formal and informal structures that underpin the current school culture. This involves identifying the management style which dominates the organization which is likely to be modelled by the head-teacher, recognizing the effective control structure – how it really works, recognizing the efficiency and effectiveness of the organizational structure or the informal networks that really work. These provide a benchmark.
2) Appoint a champion for change – the champion's credibility is of paramount importance with sufficient seniority and proven track record. It is important to be committed and energetic.
3) Build the right team for change – the team needs the range of technical com-

petencies and personal styles, not necessarily all at senior levels inside the organization. The group needs to include 'movers and shakers' as well as cynics but all with respect, trust and credibility.

4) Outline the new culture and structure – present an outline of what the school will look like at the end of the culture change. It is important to include both the structure and culture.

5) Build the case for change – it is important to communicate the sense of urgency of the need to change and to persuade others. A clear compelling case which includes quantitative and qualitative arguments. There must be a link with business objectives and the vision. If the staff understand the need for change through identifying the change factors, they will be implemented more positively.

6) Define the scope of change – these will cover the six dimensions – markets and customers, products and services, business processes, people and reward systems, structures and facilities, technologies.

7) Draw up an outline plan – vision (what is the school trying to achieve?), scope (what needs to change to realize the vision?), time frame (what will change when, and in what order?), people (who will be the change agents? who will be affected by the change and how? create a coalition for change), resources (how much will the change cost and what will be the benefits?), communications (what new communications structures will be needed?), training (management and staff in both hard and soft skills), organizational structure (what changes will be needed?)

8) Cost the change programme.

9) Analyse the management competencies – address directly those who are not enthusiastic supporters.

10) Identify the driving and restraining forces – plan to reinforce the drivers and add new ones, and reduce the restraining forces by education. This will be helped by openness and by positive successes.

11) Outline the change programme to line managers – the impact of the programme on structures, people, processes and products. Use feedback to refine the plans and build consensus.

12) Communicate – continuously with stakeholders throughout the process to avoid rumour.

13) Identify change agents – staff need to be selected who are committed, enthusiastic and command respect. Train them, use them as champions and cascade the change programme.

*Would this model for managing change be applicable in your school?*

## ORGANIZATIONAL DEVELOPMENT

Organizational development is a humanistic change process which needs to be sustained. It is

- an attempt to achieve corporate excellence by integrating executives' need for growth with organizational goals;

- focusing on organizational purpose, the human interaction process, and organizational culture; it accepts these as the areas in which problems are requiring the fullest possible integration within the organization;
- a long range effort to improve an organization's problem-solving and renewal processes, particularly through a more effective and collaborative management of the organization culture.

This is implemented by change agents who are characterised by developing self-awareness, a knowledge of organizational behaviour and change process, a transactive style of interacting with others in an organizational change situation, and a humanistic value system.

*Is organizational development, as defined here, occurring in your school?*

## REFERENCES

Hofstede, G. (1980) *Culture's Consequences: International Differences in Work-related Values*, Beverly Hills, CA: Sage.

Institute of Management (1996) *Mapping an Effective Change Programme*, Corby: IMgt.

Morgan, G. (1986) *Images of Organization*, London: Sage.

Open Business School (1999) *Changing Culture, Managing Human Resources*, Buckingham: Open University Press.

Peters, T.J. and Waterman, R. (1982) *In Search of Excellence*, New York, NY: Harper and Row.

# 16

## Strategy

### STRATEGY – THE DEFINITIONS

Strategy is the pattern of activities followed by an organization in pursuit of its long-term purposes. *Strategic issues* can be characterized as developments inside or outside the school that are likely to have an important impact on its ability to meet or determine its purposes and objectives. Strategy-making is concerned with the determination of the nature, domain and scope of the school's activities and the evaluation of their success. The pattern of activities in strategy arises from the acquisition, allocation and commitment of a distinctive set of *resources* and *capabilities* to match the challenges of the environment, and from the management of the network of relationships with and between its stakeholders.

Strategy concerns the whole school interaction with the environment and is integrative and cross-functional. This requires those managing strategy to retain a balanced vision of the functions of all parts of the school in overall planning. At the same time there will be a concentration on those areas within the school which have strategic priority. Strategy has a long time horizon, perhaps three to five years, and is concerned with projection into and the prediction of an uncertain future. The past determines the resources and capabilities available at a particular time but the main focus of strategy is in predicting and interacting with the future. The uncertainty involved comes from the unpredictability of the actions of other actors in the environment, in particular for schools the government at the macro level but also within the local community, and wider social change. Making strategy requires the assessment and integration of information about both the internal features of the school and those of its environment.

### STRATEGIC FIT

The goal of *strategic fit* is setting and managing the school's distinctive resources and capabilities. A sophisticated approach needs to take account of the following factors:

- The fit between the school and its environment is dynamic and interactive. The quality will depend on how the school develops its strategic resources and capabilities to meet the challenge of change.

- Competitors must be constantly outmanoeuvred. The aim is not only a fit between existing competitive environment and existing organizational capabilities, but also the anticipation of environmental change. Indeed, the most effective strategy will influence forces in the environment and create new sources of advantage. Schools may be reluctant to accept such language of competition.
- There is a danger that strategic fit might be used to justify an overemphasis on external analysis. It is the interaction between the distinctive set of internal resources and capabilities and the environment, rather than customer needs or actions of competitors, that should be given priority.
- Matching the resources and capabilities of the school to the environment does not imply an averaging process whereby all competitors arrive at the same conclusions and adopt the same strategies. An effective strategic fit will utilize the organization's distinctiveness in a unique interaction with a differentiated environment.

## STRATEGIC STRETCH

*Strategic stretch* is required when there is a significant gap between a school's resources and its ambitions and aspirations. A strategy of stretch (Hamel and Pralahad, 1994) can be pursued by deliberately creating a 'chasm' between a school's resources and capabilities and its *strategic intent*, the dream that drives the organization, and bridging that chasm through the leverage of the limited resources and capabilities available. Strategic stretch is about creating a sense of strategic leadership through the need to challenge the orthodoxy of accepted notions of ways to compete and operate. This will recognize the importance of managing risk through the acquisition of detailed knowledge about competitors, customers and capabilities in advance of the commitment of substantial resource allocations.

## STRATEGIC THINKING

*Strategic thinking* is central and more important than strategic planning because it is a prerequisite. Strong skills in strategic thinking require that the thinking is both relevant and realistic and rigorous. This will involve a varied and sophisticated approach to information processing – for example, at least both top down and bottom up. To be firmly embedded it will require the use of theory to explain practice and practice to check the accuracy and relevance of theory. That is there should be an insistent critical, challenging approach, and an awareness of this pluralism in thinking about strategy.

*How is strategy understood, managed or led in your school?*

## RELATIONSHIPS WITH STAKEHOLDERS

The *purposes* for a school, should reflect the values and beliefs of the main stakeholders, recognize the organizational culture and reflect the politics of managing stakeholder relationships. Purpose statements may take the form of unifying vision, mission or values summaries, and should capture the sense of identity of the school. These will not provide quantifiable measures.

The *objectives* are more specific, expressing particular expectations of stakeholder groups, or specifying particular milestones of achievement to be aimed for. At this level success or failure can be more easily measured because objectives are quantifiable. A statement of objectives will be explicit in formal strategic planning processes.

*Policies* derive from an intention that a particular pattern of strategy will be implemented over time and will lay out a programme for activities. Creating a sense of mission is about a model of congruence between organizational strategy, purpose, values and standards of behaviour.

The *stakeholders* contributing resources to the organization will seek a return. The school will need to utilize these resources to provide that return which, because it is not obviously economic, will require sophisticated consideration. Returns to stakeholders are inextricably linked over the long run to strategic responses that the school makes. Its ability to provide attractive rewards to the resource contributors, not only staff, pupils and parents but also those who contribute the financial resources is central to strategic thinking. For schools there are varied sources of stakeholder power which need to be differentiated. There is formal authority, such as that of the headteacher or the governors. There is the control of scarce resources from the DfEE, but also from parents. There are organizational structures and procedures which can be manipulated to favour teachers over parents, or vice versa. There is the control of the decision processes and of knowledge and information, with the unique role of the headteacher central in this. Boundary management becomes more important as schools have additional funds delegated and enhance their capacity to attract additional resources. The capability to manage uncertainty and to find solutions is an important source of power. Control of technology may be an important source of power. Alliances and informal networks and countervailing power structures emerge when the power becomes concentrated in relatively few hands. There is symbolism and the management of meaning – managing the messages that are conveyed by actions, and gender power based on assumed stereotypes of gender roles. The complexity of the relationship of stakeholders to the strategic planning process needs to be fully understood for implementation of strategy.

## RESOURCE-BASED APPROACHES

It is helpful to explore in a limited way the wider historical development of strategy. Porter's (1980) five forces of competition model was used to explore the profitability of an industry as determined by five sources of competitive pressure. This is perhaps the most important of the early clear and fully developed models which is recognized as relating to return on capital invested relative to the cost of capital. It is, however, worth considering and exploring the Porter model to see if schools within the education service have the secure future that may be assumed at the system level.

The five forces of competition include three sources of horizontal competition – competition from the suppliers of substitutes, the threat of competition from entrants, and competition from established producers, and two sources of vertical competition – the bargaining power of suppliers and of buyers. The strength of each of these competitive forces is determined by a number of key structural variables. Within the education service it is clear that local education authorities are already subject to many of these sources of competition. Schools need to recognize the competitive environment, and not only competition between schools, but also the threats of entry and the threat of substitutes to the education provided in schools. Porter then developed from this three generic strategies. The first is cost leadership which has application in the education service where there is inefficiency, the second is differentiation, seeking to be unique, and the third is optimizing the strategy to target segments within the market.

In this broader context the resource-based approach to strategy (Hamel and Pralahad, 1994), suggests that each organization possesses a unique bundle of assets, and that the ownership of these assets and what the firm can make of them, determines the difference in performance between, in our context, one school and another. It is an approach to strategy which emphasizes the role of school leaders in choosing among and committing to long-term paths or trajectories of competence development, a 'dynamic capabilities' route. The strategic resources are partly the capabilities of the individuals in the organization, but these will not necessarily be available long term. For a resource to be distinctive it must be hard to imitate, drawing on combinations of resources from any and every part of the school. It is the combination in bundles that creates that uniqueness – often a mixture of the hard tangible elements and the soft intangible elements, such as the internal culture or the external image. These cannot easily be copied or re-created by others. A value chain is another relevant concept, a model of a route of activity through an organization, which can be used to identify potential sources of increased efficiency. This can facilitate competitive benchmarking to see how those with comparable activities within the chain, create added value. The application of the resource-based approach to strategy in schools requires a thorough examination of what resources the school has and how it can use them more effectively and coherently.

## CAPABILITIES

The resource-based view concentrates on the elements internal to the organization, in particular the organizational processes and the organizational routines, the tangible, the intangible and the human. Capabilities are developed over time through complex interactions among the organization's resources. Uncertainty, complexity and conflict, inside and outside the organization are normal, but discretionary managerial decisions on strategy-crafting play within this context. Managers can recognize strategic assets arising from the resources and capabilities as a basis for creating and sustaining sources of advantage. The resource-based view of the school is to gather and nurture a set of complementary and specialized resources and capabilities, ideally those which are scarce, durable and difficult to imitate. Resource leverage is about focusing these resources with the greatest effectiveness, getting the most from what is available. It is about concentrating, efficiently accumulating, creatively complementing, carefully conserving and speedily recovering resources. The focus on there never being enough resources is negative and unhelpful, but schools which obtain the maximum from those available will be able to compete for the future (Hamel and Pralahad, 1994). It is important to be clear in your particular school what its resources and its capabilities are, using the skills listed below.

*How would you use this wider consideration of strategy in your school? What are your school's unique resources and capabilities?*

## LEVERAGING RESOURCE

Inevitably, resources are limited and leveraging is about obtaining the maximum benefit from them. Those with responsibility for strategic planning will need to work out how to use these processes in practice in a school.

- Converging – building consensus on strategic goals.
- Focusing – specifying precise improvement goals.
- Targeting – emphasizing high-value activities.
- Learning – fully using the brain of every employee.
- Borrowing – accessing resources of partners.
- Blending – combining skills in new ways.
- Balancing – securing critical complementary assets.
- Recycling – reusing skills and resources.
- Co-opting – finding common cause with others.
- Protecting – shielding resources from competitors.
- Expediting – minimizing time to payback.

Tacit knowledge is explored more fully in Chapter 18 on knowledge management. It is that knowledge which cannot be written down and specified, but is embedded in the interactive routines, rituals and behaviours of individuals within their organizations. Tacit knowledge is strategically the most significant resource of the organization – because it is impossible to imitate or replicate. Nonaka (1991) argues that tacit knowledge has a cognitive dimension in that it consists of the mental models that individuals follow in given situations. These internal processes of sense-making and decision-making may be personal, shared by members of a team or a department. It is the sharing which others cannot replicate because they are unique within any organization.

## CHOOSING A STRATEGY

What strategy is about at its most straightforward is seeking answers to three questions as a basis for action. Where are we now? Where do we want to go? How do we get there? Kay (1993) describes three types of distinctive capabilities:

- architecture, which describes the formal and informal relationship between internal staff, with customers and suppliers, and any collaborative arrangement, the networks. This provides an effective conduit for organizational knowledge and routines which are often the key source of competitive advantage;
- reputation, which is built on the relations with the organization's suppliers and customers. A particular reputation, perhaps for reliability or speed of service, is a source of advantage, if a parent values the school's reputation, over a competitor's, at the time they determine the child will come to the school. Reputations are wasting sources of advantage if they are not sustained. They need to be managed;
- innovation, is a source of competitive advantage when it provides a means for a school to compete more efficiently, offering something that is more valuable to the customers, or in new ways. Innovation is only sustainable as an advantage if it cannot easily be imitated, or superseded by alternatives.

## THREE DOMAINS OF STRATEGY

There are three domains of strategy: thinking, which means outwitting rivals; doing, which is outmanoeuvring rivals; and results, which is outperforming rivals. Schools which plan strategically recognize that working in a competitive environment is not about working against other schools, but that they are rivals. The three different forms of strategy are the application of the domains. These are the inventive where there are not only new products, but also radically new ways of competing; the renovative, which might involve new product–customer segments within the existing strategy serving as a platform for strategy change; and the incremental, with modest extensions of existing strategy, the fine-tuning. These may well apply to schools more fully, now we are beginning to consider the nature of schooling rather more radically and whether we are meeting the developmental and learning needs of all young people. The three complementary core elements in the marketplace are: the scope of what the school provides, the teaching and complementary learning to which pupils have access; its posture, how it competes to attract, win and retain customers, with an increasing emphasis on retaining the psychological commitment of staff, parents and pupils; and the goals, what those working for the school want to achieve, the vision. This will need radical thinking in the future which links coherently the capabilities, the domains and the core elements. Understanding the strategic context requires an interpretation of future development in education before it happens. This means describing the current changes, identifying emerging changes, projecting potential changes, and then assessing the strategic and organizational implications.

Scenario planning is a process for developing descriptive narratives of plausible alternative projections of how some future might evolve. The *future* in this model is conceptualized as an 'end-state' and the process of evolution towards it; *narrative* is defined as an explicit description of futures; *alternatives* need referent points across scenarios; *projections* are not predictions, just one view of the future that is based upon distinctive rationales. It should be plausible with some degree of evidence to support the projection. The key uncertainties are the specific factors chosen as the basis for determining the end-state and evolution towards it, that is, attempting to make sense of the future. There are many changes that have occurred in the education service, but whose consequences have not yet unfolded, most obviously curriculum development and professional development.

*How do you and how does your school explore possible future developments and their present implications?*

Johnson and Scholes (1999) state that there are three sets of generic criteria to test the appropriateness of a strategy:

1) *Suitability* – the strategy matches the needs identified in the strategic analysis, tests its consistency with the environmental or resource analysis and the fit with the organizational objectives. It capitalizes on the identified resources and capabilities.
2) *Feasibility* – how well the strategy would work in practice and how difficult it might be to achieve, though there is a danger of ignoring the challenge of strategic stretch and leverage.
3) *Acceptability* – how stakeholders might feel about the outcomes. Is the strategy likely to alienate stakeholders? The effects on the internal systems and procedures will also need to be acceptable.

## STRATEGY AND INNOVATION

Process innovation encompasses the envisioning of new work strategies, the actual process design activity and the implementation of change in all its dimensions. The successful strategic innovators spent time and effort in selling the new challenge to everyone. This has links to business process re-engineering, since it is a fundamental reconceptualization of what the business is all about that, in turn, leads to dramatically different ways of operating an existing business. This may mean destabilizing what appears to be a smooth running machine periodically. *Strategic health* is about the company's future health that could be different from today's.

## COMPETING FOR THE FUTURE

Hamel and Pralahad (1994) is probably the most germane book on strategy from outside education. Hamel (1998) later looked at competing in a non-linear world in which strategy life cycles are getting shorter and strategic innovation is the capacity to create new value for customers, wrong-foot competitors and produce new wealth for all stakeholders. Innovation has to be a deeply embedded and ubiquitous capability because of the danger that today's visionary creates tomorrow's intellectual straitjacket. The argument that competing is inappropriate since it takes energy away from focusing on pupils' learning is false; it is focusing more strongly on this learning. Schools and the wider education service need to accept the new strategy paradigm.

## THE NEW STRATEGY PARADIGM

| *Not only* | *But also* |
|---|---|
| | *The competitive challenge* |
| Re-engineering processes | Regenerating strategies |
| Organizational transformation | Industry transformation |
| Competing for market share | Competing for opportunity share |
| | *Finding the future* |
| Strategy as learning | Strategy as forgetting |
| Strategy as positioning | Strategy as foresight |
| Strategic plans | Strategic architecture |
| | *Mobilizing for the future* |
| Strategy as fit | Strategy as stretch |
| Strategy as resource allocation | Strategy as resource accumulation and leverage |
| | *Getting to the future first* |
| Competing within an existing industry structure | Competing to shape future industry structure |
| Competing for product leadership | Competing for core competence leadership |
| Competing as a single entity | Competing as a coalition |
| Maximizing the ratio of new products to old | Maximizing the rate of new market learning |
| Minimizing the time-to-market | Minimizing the time to global pre-emption |

Bringing together the earlier arguments, Hamel and Pralahad note that there had been demands for new organizational paradigms (leaner, virtual, flatter, modular) but they assert a need for new strategy paradigms. For them, strategic intent is the foundation of strategic architecture. It is an ambitious and compelling strategic intent that provides the emotional and intellectual energy for the journey. Strategic intent is the heart; strategic architecture is the brain. This is where strategic stretch is central since the current capabilities and resources are insufficient. Strategic intent is about the misfit between resources and architecture. Strategic intent conveys a *sense of direction* with a competitively unique perspective on the future. Dilemmas, paradoxes, problems and opportunities provide the raw material for creative advantage. It is about a *sense of discovery*. Strategic intent in its emotional edge implies a *sense of destiny*. It is overmanagement and underleadership that prevents this sense of direction with bureaucracy blocking creativity and innovation. Strategic intent is specific about needs not means and ensures consistency in direction. This sense of destiny is the goal that is the focus of strategic intent, and therefore is about the creation of meaning and capturing the imagination. It is only extraordinary goals that produce extraordinary effects. This is why, in the education service, we need to have strategic intent at national and local as well as at school level.

*Consider strategic intent, strategic stretch, strategic architecture as they apply to your school.*

## FOUR APPROACHES TO STRATEGY

Whittington (1993) notes that by 1993, there were 37 books with the title 'Strategic Management' which are based on essentially the same basic implausibility that the secrets of corporate strategy can be contained in a book. He argued that there were four generic approaches to corporate strategy.

1) Classical – relies on the rational planning methods. Strategy is a rational process of deliberate calculation and analysis, designed to maximize long-term advantage. Good planning is what it takes to master internal and external environments. Rational analysis and objective decisions make the difference between long run success and failure. This is Porter's approach.

2) Evolutionary – the fatalistic metaphor of biological evolution, but this substitutes the law of the marketplace for the law of the jungle. The environment is too unpredictable to anticipate effectively. Competitive processes ruthlessly select the fittest for survival. Successful strategies only emerge though managers can ensure that their organizations fit the environmental demands of the day.

3) Processualists – emphasize the sticky, imperfect nature of all human life, pragmatically accommodating strategy to the fallible processes of both organizations and markets. Strategy emerges from learning and compromise. People cannot plan rationally and the selection processes of the market are not strict. No one else will know the optimal strategy so there will be no fatal competitive disadvantage.

4) Systemic – relativistic, regarding the ends and means of strategy as inescapably linked to the culture and powers of local social systems in which it takes place. Systemic theorists are less pessimistic than the processualists about people's capacity to carry out rational plans of action, and more optimistic than evolutionists about their ability to define their strategies in defiance of market forces. The social background may give them other interests – such as the professional price of managerial power. Pursuit of these is rational even if the rationale is disguised. Deviant strategies matter because they can be carried through effectively. The particular social systems define for them the interests in which they act and the rules by which they survive.

In a discontinuous world strategy innovation is the key to wealth creation. By the mid-1970s strategy was established and the main book was Porter's *Competitive Strategy* (1980). The focus turned to quality in the mid-1980s and, in the early 1990s, to re-engineering. There is now new thinking on the content of strategy focusing on foresight, knowledge, competencies, coalitions, networks, extramarket competition, ecosystems, transformation and renewal. Strategy is now perceived to be on the border of order and chaos, of absolute efficiency and blind experimentation. The new thinking requires:

1) New voices which illuminate unconventional strategies. These are pluralistic and deeply participative; in particular this might mean young teachers, other staff and parents. It is these groups where there is greater diversity to ensure the strategy creation is pluralistic and more participative in its development.

2) New conversations creating a dialogue across traditional boundaries increase the likelihood that new strategy insight will arise. Conventionally, conversations become hard-wired over time with the same people talking to the same people about the same issues constantly. Opportunities for new insights come from breaking these conventions and juxtaposing previously isolated knowledge in new ways.

3) New passions. This is about unleashing the passion and focusing the search for challenging strategies on improving performance. People are only against change when it does not offer new opportunities. Given a chance to invent the future of the school and create a unique and exciting future in which they can share, people will commit and embrace change.

4) New perspectives. Leaders must search for new conceptual lenses to help schools reconceive themselves, customers and competitors and therefore opportunities.

5) New experiments. Launching small risk-avoiding experiments, trialling in the real world, serves to maximize learning about just which new strategies will work. The insights from talking about strategy are limited, leading only to refining insights into viable strategies.

*What are the implications of this broad consideration of strategy for you and your school now? How can the school strategy be improved?*

## A BEGINNER'S GUIDE TO STRATEGIC PLANNING

For Barry (1998) the difference between strategic and operational planning has to be clear. Strategic planning is about developing a shared vision of an organizational future and determining the best way of making this happen. As people develop this clear and compelling future they become committed to making it happen. Strategic fit is about the link between your school's mission, the outstanding opportunities and its capabilities. His simple five-step model for strategic planning is:

1) Get organized at the right time, with a steering group to keep on track, clarify which people and groups are part of the process. Obtain any support from the outside needed, define the planning steps and achieve an agreement to proceed.

2) Take stock by reviewing the history and the current situation and identify the future possibilities, focus on the most critical issues

3) Set the direction with the leaders selecting and drafting a plan which includes the school's future mission, and the overall approach for accomplishing specific goals or strategies.

4) Refine and adopt by fine-tuning and securing approval of all involved, with the target draft plan sharpened to increase the likelihood of successful imple-

mentation and broad based commitment.

5) Implement the plan with periodical monitoring and updating every year.

Good strategic planning forces future thinking, builds commitment, can refocus and reenergize a wandering organization, and can help create teamwork, promote learning and build commitment.

If you are seeking to implement Strategic Management for School Development, with full support, then as a beginner's guide the Brian Fidler (2002) book of that title provides the most thorough basis for implementing the process.

*How will you learn to be a strategic thinker?*

## REFERENCES

Barry, B.B. (1998) 'A beginner's guide to strategic planning', *The Futurist*, April, pp. 33–6.

Fidler, B. (2002) *Strategic Management for School Development: Leading Your School's Improvement Strategy*, London: Paul Chapman Publishing.

Hamel, G. (1998) 'Succeeding by making a difference', presentation at the IPD National Conference 'Managing People: Generating Success', 28 October.

Hamel, G. and Pralahad, C.K. (1994) *Competing for the Future*, Cambridge, MA: Harvard Business School Press.

Johnson, G. and Scholes, K. (1999) *Exploring Corporate Strategy: Texts and Cases*, Harlow: Pearson Education.

Kay, J. (1993) *Foundations of Corporate Success*, Oxford: Oxford University Press.

Nonaka, I. (1991) 'The knowledge creating can pay', *Harvard Business Review*, 69, November–December, pp. 96–104.

Porter, M.E. (1980) *Competitive Strategy*, New York, NY: Free Press.

Whittington, R. (1993) *What is Strategy – and Does it Matter?* London: Routledge.

# 17

## Quality Models

In this chapter we will consider a number of quality approaches and meeting the needs of customers or clients. These will include; the business excellence model (EFQM), Charter Mark, Investors in People, ISO 9000, the balanced scorecard, total quality management, the approaches of Deming and Crosby, Malcolm Baldridge National Quality Award (USA), Peters and Waterman, benchmarking and marketing. The focus is on a broader understanding of the concept of quality, which will enable your personal and professional development to be more sharply focused.

*Which quality systems or processes does your school use? How do you determine their relevance and appropriateness?*

Peter Kilfoyle, Minster for Public Services, launched the Quality Schemes Task Force in January 1999, with representatives associated with the Excellence Model, Charter Mark, Investors in People and ISO 9000, together with government officials

### EUROPEAN FOUNDATION FOR QUALITY MANAGEMENT (EFQM)

The European Quality Award was developed by the European Foundation for Quality Management. The UK Quality Award for Business Excellence (British Quality Foundation) was established in 1994. A clear distinction is drawn in the model between the Enablers (*how* results are being achieved) and the Results themselves (*what* the organization has achieved and is achieving) (See Figure 17.1). Both are equally important, which is significant given the debate about whether the focus for school improvement should be on the inputs or the outputs. The self-assessment process against the Excellence Model, the first part of the application process, identifies strengths and areas for improvement; identifies priority areas to address; provides year-on-year assessment of performance against a widely recognized model; provides a framework that makes sense of all quality and improvement activities; generates fresh motivation for improvement; gives an insight into world-class practice; and, enables comparison with a wide range of other organizations. The application process increases awareness of business excellence, motivates staff to focus their effort on self-analysis and continuous improvement, fosters teamwork in operating to tight deadlines, and provides an exceptional development opportunity for all involved in preparing the submission. That is it provides a rigorous basis for school self-evaluation.

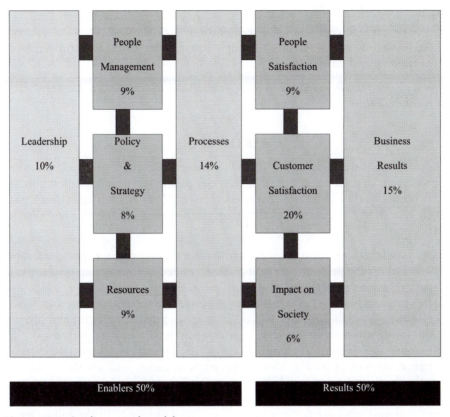

**Figure 17.1** Quality award model

*People Management* and *People Satisfaction* are similar to the Malcolm Baldridge National Quality Award Award Human Resource Management criteria (see below) and Investors in People.

*People management* (9 per cent) is about how the organization releases the full potential of its people to improve its business continuously. Evidence is needed of how:

1) people resources are planned and improved;
2) the skills and capabilities of the people are preserved and developed through recruitment, training and career progression;
3) people and teams agree targets and continuously review performance;
4) the involvement of everyone in continuous improvement is promoted and people are empowered to take appropriate action;
5) effective top-down, bottom-up and lateral communication is achieved.

*People satisfaction* (9 per cent) is what the organization is achieving in relation to the satisfaction of its people (all the individuals employed by it). Self-assessment should demonstrate the organization's success in satisfying the needs and expectations of its people:

1) The people's perception of the organization.
2) Additional measures relating to people satisfaction (e.g. staff turnover, levels of training and development).

*How well are people managed in your school and how satisfied are they? How do you know this?*

## CHARTER MARK

Charter Mark is the government's award scheme for encouraging and rewarding improvement in public services. It is the only public service award that concentrates on the quality of service that users receive. There is a self-assessment pack which reveals the organization's level of performance against the ten Charter Mark criteria.

1) *Set standards* – set clear standards of service that users can expect, and monitor and review performance and publish results, following independent validation, wherever possible.
2) *Be open and provide full information* – be open, and communicate clearly and effectively in plain language to help people using public services; and provide full information about services, their cost and how well they perform.
3) *Consult and involve* – consult and involve present and potential users of public services as well as those who work in them; and use their views to improve the services provided.
4) *Encourage access and the promotion of choice* – make services easily available to everyone who needs them including using technology to the full, offering choice whenever possible.
5) *Treat all fairly* – treat all fairly, respect their privacy and dignity; be helpful and courteous, and pay particular attention to those with special needs.
6) *Put things right when they go wrong* – put things right quickly and effectively; learn from complaints; and have a clear, well publicized and easy-to-use complaints procedure, with independent review whenever possible.
7) *Use resources effectively* – use resources effectively to provide best value for taxpayers and users.
8) *Innovate and improve* – always look for ways to improve the services and facilities offered, particularly the use of technology.
9) *Work with other providers* – work with other providers to ensure that services are simple to use, effective and co-ordinated, and deliver a better service to the user.
10) *Provide user satisfaction* – show that your users are satisfied with the quality of service they are receiving.

For each criterion there are a number of subheadings with guidance on what you will need to show the judges.

*Could your school produce evidence to match these criteria?*

## INVESTORS IN PEOPLE

Investors in People is the basis of much quality work that has occurred in schools. The distinctive focus is on the development of people. In many schools the new Department for Education and Skills (DfES) performance management framework has been extended to all staff. The Investors in People approach might be said to complement and provide external validation for the successful implementation of whole-school performance management.

1) *Commitment* – an Investor in People makes a public commitment from the top to develop all employees to achieve its business objective.
   (a) There is a public commitment from the most senior level within the organization to develop people.
   (b) Employees at all levels are aware of the broad aims or vision of the organization.
   (c) There is a written but flexible plan which sets out business goals and targets.
   (d) The plan identifies broad development needs and specifies how they will be assessed and met.
   (e) The employer has considered what employees at all levels will contribute to the success of the organization and has communicated this effectively to them.
   (f) Where representative structures exist, management communicates with employee representatives a vision of where the organization is going, and the contribution employees (and their representatives) will make to its success.
2) *Planning* – an Investor in People regularly reviews the training and development needs of all employees.
   (a) The written plan identifies the resources that will be used to meet training and development needs.
   (b) Training and development needs are regularly reviewed against business objectives.
   (c) A process exists for regularly reviewing the training and development needs of all employees.
   (d) Responsibility for developing people is clearly identified throughout the organization, starting at the top.
   (e) Managers are competent to carry out their responsibilities for developing people.
   (f) Targets and standards are set for development actions.
   (g) Where appropriate, training targets are linked to achieving external standards and particularly to National Vocational Qualifications (or Scottish Vocational Qualifications in Scotland) and units.
3) Action – an Investor in People takes action to train and develop individuals on recruitment and throughout their employment.
   (a) All new employees are introduced effectively to the organization and are given the training and development they need to do their jobs.
   (b) The skills of existing employees are developed in line with business objectives.
   (c) All employees are made aware of the development opportunities open to them.

    (d) All employees are encouraged to help identify and meet their job-related development needs.

    (e) Effective action takes place to achieve the training and development objectives of individuals and the organization.

    (f) Managers are actively involved in supporting employees to meet their training and development needs.

4) Evaluation – an Investor in People evaluates the training and development to assess achievement and improve future effectiveness.

    (a) The organization evaluates how its development of people is contributing to business and goals and targets.

    (b) The organization evaluates whether its development actions have achieved their objectives.

    (c) The outcomes of training and development are evaluated at individual, team and organizational levels.

    (d) Top management understands the broad costs and benefits of developing people.

    (e) The continuing commitment of top management to developing people is communicated to all employees.

*You could again explore whether your school could produce evidence for these indicators.*

## ISO 9000

ISO 9000 originated in the UK as BS 5750, the British Standard for quality management systems. ISO 9000 is now the global standard for quality management systems that support organization and customer relationships, with accreditation in over 340,000 organizations in 150 countries. The generic nature and much reduced documentation published in December 2000 has significantly increased its applicability in the public sector. ISO 9000 supports quality by clearly defining and documenting an organization's procedures and processes. The Standard is based on the Plan-Do-Check-Act continual improvement cycle. Independent third party assessment highlights product or service deficiencies and aids the development of improvements. The latest version, by validating the procedures and processes, allows managers to focus more on outcomes.

Schools have achieved quality accreditation in all four of these models.

## BALANCED SCORECARD

The Balanced Scorecard is a multidimensional framework for describing, implementing, and managing strategy at all levels of an enterprise by linking objectives, initiatives, and measures to an organization's strategy. The scorecard provides a view of an organization's overall performance by integrating financial measures with other more subjective key performance indicators around customer perspectives, internal business processes, and organizational growth, learning and innovation. The Balanced Scorecard is a framework for implementing and aligning complex programmes of change and indeed for managing strategy-focused organizations. Organizations are asked to select several critical indicators in each category linked to the overall strategic vision and competitive situation, to determine future success indicators. There is a need for a mix of different measures including non-financial, even if they are less sophisticated, to capture the important softer issues. For schools this gives the financial imperative a clear significance.

## TOTAL QUALITY MANAGEMENT

Total quality management (TQM) is a metaphor for the process and management of change, designed to realign the mission, culture and practices of a school to the pursuit of continuous quality improvements. Total quality management is founded on the belief that quality begins and ends with individual effort and attitude. It is a rigorous, highly disciplined and skilled procedure designed to challenge current practice and performance, and achieved by an all-pervasive training or coaching programme. Organizational, team and professional cultures are challenged though feedback. A TQM culture is predicated upon a commitment to customers' interests, needs, requirements and expectations, and upon the commitment of everyone to the constant improvement of the quality of everything that an organization does and provides for its customers. The resultant culture and working practices are designed to continually improve inputs and outcomes. For West-Burnham (1992, p. 26) total quality management as practised in schools can be defined as follows:

1) Quality is defined by the customer, not the supplier.
2) Quality consists of meeting stated needs, requirements and standards.
3) Quality is achieved through continuous improvement, by prevention, not detection.
4) Quality is driven by senior management but is an equal responsibility of all those involved in any process.
5) Quality is measured by statistical methods; the 'cost of quality' is the cost of non-conformance. Communicate with facts.
6) Quality has to pervade human relationships in the workplace; teams are the most powerful agents for managing quality.
7) Quality can only be achieved by a valued workforce; education, training and personal growth are essential to this.
8) Quality has to be the criterion for reviewing every action and every process.

*How is quality understood in your school? What is it applied to?*

## THE QUALITY GURUS

### Deming

Deming was a statistician who is credited with playing a significant part in the Japanese post-war boom. His focus is on the reluctance of managers to accept their management role. His 14 points are targeted to overcome the 'Deadly diseases' of

Western managers. He argued that a long-term commitment to a major change in values and philosophy at societal level was also required (Deming, 1986).

1) Create constancy of purpose – to improve product and service.
2) Adopt new philosophy – for new economic age by management learning.
3) Cease dependence on inspection – to achieve quality; eliminate the need for mass inspection by building quality into the product.
4) End awarding business on price – instead, minimize total cost and move toward single suppliers for items.
5) Improve constantly and forever the system of production and service – to improve quality and productivity, and to decrease costs.
6) Institute training on the job.
7) Institute leadership – supervision should be helped to do a better job; overhaul supervision of management and production workers.
8) Drive out fear – so that all work effectively for the organization.
9) Break down barriers between departments – research, design, sales and production must work together to see problems of production and use.
10) Eliminate slogans, exhortations and numerical targets – for the work force such as 'zero defects' or 'new productivity levels'. Such exhortations are diversory, as the bulk of the problems belong to the system and are beyond the power of the workforce.
11) Eliminate quotas or work standards, and management by objectives or numerical goals – substitute leadership
12) Remove barriers that rob people of their right to pride of workmanship – hourly workers, management and engineering; eliminate annual or merit rating and management by objective.
13) Institute a vigorous education and self-improvement programme.
14) Put everybody in the company to work to accomplish the transformation.

This approach is said to have contributed significantly to the post-war Japanese boom but may have had implications for the last ten years' stagnation in Japan also. The implications for schools might be a renewed focus on whole-staff commitment to transformation, the encouragement of pride in teaching, self-improvement training and leadership, school self-evaluation rather than inspection.

*How do you respond to this model?*

## Crosby

For Crosby (1978) there are four absolutes for quality management, defined as a systematic way of guaranteeing that organized activities happen the way they are planned:

1) Quality is conformance to customers' requirements not intrinsic goodness.
2) The quality system rests on prevention not detection.
3) The ultimate standard is zero defects.
4) The criterion of measurement is the measure of non-conformance.

The Crosby, Fourteen Steps to Quality improvement, has differences in emphasis from Deming. These are presented in full because they have been the basis of specific quality initiatives in the education service in the UK.

1) Make it clear that management is committed to quality.
2) Form quality improvement teams with senior representatives from each department.
3) Measure processes to determine where current and potential quality problems lie.
4) Evaluate the cost of quality and explain its use as a management tool.
5) Raise the quality awareness and personal concern of all employees.
6) Take actions to correct problems identified through precious steps.
7) Establish progress monitoring for the improvement process.
8) Train supervisors to actively carry out their part of the quality improvement programme.
9) Hold a Zero Defects Day to let everyone realize that there has been a change and reaffirm management commitment.
10) Encourage individuals to establish improvement goals for themselves and their groups.
11) Encourage employees to communicate the obstacles they face in attaining their improvement goals.
12) Recognize and appreciate those who participate.
13) Establish quality councils to communicate on a regular basis.
14) Do it all over again to emphasize that the quality improvement programme never ends.

*After considering these two models is there an agreed understanding of quality in your school?*

## Malcolm Baldridge Quality Award

The Malcolm Baldridge Awards are the most prestigious quality awards in the USA. In 1995 there was a carefully prepared education pilot, though the cost of assessment has meant that there has been no significant implementation. Given the status of the award, and the research that went into devising the pilot, it is worth examining the model in some detail. The core values and concepts are learning-centred education, leadership, continuous improvement and organizational learning, faculty and staff participation and development, partnership development, design quality and prevention, management by fact, long-range view of the future, public responsibility and citizenship, fast response and results orientation. These are explained in detail and embodied in the seven categories presented in the model in Figure 17.2. The language through which this is presented demonstrates a profound commitment to high-quality education. The model shows a rigorous understanding of the context and a sensitive application of the criteria to allow schools to assess their own performance.

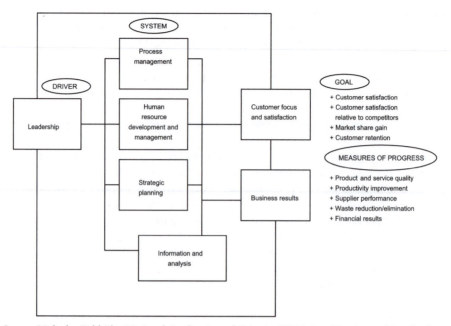

*Source:* **Malcolm Baldridge National Quality Award Criteria, US National Institute of Standards and Technology.**

**Figure 17.2** Baldridge award criteria framework

There are four criteria for human resource development and management.

1) *Human resource planning and evaluation* – describe how the school's human resource planning and evaluation are aligned with the school's overall performance improvement plans and address the development and well-being of faculty and staff.
2) *Faculty and staff work systems* – describe how the school's faculty and staff positions promote a student focus, cross-functional co-operation and high performance. Describe also how evaluation, compensation, promotion and recognition reinforce these objectives.
3) *Faculty and staff development* – describe how the school's faculty and staff development advances school plans and contributes to faculty and staff performance improvement, development and advancement.
4) *Faculty and staff well-being and satisfaction* – describe how the school maintains a work environment and a work climate conducive to the well-being and satisfaction of faculty and staff and focuses on the school's performance objectives.

This model has been presented in some detail because it is about self-assessment and an interesting international quality model directly focussed on the education service.

## Peters and Waterman

Peters and Waterman (1982) suggested that it was possible to define the attributes which characterize excellent American companies. The non-rational quasi-religious thought and behaviour which characterized this approach to quality became extremely popular in the 1980s. The characteristics were of companies which were *In Search of Excellence*, the best selling business book ever with over 5 million copies sold. The eight characteristics they identified have become central to an understanding of quality.

1) A bias for action: getting on with it.
2) Close to the customer: learning from the people they serve.
3) Autonomy and entrepreneurship: fostering innovation and nurturing 'champions'.
4) Productivity through people: treating the rank and file as a source of quality
5) Hands-on, value-driven: management showing its commitment.
6) Stick to the knitting: stay with the business you know.
7) Simple form, lean staff: some of the best companies have a minimum of headquarters staff.
8) Simultaneous loose–tight properties: autonomy in shop floor activities plus centralized values.

The application of these characteristics to education was explored in the 1980s and 1990s. The second most influential of Peters's books was *Thriving on Chaos* (1987), with another title that was appropriate for the time. This opened with the statement 'There are no excellent companies'. This was about the move from hierarchical management pyramid to a horizontal, fast, cross-functional, co-operative one. In *Thriving on Chaos* the five chapters illustrate the approach: 'Creating total customer responsiveness'; 'Pursuing fast-paced innovation'; 'Achieving flexibility by empowering people'; 'Learning to love change: a new view of leadership at all levels'; and 'Building systems for a world turned upside down'. These two books contain the most energetic of Peters's work, and the enthusiasm and self-belief that characterize his message. His 12 attributes of quality revolutions (Peters, 1987) are:

1) Management obsession with quality – practical action to back up the emotional commitment.
2) Passionate systems – failure is due to passion without system or system without passion. There has to be a belief system.
3) Quality is measured – from the start, carried out by those involved and displayed.
4) Quality is rewarded.
5) Everyone is trained for quality – every person should be trained in the appropriate technologies for assessing quality.
6) Teams involving multiple functions/systems are used – including quality circles.

7) Small is very beautiful – every improvement is significant.

8) There is constant stimulation – new goals, new events, new themes.

9) There is a parallel organization structure devoted to quality improvement.

10) Everyone is involved – suppliers especially, but distributors and customers too, must be a part of the organization's quality process, possibly in joint improvement teams.

11) When quality goes up, costs go down – quality improvement is the primary source of cost reduction. The elementary force at work is simplification – of design, process or procedures.

12) Quality improvement is a never-ending journey – all quality is relative. Every product or service is constantly getting better or worse, but never stands still.

Peters has a restless energy and changes his views, but presents models that challenge and help clarify what we mean by quality.

   *Given these considerations of quality, what is an appropriate model for your school?*

## BENCHMARKING

Benchmarking is a process of learning about your own practices, learning from the best practices of others with a reputation for outstanding performance and then making changes to meet or beat the best in the world. It is a systematic analytical approach to improving performance by understanding and learning from the success of others. Successful benchmarking entails:

* identifying your organization's present level of performance;
* comparing your organization against others with similar organizational challenges, as well as others who have achieved the successful performance one aspires to;
* identifying the gap between current practice and the benchmark.

The challenge then is discovering and understanding the best practice to reach new goals and closing the gap. Benchmarking can be applied to management practices as well as more technical processes.

   Best practice is a high-performance way of achieving business objectives, which solves problems, creates opportunities, and improves business results. Benchmarking provides a direct link between learning and taking action. Beacon Schools provide such a government benchmark. The benchmarking process builds support for change by demonstrating what can be done through real-life examples and involving the people who will be making the changes (Tucker, 1996).

1) Benchmarking is a focused structured process of self-evaluation, adapting and learning fast through finding leading organizations' secrets, and implementing improvements.

2) You do not mindlessly copy others when you benchmark. You must adapt and

tailor their successful strategies to fit your own unique circumstances

3) You should reach outside the world of education to capture richer ideas and experiences. They are usually very transferable and therefore encourage innovation.

4) The key to successful benchmarking is, simply, sharing. Your willingness to exchange information increases others' willingness to be open and share their experiences.

5) Benchmarking is not expensive. Most benchmarking can and should be done via e-mail and telephone. Best practice information can be collected in many highly productive ways. Site visits are only necessary in special situations.

6) The key to successful benchmarking is involving the people who will have to implement the changes. People commit to change when they seek out, learn and adapt new ideas to their own situation.

7) Benchmarking is, arguably, the single most powerful tool for ensuring that your school has set its sights on excellence and the pursuit of innovation.

*What does and should your school benchmark against best practice for improving performance? How can this be best achieved?*

## QUALITY AND MARKETING

A marketing orientation is

> a management orientation that holds the key tasks of the organisation is to determine the needs, wants and values of a target market and to adapt the organisation to delivering the desired satisfactions more effectively and efficiently than its competitors. (Kotler and Armstong, 1994)

> 'relationship marketing' emphasises that the 'provider' seeks to develop a connection with the 'customer' which extends far beyond the ideas of simply selling a product. It seeks to establish a multi-sided relationship between partners, identifying and meeting the needs of parents, pupils and other stakeholders who actively recommend each other to a wider audience and continually seek to further the relationship. (Foskett, 1997)

Best marketing practice is made up of:

- genuine marketing orientation – the identification and satisfaction of customers' needs;
- heightened environmental sensitivity – a commitment to monitoring, scanning and assessing changes in the marketplace;
- organizational flexibility and adaptability – the need to avoid an over-rigid structure within the school and a mechanism for changing this structure in line with changes in the environment;
- increased marketing professionalism – a commitment to the recruitment of trained marketing professionals and the realization of the benefits of ongoing training.

The marketization of education (Bridges and McLaughlin, 1994) has a very different focus. The school marketing plan is the most visible organizational symbol of a marketing orientation and implies that marketing is manageable though systematic planning. The marketing function has been about managing the four Ps of product, price, promotion and place. The marketing mix is suited to a systems design approach for integrating the different elements of the mix. One of the distinctive skills of professional marketers is their ability to create, maintain, protect, reinforce and enhance brands, which for a school would be its identity. If the real value of a company lies outside the business itself, in the minds of potential buyers, then the reality of the schools lies in the minds of parents. The marketing mix requires an appropriate communications mix. Some 'marketing' has been too directly focused on recruiting to the school, hence the links to marketization. Marketing for business has shifted to building short- and long-term relationships through networks. The idea of developing brands is now being extended to deal with the intangible values of brands. The school brand, its institutional identity, is increasingly the focus of external relations in schools (Foskett, 1992).

*Does your school have a marketing strategy and a marketing plan? How do you evaluate their effectiveness?*

## REFERENCES

Bridges, D. and McLaughlin, T.H. (1994) *Education and the Market Place*, London: Falmer.

Crosby, P.B. (1978) *Quality is Free*, New York, NY and London: McGraw-Hill.

Deming, W.E. (1986) *Out of the Crisis*, Cambridge, MA, and London: MIT Press.

Foskett, N. (ed.) (1992) *Managing External Relations in Schools*, London: Routledge.

Foskett, N. (1997) 'Marketing for schools', *Management in Education*, **11**(5), November–December.

Kotler, P. and Armstrong, G. (1994) *Principles of Marketing*, Englewood Cliffs, NJ: Prentice-Hall.

Peters, T.J. (1987) *Thriving on Chaos*, London: Macmillan.

Peters, T.J. and Waterman, R.H. (1982) *In Search of Excellence*, New York, NY and London: Harper and Row.

Tucker, S. (1996) *Benchmarking: A Guide for Educators*, Thousand Oaks, CA: Corwin Press.

West-Burnham, J. (1992) *Managing Quality in Schools*, London: Longman.

# 18

## The Learning Organization and Knowledge Management

### THE LEARNING ORGANIZATION

A learning organization is one which facilitates the learning of all its members and continuously transforms itself. Some organizations have explored what strategies they need to survive or more positively to influence the direction of change through their capacity to learn. They have learned to scan the environment attentively, to adapt and change quickly and intelligently and to generate new ideas which question established values and icons. They have a capacity to learn and to unlearn. Poor performance often results from persisting with failing strategies despite evidence of the failure of these polices. Individuals learn by a process of experience and reflection; groups learn by a process of sharing of individual experiences; organizations learn by a process of sharing individual and group experiences

Schools like other organizations differ profoundly in their capacity to learn, change and improve. Educational leaders need to identify the current everyday routines, structures and system barriers to organizational learning. Effective strategic human resource management ensures that internally – through structures and processes aligned to current strategies – and externally – with strategies adapted to the environment, the strategic 'fit' ensures organizational learning. Organizational learning is about learning, responsiveness, flexibility, commitment and quality. The external pressures for change that require learning are the cultural dimension – at the level of public ideas and values, and policy, that is, the received wisdom; and the institutional dimension – when these ideas have become embodied in sets of institutionalised practices, such as Investors in People and the business excellence model.

*How well does your school learn, change and improve? How do you learn, change and improve?*

### SENGE

Senge (1990) defined the learning organization as a model of how organizations should be structured if they are to achieve maximum learning. The concept emerged in the late 1980s in the USA though much of the thinking is built on earlier systems theory. The learning processes are growth, development, adaptation and learning which underlie healthy, adaptive survival. Senge argues that superior performance depends on superior learning. He makes much of the role and attributes of the leader in the learning organization, identifying in some detail the qualities and skills required: an overarching view of the whole system, developing a personal vision, patience, the releasing of energy, devolving leadership and the periodic reframing of vision through teamwork.

Executive leaders develop strategies for creating an environment where people are open to new ideas, responsive to change, and eager to develop new skills and capabilities (Senge, 1992). He defined learning organizations as 'organizations where people continually expand their capacity to create the results they truly desire, where new and expansive habits of thinking are nurtured, where collective aspiration is set free and where people are continually learning how to learn together' (*Ibid.*). This is a vision for a school. The Senge model is based on five disciplines:

- Systems thinking is about understanding the relationship and patterns within the whole in order to change them.
- Personal mastery is about focusing energies, operating as an artist, continually learning and clarifying and deepening personal vision.
- Mental models are images, often unconscious that influence the way we act. In order to grow it is essential to unearth these pictures and understand them to be able to use them productively.
- Building shared vision through creating a commitment to a shared understanding of the future ideal, not a mere vision statement. It is about having skills in achieving pictures of the future that foster genuine dedication and energy.
- Team learning is developing skills in ensuring the intelligence and performance of the whole is greater than the sum of the individuals through genuinely thinking together as a team.

These five disciplines characterize the learning organization which is a concept to focus aspiration. For schools the importance of unlearning old habits, old beliefs and old behaviours may be as critical and more difficult since school cultures are frequently profoundly embedded.

*Given this definition, is your school a learning organization?*

## THE LEARNING COMPANY

Pedler, Burgoyne and Boydell (1991) presented a profile of the learning company with 11 interlocking elements of a jigsaw, for which scores can be allocated between 1 and 5 for each characteristic to provide an intuitive diagnosis of your school as a learning organization. A score of 40 or above suggests your school may have many of the virtues of a learning organization. You will need to interpret the business language to meet your own needs. If the score is below 20, sporadic learning only may be taking place. The original model has significantly more information than is shown here. The 11 characteristics of a learning organization are:

- The learning approach to strategy – policy and strategy formulation are structured as learning processes.
- Participative policy-making – appraisal and career planning discussions often generate visions that contribute to strategy and policy.
- Informating – information is used to understand, not for reward or punishment.
- Formative accounting and control – systems of accounting, budgeting and reporting are structured to assist learning.
- Internal exchange – departments speak freely and candidly with each other both to challenge and give help.
- Reward flexibility – the basic assumptions and values underpinning reward systems are explored and shared.
- Enabling structures – roles and careers are flexibly structured to allow for experimentation, growth and adaptation.
- Boundary workers as environmental scanners – there are systems and procedures for receiving, collating and sharing information from outside the school.
- Inter-organizational learning – using benchmarking in order to learn from the best practice in other schools and businesses.
- Learning climate – there is a general attitude of continuous improvement – always trying to learn and do better.
- Self-development opportunities for all – the exploration of an individual's learning needs is a central focus of appraisal and career planning.

*Using this more technical model, in which areas does your school not have the characteristics of a learning organization?*

## LEARNING AT THE INDIVIDUAL, TEAM AND ORGANIZATIONAL LEVELS

We know much about individual learning, though this is being greatly enhanced by developments in understanding the brain discussed earlier, but there is also more recent evidence about how the learning and generic problem-solving capacity of an organization can be enhanced. Professional development may concentrate on learning to do things better technically, as opposed to learning about the assumptions underlying what you do and why you do them. The former may actually inhibit the radical fundamental learning because it is based on fire fighting, not a thorough analysis and challenge of deep organizational assumptions and values. There is a danger of concentrating learning at the individual level, and even at this level of concentrating on simpler forms of learning. Senge talks about 'adaptive' or 'generative' learning. Argyris (1990) makes a similar distinction between single- and the double-loop learning which is about questioning established mindsets. However, schools may create learning systems that inhibit double-loop learning because they inevitably call into question the school's norms, objectives and basic policies.

The two sets of variables Argyris (1990) identifies that affect the effectiveness of learning are the nature and flow of information within the organization and the willingness of those who receive information to analyse and interpret it openly and thoroughly. In many organizations data is distorted and the reception of it interrupted. The three factors, for Argyris, which are necessary for the achievement of organizational learning, are at the individual level; the structure and culture; and the organizational decision-making systems and processes. Individuals have significant variations in their individual learning skills, attributes and behaviour. At the structural level the focus is on the relationship between stability and responsiveness to change. The capacity of schools to perform complex tasks extremely well depends on the processes of work differentiation and their subsequent reintegration and co-ordination, all of which involve forms of political behaviour. Schools are occupational organizations in which certain states of mind are encouraged to exist and thrive. Though every school is different, the dimensions and nature of those differences need to be recognized. A learning organization must develop the ability to recognize the nature and role of the frameworks, normative as well as cognitive, that they currently use.

> At the heart of a learning organisation is a shift of mind – from seeing ourselves as separate from the world to connected to the world, from seeing problems as caused by someone or something 'out there' to seeing how our actions create the problems we experience. A learning organisation is a place where people are continually discovering how they create their reality, and how they can change it. (Argyris, 1990, pp. 12–13)

*Consider the links between culture and the learning organization.*

The difficulty in establishing a learning school is in identifying precisely the cultural blockages inhibiting learning. Those with responsibility may respond with culturally based ways of evaluation and sensible thinking. The may not react positively to attempts to identify and critique values which they regard as central. Their responses may be formulated in terms of the particular cultural values and mindsets being analysed and challenged. Identifying and mobilizing the support of cultural deviants therefore is particularly important.

Morrison (2002) provides a self-assessment scale for the types of learning in a school as a learning organization – maintenance learning, benchmark learning and creative learning. He refers to Senge's model that in schools as learning organizations involves:

- Learning which is learner-centred rather than teacher-centred.
- Encouraging diversity rather than homogeneity – embracing multiple intelligences and a diversity of learning styles.
- Understanding interdependency and change rather than the memorization of facts and striving after 'right answers'.
- A continuous exploration of the theories in use by all those involved in education.
- A reintegration of education within webs of social relationship, e.g. linking families, friends and whole communities.

## LEARNING AND DECISION-MAKING

The elements of the decision process – problems, models, decision-maker, solutions, opportunities, become mixed together fortuitously and lie randomly like rubbish in a dustbin. Decision-making is not classically rational but the ground on which organizational conflicts and differences are played out, and may be unrelated to learning. There is a complementary danger of groupthink (Janis, 1972) which creates subtle anti-learning group dynamics. To overcome this will require: disinterested leadership because the leader normally makes her/his preferences clear; more methodical group processes such as information search and systematic decision-making; recognizing the manifestations of patterns of group behaviour which lead to overestimating the group's competence; challenging the illusion of the group's invulnerability and unanimity; and testing the collective rationalism and pressures towards conformity such as self-censorship rather than the encouragement of safe dissent. The learning group will make better decisions.

The capacity of the school to learn through double-loop learning, going beyond existing boundaries and routines, is increasingly crucial to the school's survival. Schools that are not interested in thinking about how they learn, and in addressing the barriers to learning, will not learn, and if they do not learn will probably not perform. All those working within a school can enhance its capacity to engage in the learning process by recognizing the forces, structure and culture that undermine learning and identifying some of the positive practical steps that can be taken. This means that a learning organization as for Senge, in a period of globalization, the knowledge era and with access to all the information technology, is continually expanding its capacity to create its future.

## CREATING A LEARNING ORGANIZATION

Braham (1995) lists the characteristics of an almost obsessional approach to learning that will lead to the creation of a learning organization. There are clear links across to some of the other themes explored in this book.

1. Learning is incorporated into everything people do.
2. Learning for learning's sake is encouraged and rewarded.
3. The organization supports teamwork, creativity, empowerment and quality.
4. Employees are trusted and encouraged to choose courses that they need.
5. People with different job titles from different departments learn together.
6. The organization promotes mentoring relationships to enhance learning.
7. Learning is an integral part of meetings, work groups, and work processes.
8. Everyone in the organization has equal access to learning.
9. Mistakes are learning opportunities.
10. The organization encourages cross-training and rewards employees that learn a broad range of skills.
11. Continuous learning must become a ubiquitously shared, core value of the organization. (*ibid.*)

The use through learning of concepts (best and latest ideas), competence (ability to operate at the highest standards) and connections (relationships that provide access to the best people) grow from such investments in innovation, training and collaboration. Learning organizations are ultimately where people develop both personal and organizational perspectives for both immediate and long-term sustainable performance improvement.

*How can your school learn more profoundly? How can you contribute to enhancing its capacity to learn?*

## KNOWLEDGE MANAGEMENT

For Rajan (1998), Chief Executive of CREATE (Centre for Research in Employment and Technology in Europe) knowledge management is about leveraging existing knowledge inside an organization and creating new knowledge in the process. The five categories of knowledge are:

- Data – raw numbers or anecdotes which are not in themselves revealing.
- Information – the key messages from the data once analysed for their meaning.
- Explicit knowledge – transmittable in formal, systematic language and about making enough sense out of information to be able to propose action.
- Tacit knowledge – personal, context specific but hard to formalize and communicate – in oral or written form – because it comprises insights, hunches and intuitions.
- Wisdom – combines all categories of knowledge to the extent that its deployment requires mental and emotional intelligence, learning and experiencing, thinking and doing.

For Rajan, in the corporate context the tacit knowledge and its refined version, wisdom, derived from accumulated insights and experiences, are converted from individual learning to organizational learning.

- Intuitive knowledge – spreading individual insights and intuitions from some to many people.
- Conceptual knowledge – translating individual insights into words or concepts which can be disseminated widely through oral, written or visual means.
- Operational knowledge – internalizing a formal body of knowledge into an individual's subconscious by its repeated application.
- Systematic knowledge – creating a library of knowledge using words, concepts and numbers in ways that provide easy access to all.

*How do the leaders in your school understand this kind of knowledge?*

Knowledge management, a more recent development, is the engine room of the learning organization. Knowledge management is the management of the information, knowledge, and experience available to an organization – its creation, capture, storage, availability and utilization, in order that organizational activities build on what is already known and extend it further. Organizations know they have vast reservoirs of knowledge vital for future success but may lack the ability to tap into them and to create a culture of knowledge sharing, capturing and rewarding the knowledge potential of everyone. A knowledge management system will include the following processes, which show the links with learning organizations:

- managing the generation of new knowledge through learning;
- capturing knowledge and experience;
- sharing, collaborating and communication;
- organizing information for easy access;
- using and building on what is known.

*Given this definition does your school manage knowledge effectively?*

## NETWORKS AND KNOWLEDGE MANAGEMENT

The key to knowledge management is to unlock the flow of knowledge and to help it flow faster. It is about the new technologies – intranets and the Internet which will help shift control of knowledge away from the organization and towards the learner. For the education service it is important to be clear what the organization is – the whole education service, the local education authorities, networked learning communities or schools. Network analysis enables the measurement and visualization of organizational knowledge in its early evolutionary or tacit stages at any level. Leveraging the knowledge capital in the educational service, or an institution, is a complex process. A network analysis can identify leverage points for change, map and measure the required action steps and identify hot spots for future development.

Those who determine which knowledge is to be retained, for example on the various parts of the National College for School Leadership website need high level skills in knowledge management. The DfES website could provide an opportunity to manage this process, through the National Grid for Learning, with proper strategic planning. There is a need, however, for knowledge champions to determine what the knowledge culture within the education service is, and they may come through different routes. They need shared mindsets, visions and strategies; new values and attitudes; networking and teamworking; recognition and reward for knowledge-sharing; and trust. The market value of a company depends increasingly on the valuation of its intellectual capital. Teacher professional development will be about skilfully accessing the knowledge that will be increasingly more directly and easily available. It is important for the education service to learn from good practice in knowledge creation and exchange (Rajan, Lank and Chapple, 1999) and to know that tacit knowledge is about skills, attributes and behaviour.

*Are you a member of any networked learning communities?*

## STRATEGIC KNOWLEDGE MANAGEMENT

If intellectual capital is a combination of competence and commitment, knowledge management is about the transformation of human capital into structural capital. The important part is to build on the learning and convert the learning into action. The role of senior management is to make sure that after learning, there are mechanisms in place for transferring this learning. In knowledge management, strategic advantage lies in the sense-making capabilities of the brain that interpret information and data more than the electronic information highways. New knowledge is created by and through people. Smart organizations work out how to capture as much as possible and make it available to everyone. Within strategic knowledge management there are links to:

- strategy development – master concepts, the road map process, standards, structure and security;
- promotion and co-ordination – best-practice sharing, community of practice, knowledge management, knowledge culture and knowledge management process;
- provision of services – support for communities of practice, evaluation tools for knowledge management and observing future development of knowledge business.

## TACIT KNOWLEDGE – A PRELIMINARY CONSIDERATION

Nonaka and Takeuchi in *The Knowledge Creating Company* (1995) suggest that such a company focuses on developing intangible assets and tends to emphasize the part of IT only in facilitating knowledge transfer. Ideas, intellect and information have replaced land labour and capital. They describe knowledge management as 'the capability of the organization as a whole to create new knowledge, disseminate it through the organisation and quickly embody it in key products, services and systems' (*ibid.*). They emphasize the importance of tacit knowledge, the informal unconscious skills and understandings, and the four processes to assist making tacit local knowledge explicit:

- Socialization – encouraging teams to share their tacit experiences and mental models through observation and imitation.
- Externalization – articulation of explicit knowledge through iterative dialogue to clarify meaning.
- Combination – standardizing knowledge, combining new ideas with existing knowledge.
- Internalization – reframing their implicit understanding to take account of new knowledge and enrich tacit knowledge.

They argue that the Japanese recognize the importance of intuition and tacit knowledge and use tools like metaphor and analogy to elucidate tacit knowledge, with information available on one integrated database accessible by all and employees rotating around departments. Several teams will develop ideas for a single project with the apparent redundancy forcing people to think from different perspectives. Middle managers 'orient this chaos towards purposeful knowledge creation, as knowledge engineers who synthesise and make explicit the tacit knowledge' (*ibid.*). The West, and this may include your school, focuses on externalization and combination, placing faith on explicit records of outcomes, but this can incline to paralysis by analysis.

*Consider the concept of tacit knowledge as it applies to your school.*

## THE BENFITS OF KNOWLEDGE-SHARING AND THE USE OF IT

Knowledge management is a process not a technology linked to changes in the ways that people work. The need is to focus on the process – the way people are involved and the way implementation is managed, underlined by the limitations of technology. It is important to ensure that there are rewards for knowledge-sharing even if these are symbolic. Knowledge workers may find that opportunities to work on challenging projects are their own reward, with professional recognition or influence in the future as the result. The IT community in the education service needs to be addressing the real and growing need to convert knowledge into a genuine asset. The key to the value of many companies is their intangible assets. Knowledge management is about sustaining and developing this capital. In businesses the widely accepted divisions are:

- externally related or customer assets, including brands, customer relationships and reputation;
- internal or structural assets, such as systems, patents, processes, culture, documented experience and knowledge;
- human assets – the people available to the organization, their intelligence, skills and experience – and how they are led and motivated.

Knowledge management is about transferring the skills and attitudes that are essentially personal to the second category, the knowledge, wisdom and experience that can be captured for all employees. The interest in intellectual assets is one of the driving forces behind the development of knowledge management. A second factor is the learning organization. As shown above, learning organizations have found that their greatest need is to capture and use the knowledge available to them. Change means that teams and relationships are broken up, including the staff who used to co-ordinate corporate synergy of knowledge and resources. This can lead to wasted effort and repeated mistakes from the failure to manage knowledge and experience across an organization. The third significant development is information technology. The potential for such systems to enhance organizational learning is being rapidly realized in some companies.

## COMMUNITIES OF PRACTICE

Some organizations make knowledge-sharing part of the work process; others are developing specific knowledge-sharing competencies for use during recruitment and appraisal processes. A significant element of recruitment is to begin the process of accessing the knowledge that interviewees have to evaluate their possible contribution to the organization. What is important while they are with the school is getting them to share their insights and experience so projects can be completed faster and more effectively. A sophisticated approach would persuade staff that effective knowledge-sharing can make their jobs easier and more satisfying, and can enhance their reputations. Rather than attempting to capture what other people might want to know, the emphasis should be on finding ways to connect people within 'communities of practice' and promote collaboration between them.

The relationship between the learning organization and knowledge management was summarized at the 1999 IPD People Mean Business Conference by the Assistant Director General of the IPD (Ward Griffiths) as shown below. To achieve a learning organization and knowledge management the following are required.

- Emphasis on culture management and organization design.
- Emphasis on maintaining and managing tacit knowledge embedded as organizational culture and value systems.
- Strategic/HR managers responsible for change.
- Emphasis on information systems management and systems design.
- Emphasis on changing tacit knowledge into explicit knowledge.
- IS/IT managers and chief knowledge officers responsible for change.

*How important will knowledge management be in your professional development? How important will it be for the education service?*

## KNOWLEDGE MANAGEMENT IN EDUCATION

The sections above have sought to link the learning organization and knowledge management in business to education. Sallis and Jones (2002) have clarified the implications of knowledge management in education in the first book which has concentrated on this subject. This merits a fuller reading. The book explores what knowledge management is, making the most of what you know, developing value-creating knowledge, adapting management processes to meet the challenges of the knowledge era, using knowledge to strengthen institutional performance, and enhancing the learning of pupils, students and staff. There is a useful knowledge management self-assessment checklist with scoring for elements which relate to vision and mission, strategy, organizational culture, intellectual capital, learning organization, leadership and management, teamwork and learning communities, sharing knowledge, knowledge creation, digital sophistication for the organization. This provides an excellent foundation for developing an understanding.

## DEFINING TACIT KNOWLEDGE AND KNOWLEDGE COMMUNITIES

The two lists below from Sallis and Jones (2002) illustrate the explanatory practicality and clarity of their approach.

*Tacit or personal knowledge* (ibid, *p. 14*):

- is about 'knowing how' (procedural knowledge);
- is socially constructed knowledge;
- has two strands – technical knowledge of *know-how* and cognitive knowledge
- contains the folklore of the organization;
- is stored inside people's heads;
- can be the knowledge of the mastery of a skill;
- contains values, insights, hunches, prejudices, feelings, images, symbols and beliefs;
- can be chaotic;
- is difficult to codify and to store on databases and intranets;
- is often difficult to communicate and share;
- is valuable and a rich source of experience and learning.

*Knowledge communities (ibid., p. 26):*

- are self-organized informal groups;
- have social meaning to members who value the relationship formed in the community;
- are learning communities;
- are built around common purposes and things that matter;
- involve the common pursuit of problems and solutions;
- operate across functions and divisions;
- can be supported by nurturing management or leadership styles;
- have a life cycle that depends on the value of the task to the group;
- are repositories of tacit knowledge;
- can make tacit knowledge explicit;
- can keep organizations at the leading edge of knowledge creation;
- can effectively use the emotional IQ (EQ) of their members;
- have a strong resonance in education.

Those taking seriously their personal and professional development will need to be members of learning organizations and to develop the skills to work with whatever knowledge management processes are now accessible. In future these will be essential skills in the professional teaching career.

*How is tacit knowledge of your school used? How, in practice, do you belong to knowledge communities?*

## REFERENCES

Argyris, C. (1990) *Overcoming Organisational Defences: Facilitating Organisational Learning*, Boston, MA: Allyn Bacon.
Braham, B. (1995) *Creating a Learning Organization*, Menlo Park, CA: Crisp Publications.

Drucker, P. (1998) 'The future that has already happened', *The Futurist*, November. pp. 43–5.

Janis, I.L. (1972) *Victims of Groupthink*, Boston, MA: Houghton-Mifflin.

Morrison, K. (2002) *School Leadership and Complexity*, London: Routledge Falmer.

Nonaka, I. and Takeuchi, H. (1995) *The Knowledge Creating Company*, Oxford: Oxford University Press.

Pedler, M., Burgoyne. M.J. and Boydell, T. (1991) *The Learning Company: A Strategy for Sustainable Development*, 2nd edn, New York, NY and London: McGraw-Hill.

Rajan, A. (1998) 'Knowledge workers: improving performance' presentation synopsis, CIPD HRD week.

Rajan, A., Lank, L. and Chapple, K. (1999) *Good Practices in Knowledge Creation and Exchange*, London: CREATE.

Sallis, E. and Jones, G. (2002) *Knowledge Management in Education: Enhancing Learning and Education*, London: Kogan Page.

Senge, P. (1992) *The Fifth Discipline: the Art and Practice of the Learning Organisation*, London: Doubleday.

# 19

## Business Process Re-engineering: Achieving Radical Change

### WHAT IS BUSINESS PROCESS RE-ENGINEERING? HOW IS IT RELEVANT FOR SCHOOLS?

Business process re-engineering (BPR) is the fundamental rethinking and radical redesign of business processes to achieve dramatic improvements in critical, contemporary measures of performance, such as cost, quality, service and speed. 'Business re-engineering means starting all over, starting from scratch ... At the heart of business re-engineering lies the notion of discontinuous thinking – identifying and abandoning the outdated rules and fundamental assumptions that underlie current business operations' (Hammer and Champy, 1993). The argument is that change, competition and customer expectations are changing so rapidly that incremental quality improvements are inadequate. This, it might be argued, applies increasingly to schools. 'Re-engineering takes 40% of the labour out of most processes. For middle managers, it is even worse; 80% of them either have their jobs eliminated or cannot adjust to a team-based organisation that requires them to be more of a coach than a taskmaster' (Hammer and Champy, 1993).

The Chartered Institute of Management (CIMgt) (2000) characterizes organizations as process driven and distinguishes BPR as convulsive and revolutionary. The essence of BPR is that change has to be discontinuous because it challenges current assumptions, received wisdom and routine thinking. This model for radical and creative change has brought about some spectacular gains in performance, productivity and profitability. However, there has been no guarantee of success and frequently internal resistance depending on how well the process has been managed. The CIMgt understanding of the BPR process is the development of the vision; the identification of objectives; undertaking the preliminary planning; analysing the existing processes; establishing performance indicators against which improvement can be measured; collecting data for analysis; redesigning the processes; finalizing the implementation process; and, monitoring and evaluating progress. This change process model itself is traditional.

Business process re-engineering is now sometimes perceived as a fad from the mid-1990s because the process was not always effectively carried through. The reason for most of the failures was because people were ignored. Now (2003) that the DfES has a Minister for Children and Young People, this provides a new opportunity for re-engineering support for families with children not normally coherently supported by the education and training services, social services, the health service, the police, the tax and benefits system and employment. This new ministerial role illustrates central government recognition of the potential of BPR to impact on children and young people. The proposed Children's Commissioner and local authority Directors for Children's Services (2003) demonstrate the same policy thrust.

*Consider a child you know who is involved with a number of agencies and explore how coherent is the family support from the state.*

## PREPARING FOR THE LONGER VIEW

Kanter (1998) explores what leads to the longer view within which BPR, 'traumatic restructuring', exists. Schools that are to improve their performance dramatically need to work within this longer term.

1) Understanding the dynamics of systems – people take the long view when they have a deep understanding of system dynamics. Learning from experience and the past enables people to uncover root principles, cause-and-effect relationships, and insight into dynamics, trajectories and consequences. Knowledge is central to the new information-based organizations. Learning comes from respect for experience and desire to improve.

2) Commitment to one's successors – people take a long view when they feel a commitment to those who come after them so they want to build enduring institutions and leave a legacy for the future. Rekindling idealism involves a reminder that the present is another step in history. People care about their place in history when the past is valued. History is an antidote to arrogance, through a sense of responsibility ensuring that assets do not deteriorate

3) Belief that the rules are fair – people take the long view when they believe that the rules of the game are fair. They believe they will share equitably in the returns. It is hard to do this alone deferring gains when others are cashing in.

4) Trusting the leaders – people take the long view when they perceive leaders as trustworthy. When decisions take their needs into account, they feel included. Trust is a bet about future actions based on experience. A track record of keeping promises is a good predictor. Realigning interests and rebuilding commitment after traumatic restructuring involves making short-term promises and keeping them to restore faith. Leaders erode their credibility by violating agreements or pressurizing stakeholders to make greater concessions. The long view must be shared embodying wisdom and values from the past as well as hopes and dreams for the future.

*School leaders need to achieve this culture as a basis for radical change. Is there a widespread commitment to this longer view in your school?*

Business process re-engineering, the fundamental redesign of organizational processes cross-functionally around outcomes, draws on IT to support these changes. Schools are increasingly accessing high-quality data to evaluate individual performance. In seeking to identify how best to satisfy or excite this individual customer, BPR frequently uncovers redundant processes that no longer add value. The original model (Hammer and Champy, 1993) was interpreted as requiring that large numbers of staff had to be made redundant. The intention had been to streamline or remove bureaucratic procedures and to make work processes more efficient. The practice, however, was not to improve through reorganization but to reduce costs through staff cuts, and without the managers having to accept direct responsibility. There were dramatic improvements in individual processes but frequently a significant decline in overall results. People and values were ignored (Snyder, 1996). The short-term expedient managerial behaviour, protecting their own positions, resulted in short-term contracts for some and longer working hours and increased stress for others, producing alienated workforces which had little or no identification with the employer. If there is to be a radical transformation, it will require a cultural change which demands sophisticated change leadership skills. This was difficult to achieve in practice without replacing the intransigent senior staff, changing work procedures and making new demands on the workforce.

## THE FAILURES DUE TO IGNORING THE PEOPLE DIMENSION

As early as 1994 this reason for failure was recognized (Obeng and Crainer, 1994). Though the need to change was high, the practical implementation of re-engineering was held back because the human implications were ignored, overlooked or underestimated. The revolution did not reach out to the attitudes and behaviour of managers. This exacerbated the problems caused by underestimating the human implications of the re-engineering process. It is easier to redesign procedures and invest in technology than to take up the more profound challenge of changing people's attitudes, beliefs and values. The changes involved in re-engineering are significantly greater than those contemplated in the more incremental total quality programmes. Such active change management is harder to rationalize and achieve than reactive change.

*How does business process re-engineering as a concept apply to your school? Would your educational processes benefit from a fundamental reconsideration? How well do your leaders manage change?*

The reduction of the number of management levels this requires is inevitably supported by a system of competency assessment and performance related pay which schools are moving towards. When the repetitious and needless activities are recognized and removed, tackling the teacher workload, a process necessary to enhance the quality of the core purpose of learning can be driven forward. However, the security of some specialists, including middle managers, and set procedures will be lost since it is essential not to fall back on functional hierarchies or traditional ways of doing things.

## RE-ENGINEERING MANAGEMENT PROCESSES

The managers who drove through these processes in business in the mid-1990s underestimated the human side of re-engineering. Cultural and personnel issues were relegated below technical processes and the associated IT. Managers were loath to re-engineer their own activities, espousing revolution but practising conservatism, so problematic management practices escaped demolition – and this undermined the very structure of the rebuilt enterprises. This may apply to school leaders in similar circumstances (Fletcher, 1994). The re-engineered organization is elusively intangible but is about performance management and the disappearance of traditional career ladders. For the manager whose skills are built on the old functional certainties the process-based organization is difficult to manage. This destruction and disruption of their power bases may cause senior and middle managers to focus on their loss of control and authority. Becoming process owners can be difficult for school leaders who may be uncomfortable with the rigorous and ceaseless questioning which re-engineering brings – particularly from the pupils. The potential for dissension and conflict is high and organizations and managers have to acknowledge their own need to change radically if they are to break ingrained habits. The re-engineering of learning and assessment for each pupil in partnership with other agencies is what BPR is about for local education authorities and schools.

## CHANGING THE CULTURE, SYSTEMS, STRUCTURE AND HIERARCHY

The change from the traditional functional hierarchy to process requires changes in the culture, systems, structure and technology which all demand the identification of the new skills and competencies required. The technology here is teaching. The hierarchies, boundaries and internal focus are refocused on teams, cross-sections and externally. The culture of smothering, second guessing and controlling is changed to one of empowering, trusting and supporting. There is a change from an upward focus to downward focus and from analysis and a fear of mistakes to action and calculated risk-taking (Barner, 1996). Re-engineering requires many of the other skills we have considered in this book – managers as leaders, coaches or facilitators; cross-functional teams; roles and responsibilities redesigned to focus on project teams; status related to contribution; communication using all channels and functions; and individual creativity and initiative.

Business process re-engineering, the business panacea of the 1990s and now being applied practically in the 2000s, remains about three forces – customers, competition, and change. The application of the language of 'marketing' and 'customers' in education is healthy in a world where customers have a more empowered relationship with those who provide for them. Pupils' learning with parental and teacher support is the school's core purpose achieved through new ways that ensure standards and the quality of learning are improved not just marginally and incrementally. If BPR is to achieve dramatic improvements in the critical contemporary measures of performance, the cost, quality, service and speed indicators for every individual pupil's performance and school performance need to be measured. The current structures of the businesses and schools have often been built over time, usually by a series of independent and uncoordinated decisions (Aldritch, 1994). This accretion process may have distorted the structures from those that effectively met customers' needs in the past. Indeed, when the original structures were established the needs of customers would probably not have been given adequate priority. The role of parents in schools has changed significantly, though more in theory than in practice, since the traditional school management structures, particularly in secondary schools, were determined. These structures may meet the needs of the school management or of the teachers but may not have been radically reconsidered and changed to make pupil and parent needs pre-eminent.

*Does the strengthened focus on meeting pupil and parent needs undermine teacher professionalism? How could your school's performance be dramatically improved? How do you know how well every child is learning in every lesson?*

Business process re-engineering concentrates precisely on delivering value to the customer, client or parent. This process will lead to competitive superiority in the marketplace and greater commitment from parents to the school. The traditional understanding of teacher professionalism, which may be interpreted as teachers know best, is inimical to such a focus on the customer. The child's total learning experience at the individual level is arguably insufficiently the focus of school processes, even in primary education. This becomes increasingly the case as children get older. Secondary schools have rarely re-engineered the learning processes to provide an individualized coherent learning experience for individual children, despite mapping exercises across the curriculum. Each child has to cope with at least a dozen teachers and an academic and pastoral hierarchy above them.

## CHALLENGING TRADITIONAL SCHOOL STRUCTURES

Traditional school structures, with separate and occasionally almost tribal key stages or departments, may create co-ordination problems. This is manifested in secondary schools by the separate academic and pastoral systems. These were created, it could be argued, to solve the staffing and educational problems which occurred when grammar schools and secondary modern schools amalgamated (Tomlinson, 1994). This problematic structure has not been seriously challenged in comprehensive schools for 30 years. These and other separate functions in schools are like departments with the salary allowances based on responsibilities but which only infrequently relate to the quality of service. Such traditional systems are being replaced in business by new technologically based management systems. In schools parallel developments will require much more sophisticated measurement of individual progress in learning and 'added value'. Imagination and courage are required to develop and use such information systems at the individual pupil level. More important is the use of 'non-teaching' staff whose skills, particularly leadership and management skills, continue to be underused.

Schools created roles with some parallels to the functional structure of companies when they responded to local management of schools (LMS). Marketing, finance and personnel were established as new distinct functions, often with senior teacher-managers given responsibility for carrying them out when non-teachers could have more effectively carried out all these responsibilities. This meant the establishment of new power bases for which the management team may now fear loss of control and authority. Business process re-engineering requires a change from the traditional functional hierarchy to independent multi-skilled individuals taking responsibility for the entire process. Even the more net-worked, more self-managing primary school class teachers, where they succeed in being open and co-operative with high levels of trust, need to connect effectively. Every child as customer will need to be treated as an individual learner. Core processes in schools, which means the highest possible quality learning for each learner, need to flow creatively across functions and departments. Re-engineering requires a dismantling of the functional boundaries which inhibit the achievement of these core processes.

*Do you see possibilities for applying business process re-engineering in your school?*

## THE TECHNICAL PROCESS FOR DELIVERING BPR

The current processes need to be mapped to find bottlenecks, shortfalls, duplication and incorrect routing. These will be the legacies of policies, traditions and systems of past years. The processes need to be remapped to produce the best way in which learning can be achieved. Any processes that do not add value should be eliminated, and all others monitored and managed. The next stage is to design the flattest structure that will support the newly redeveloped processes. This may mean that significant promotions occur only every ten years even for the person who reaches the top. This has implications for career management. Before long there may be teachers, team leaders and the leadership team only, even in large secondary schools, and the leadership team may include very few teachers. Team leaders in business have been loath to engineer their own activities, espousing revolution and practising conservatism.

Business process re-engineering is about setting ambitious targets for improvement, rule-breaking and the creative use of IT. The emphasis in the new culture has to be on quality, productivity, innovation, empowerment, teamworking, flat structures, multiple skills and cross-disciplinary working. The leader needs to create and sustain the vision while moving towards the new organization with its flatter hierarchy and multifaceted, cross-functional process teams. The leader, the senior executive, who authorises and motivates, has to be strong, assertive, committed and knowledgeable. The more feminine characteristics, increasingly recognized as appropriate for leadership, may achieve these ends even more effectively.

## THE ROLES IN BPR

The following roles have emerged in organizations which have successfully implemented BPR.

- The leader who authorizes and motivates the re-engineering process.
- The steering committee which makes the overall strategy and monitors its progress.

- The process owner is the manager for a specific process and re-engineering effort focused on it.
- The re-engineering team which carries out the diagnosis and redesign of a particular process.
- The 're-engineering czar' is responsible for developing re-engineering techniques, tools and for achieving synergy across the separate re-engineering processes. This is a more rigorous and certainly more focused form of change leader.
- Cross-functional teams should carry out the radical redesign of business processes and their implementation.

In schools these roles will be necessary to ensure a reconfiguration of entire processes and the redesign of subprocesses. The headteacher's role may need detailed reconsideration and all other leaders and managers may need to reconsider the strategic significance of their current jobs and the implications for their planned careers.

*If you have been involved in a restructuring was the process similar to this?*

## THE FORMAL PROCESS

The first phase of BPR is discovery, the seeking of a strategic vision for leadership in the competitive environment (Kearney, 1994). The current culture needs to be assessed to provide a basis for understanding how it can be changed. This requires a critical appraisal of the current school performance. The quality of education and learning that the school provides may indicate a culture of complacency, particularly in the apparently high-performing and Beacon schools. This is followed by a decision about which approach to core business process modelling will work.

Next is the redesign process itself which has to be detailed, planned and engineered. The focus will be on data collection, analysis, concept development and the specification of alternatives. At this stage all assumptions, principles and purposes need to be challenged. This may be difficult when schools judge there are already too many initiatives that they have to cope with. A more detailed vision of what the core business process will look like after re-engineering has to be worked out so the individual pupil really is the focus. A progressive refinement of the activities within each core business process is necessary to get to this level of analysis. There is always the problem of achieving a balance between the level of detail and usefulness of the analysis. The process uses the tools of innovation and creativity discussed earlier to build a bridge from blue-sky vision to realistic conceptual design. Finally there is the realization, the implementation, of the redesign to deliver the strategy. The process improvement has to be taken to the marketplace to capture and control the market, and indeed to seek out new markets. This means centrally the hearts and minds of parents and pupils. Children need to be learning at the limit of their capabilities throughout the school day.

*How do you know how well every pupil is learning in your school?*

## LEARNING TO CHALLENGE THE RECEIVED WISDOM

The lessons of experience are perhaps surprising in view of the technical language. Those who are not experts can redesign processes. Being an outsider is helpful. Preconceived notions have to be discarded. It is essential to see things through the eyes of customers. Redesign is best done in teams. It is not necessary to know a great deal about the current process. Valuable ideas can be discovered. The redesign process can be enjoyable. In practice there needs to be an analysis of the entire core process from the initial customer connection through to suppliers and back to the customer. This analysis must challenge everything and focus on process improvement, not push problems upstream – that is, to school leaders, the LEA or the government. It is similarly necessary to take the process improvement to the marketplace. All those involved may have to unlearn the principles and techniques that may have brought them apparent success for so long.

*Seek information about the school management structure in your school ten years ago and the changes that have occurred in this period. How effective have they been?*

Classical business structures that specialize work and fragment processes have become self-perpetuating precisely because they stifle innovation and creativity. A process orientation is about ambition, rule breaking and the creative use of information technology. After the BPR process several jobs may be combined. The employee becomes both customer service representative and caseworker. The case manager provides a single point of contact as an empowered customer service representative. This language is almost applicable in some primary schools, if only for the year the teacher has responsibility for the pupil. Secondary schools have more to change. Work is performed where it makes most sense. Checks and controls are only maintained to ensure that people are not abusing the process or adding no value. This will result in a change in the shape of work units, with some operations centralized and others decentralized. Jobs change from simple tasks to multidimensional work. Job preparation changes from training to education. This is particularly important for staff development which had moved towards a more technical training for new developments.

*Is the learning of every child coherent throughout each day?*

The focus of performance measures and compensation is changing from activity to results. The current reconsideration of salary structures and the principle of higher payment for those who ensure that the learning process is successful is a subject of debate. The BPR approach would provide substantial rewards for outstanding performance as additional payments not permanent pay rises. Contribution and performance are the primary bases for compensation. The criteria for advancement or promotion, however, are not directly related to performance in the present job. The criteria for promotion concentrate on the ability to carry out the next job. This salary model provides a rationale which is insufficiently evident in the present system, still a classic example of inertia and accretions over time. The values change through BPR from the protective to the productive.

*How effective is the hierarchical management structure in your school in carrying through core processes? Would you describe it as traditional?*

The existing corporate culture and management attitudes may prevent the implementation of BPR. School cultures are particularly intense, and some management attitudes particularly conservative. Business process re-engineering cannot happen from the bottom up. The leader must understand re-engineering, not skimp on resources, or bury it in the middle of the corporate or school development agenda. Energy must not be dissipated across too many re-engineering projects. Business process re-engineering should not be attempted when the head-teacher is within two years of retirement, or the effort will be wasted. The translation of the new design into practice is more important than the preliminary analysis. Schools are arguably frequently better at policy-making than at implementation. Business process re-engineering will inevitably make some people dissatisfied, but trying to please all the staff is a hopeless ambition if this gets in the way of pupil learning. Indeed, the failure to grasp the need to change may result from a weakness which in the end will be self-destructive, a culture of complacency. If staff resist necessary changes it may be essential to push forward and not drag the effort out.

*The design of school management structures it is argued needs to be more strongly reconsidered than has been the case. How do you respond to the analysis in this chapter? Does it require any action from you?*

## CONCLUSION

Eight critical success factors for BPR derived from the above, on the basis that schools must change radically, are:

1) Establish strategic purpose.
2) Ensure top management direction and support.
3) Set stretch goals (ambitious targets to exceed significantly current performance levels).
4) Define core processes.
5) Re-design and create higher level processes (i.e. major end to end activities in an organization such as bringing new products to market).
6) Conduct effective change management.
7) Establish systems to ensure that staff from different functions (e.g. marketing, IT – or teaching and administration) work together.
8) Promote stakeholder involvement with effective planning and project management.

# REFERENCES

Aldritch, M. (1994) 'Work process improvement', *Training and Development*, **12**(3), March, p. 3.

Barner, R. 'Seven changes that will challenge managers – and workers', *The Futurist*, March–April, pp. 14–24.

Chartered Institute of Management (CIMgt) (2000) *Business Process Re-engineering*, London: CIMgt.

Fletcher, J. (1994) 'Learning from business: core process re-engineering', BEMAS Conference Papers.

Hammer, M. and Champy, J. (1993) *Reengineering the Corporation: A Manifesto for Business Revolution*, London: Nicholas Brealey.

Kanter, R.M. (1998) 'Managing for long term success', *The Futurist*, August–September, pp. 43–6.

Kearney, D. (1994) 'Business process re-engineering', *Training and Development*, **12**(3), March, pp. 14–17.

Obeng, E. and Crainer, S. (1994) *Making Re-engineering Happen*, London: *Financial Times*/Pitman.

Snyder, D.P. (1996) 'The revolution in the workplace: what's happening to our jobs?', *The Futurist*, March–April, pp. 8–13.

Tomlinson, H. (1994) 'More value for less effort', *Education*, 183(22), 3 June, pp. 442–3.

# 20

## Work and Life: Achieving a Balance and Planning for the Future

The *Observer*, in association with the Department of Trade and Industry (www.dti.gov.uk/work-lifebalance) published a special supplement on 3 March 2002 entitled *Work Life Balance: Redressing an Imbalance*. The government had launched its Work Life Balance campaign in March 2000 making it a priority to promote the benefits of flexible working practices. The problem caused by excessive hours is not only an issue in education as evidenced in the Teacher Workload Study, but requires a change to the pervasive UK work culture which makes people feel they have to be seen to work very long hours. The initiative is aiming to cultivate conditions where employers can see the benefits of adapting traditional working practices to enable workers to ask for alternatives. Increased flexibility means happier, healthier, more motivated and more productive staff. Current practice in schools needs to be reformulated to make this possible. The pace of change will not reduce nor will the need to perform better in a context in which transformations in technology require schools to meet the pace of change head on. Overwork and inflexible working practices mean a less productive teaching force with recruitment and, particularly, retention problems. A better work–life balance can support developments associated with many of the issues we have addressed in this book – productivity, motivation, performance, morale, loyalty and creativity – to help staff with family and caring responsibilities. If a school can retain its staff by looking after them better they will contribute more positively. The European Working Time Directive (1998) which limited working hours in the European Union (EU) to 48 hours, with an opt-out clause for the UK, needs to be explored more fully in the education context. A new issue which is emerging is for fathers who want quality time with their children, not just paternity leave.

*Are there staff in your school whose work–life imbalance is impacting on their effectiveness as staff and as people? How do you know if this is the case? Has the school policies or practice to manage this?*

### EXPECTATIONS OF EMPLOYEES AND THE LONG HOURS CULTURE

The work–life balance originally developed as an issue for women with the recognition that significant numbers of married women and women in long-term relationships worked full time and managed the home largely on their own.

207

Single-parent mothers had even greater problems. Changing expectations and growing employment instability in business has meant that all employees have been more inclined to change employers to seek promotion and salary increase but now place greater emphasis on comparing the other benefits in employment. Effective work–life policies help recruit and retain good employees. There is a concern in the education service that such developments have not kept pace with those in other forms of employment, though there may be much greater security of employment. Employees do not want the long hours culture, and working hours are longer in Britain than in most of Europe (ISR, 1998). Attitudes towards efficiency and quality and feelings of job satisfaction and job security are lower in the UK than almost every other European county. United Kingdom management is rated less favourably by employees than management in any other country, and UK employees feel less committed to their companies than employees anywhere else in Europe. Teachers' hours appear to be increasing significantly, and teacher workload is a major issue because, despite the rhetoric of cutting bureaucracy, it is increasing. This is in a context where it is recognized that motivated and committed staff are a major determinant of organizational success.

A work–life redesign will involve matching individual life goals with new work goals which will involve prioritizing and may involve releasing work, achieving a better balance and reducing the working hours from 70 to 40 per week by working smarter in employment. Teaching is only one form of employment where this is an issue. There needs to be action to combat a 'long hours' culture, and improved arrangements for maternity, paternity and parental leave without alienating those who may not receive these benefits. Coopers and Lybrand in a 1997 survey found 45 per cent of students saw a rewarding life outside work as a top priority. Ashridge Management College (1999) showed that 93 per cent of male managers say they are increasingly committed to spending time with their family. The teaching profession is not alone in needing to make work more attractive. Two-thirds of managers believe they are expected to ask more and more from their staff, and only one-third would deny that they push staff too hard. This may well be true of headteachers also. This is a national problem therefore not simply one for the education service.

*Has the response to the Teacher Workload Study impacted on your school in any significant way yet? How satisfactory is your own work–life balance now?*

## ACHIEVING COMPLEMENTARY VALUE FROM WORK AND HOME

Parental responsibilities and employment patterns are changing. More employees are carers. Family life is more complex and diverse. There is a new legal context with the Working Time Directive, significant improvements to the statutory maternity leave scheme, the right to parental leave, the Part-time Workers Directive, and case law associated with the Sex Discrimination and Equal Pay Acts. The legal context is requiring highly skilled management to ensure that this new context produces higher levels of customer service. We need to find ways of evaluating and improving teacher satisfaction, which are accepted as genuine. You will need to manage your own career and life in this context.

An IPD survey (Guest and Conway, 1998) explored fairness at work, working hours and the balance between home and work and performance at work. The psychological contract, which has been discussed elsewhere in this book, is a way of interpreting the state of the employment relationship, a set of unwritten reciprocal expectations between an individual employee and the organization. It is the perception that a promise of future commitment has been made and a contribution given by the individual, and hence there is an employer obligation to provide complementary future benefits. The survey shows that three modern myths are undermined. Over two-thirds of employees believe employers have kept their promises with regard to job security. Less than 5 per cent are very worried about their own job security. High levels of loyalty to employers have been sustained; indeed there has been a small increase, despite the perception that there is a new breed of employees willing to sell their services to the highest bidder. Thirdly, the idea that people look to work rather than home for their satisfaction is not sustained. People look to work for challenge and to home for relaxation. What is significant about this survey is its realism. British workers have high levels of satisfaction with life as a whole. Young workers still expect a career. However, 55 per cent of those working beyond their contracted hours get no extra pay and are mainly responding to the demands of their workload, with this work tending to squeeze out home life.

*Is your experience that friends outside the teaching profession have the same issues with the work–life balance as teachers?*

## TEACHING AS MEANINGFUL WORK

In contrast a *Management Today* survey (August 1999) found that over 40 per cent of respondents were likely to look for a job within the next 12 months, 49 per cent think morale is low in their organization, 55 per cent face frequent stress at work; 30 per cent think their health is suffering because of their work, while 28 per cent think their sex life is being affected; half have too little time to build relationships out of work and 20 per cent sometimes drink to ease the pressure of work, with 8 per cent having turned to therapy or counselling. This chapter concludes the book, therefore, with the implication that, although there are considerable pressures on teachers, the work itself is intrinsically worthwhile and the problems that teachers and teaching face are not significantly different from those in other forms of employment. The miseries of the dissatisfied do affect the welfare of the apparently contented majority. Though 81 per cent claim to be 'very loyal', 31 per cent claim not to trust their employer and 40 per cent believe their organization does not respect its staff. There is an argument that if performance is not rated against some absolute yardstick evaluating how productive they are, the pathology of the workplace is such that everyone ends up working harder, longer and under more stress than they would like. The desire to demonstrate commitment means people end up working miserably long hours even when the results do not justify the effort put in. This survey represents the view of managers themselves who have the power to shape company policy in a more benign direction. Though the median employee is broadly satisfied, that does not mean that life could not be improved. There may be a confusion between 'confronting a challenge' and sitting at a desk for 15 hours. More important is the belief that long hours and stress-induced effort is needed to generate the extra output. If staff are worked too hard they will inevitably end up underperforming, leaving, or requiring more pay to keep them whilst they are probably contributing less.

*In this context how do staff perceive your school, your LEA and the DfES? How many hours do you work each week in term time? How could this be reduced and make you more effective?*

## THE PERFORMANCE OF KNOWLEDGE WORKERS IN TEAMS

The retention and motivation of 'knowledge workers' such as teachers is now recognized as crucial throughout business. Knowledge workers are assets who appreciate in value through the knowledge, skills and experience they acquire during their time in the organization. When they leave it is a loss of intellectual capital. The evidence suggests (Buckingham and Coffman, 1999) that employees leave managers not companies, that is, if it can be translated, teachers leave heads of key stage or heads of department and headteachers, not schools. A key expectation of workers is that managers care about them as individuals. There is an enormous variation on this dimension within companies and, no doubt, within the education service. The link in the retail trade of quality of performance and working for a manager who cares about them as individuals is strong. One multinational found that within the organization one team matched the top 1 per cent in the world and another similar team the worst 1 per cent. The Gallup Organization evidence shows that four dimensions affect staff turnover, customer satisfaction and performance:

- having a manager who shows care, interest and concern for each of them;
- knowing what is expected of them;
- having a role that fits their abilities;
- receiving positive feedback and recognition regularly for work well done.

The Gallup focus on natural talents and personal qualities rather than experience or skills at the selection stage has been a feature of this book. One solution to the work–life problem is to work for a manager who her/himself is talented and naturally embraces the foundations of good, caring management with all the implications this may have. They will have the skills of defining the role objectively and clearly, but let employees find, as far as possible, their own routes to achievement. Headteachers need to know the personal qualities that are available to fit teachers to roles. The recognition and reward policies need to become a strong feature of the school culture. This evidence suggests that good headteachers will retain good staff.

*What are the psychological rewards that are offered in your school? How successful is this in practice? How do staff in your school look forward to the future?*

## CHANGE FORCES

At the same time teachers need to work with what Fullan (1993) describes as the changes forces.

1)  Teachers of the future will make their commitment to moral purpose more prominent, more active, more visible, more problematic.
2)  Teachers must substantially deepen their knowledge of pedagogy.
3)  Teachers must be cognizant of the links between the moral purpose of the school level and larger issues of educational policy and societal development.
4)  Teachers must work in highly interactive and collaborative ways.
5)  Teachers will work in new structures.
6)  Teachers must develop the habits and skills of continuous inquiry and learning.
7)  Teachers must immerse themselves in the mysteries, the highs and lows of the dynamic complexity of the change process – how conflict is inevitable, how vision comes later, how individualism and collectivism co-exist in dynamic tension, how arbitrary disturbances in the environment are par for the course, how you never arrive, and how sometimes things get worse, despite your best efforts (*ibid.*, p. 80).

*Do your teachers look forward to this world?*

## FROM THE CURRENT WORK–LIFE BALANCE TO CREATING THE FUTURE

*Scenario planning* is a technique for projecting into and talking about the future. It is useful because it shifts us from the 'day-to-day' mindset into neutral or objective territory so that we can take a more strategic view of the challenges that each one of us will face. The emotional dimension of future trends in information industries, which education might be characterized as, has a potential impact on strategy. These trends need to be integrated into existing strategy in collaboration with partners in the education service. Teachers, as individuals, need to understand these scenarios.

David Mercer of the Open Business School and the Strategic Planning Society organized, for the Futures Observatory, a Millennium Debate. In the education service we need to be more alive to such changes and the implications for education and in particular here for the work life balance. Information and communications technology will have a profound impact on education and teachers' lives and careers. Two presentations from this conference have profound implications for schools and education. The first, Ian Pearson's, explored information technology, the second, David Mercer's starts from the individual and reaches out to the world.

Ian Pearson, BT's futurologist, explored *long-term drivers in IT* in this debate. This is the context in which future schools and the future of educational leadership and teachers' careers are now being redefined. This future, where the work–life balance needs to be achieved, includes:

- Total connectivity – it will be assumed that everything that should be connected is connected.
- Ubiquitous access – we will be able to access the network from almost anywhere at an acceptable cost. High-speed mobile networks will provide us with all the information services we need even when we are on the move.
- Improving interfaces – dealing with anything in IT will be easier and more pleasant than dealing with another person. Eventually we will be able to make links to the nervous system and brain with full thought recognition. This will catapult humankind into the evolution fast lane.
- Increasing machine intelligence – making for a more pleasant and useful contact with the machine world, eventually making people obsolete in most roles. Machines will surpass human intellectual capability before 2020. At some point machines will have genuine self-awareness and consciousness
- Every human institution will be disassembled and reconstituted to serve people better. Geography and physics will be greatly reduced constraints. Politics, business and society will be totally restructured.
- Accelerated development through machine enhanced intelligence, together with the convergence of IT with other technologies, will enable the anticipated breakthroughs in biotechnology, material, genetics, nanotechnology, energy and travel. The twenty-first century will be that one when we achieve mastery of ourselves and the world around us.
- People can affect and direct change but, barring worldwide catastrophe, there are no human institutions that can prevent them happening. People are deluded if they think these are only possibilities.

In this future world, and this is one interpretation only, teachers, and increasingly other professionals in schools, will need to achieve an appropriate work–life balance in this very different context.

*How has technology impacted on and changed your life and work to date? How much of your professional development is exploring preparation for the future?*

David Mercer from the Open Business School and the Strategic Planning Society explored *six drivers for the future*, key forces shaping the future of society over the next 25 years. These drivers provide the context in which work and life will need to be better balanced.

- Individual empowerment. This will focus on: Women's century – women are better qualified to work in the new information society and to provide the more caring management leadership now demanded. Different forms of family – new extended forms which are emerging from the breakdown of the nuclear family will offer many women sole charge of the family. There will be a focus on smaller communities rather than nation-states. New politics – the decline of political parties will accelerate. People will want the right to determine their own destinies, as evidenced by the growth in consumer power; this will extend to the replacement of political parties. New values and search for meaning – the move to individual empowerment will result in a comparable shift in values. The emerging reality of personal fulfilment will stimulate the search for new meanings in life which marketers and employers will need to address.

- Symbiosis with the computer – the most revolutionary outcome of the PC revolution. In recent years society has been evolving. With a form of symbiosis emerging, there is the possibility of evolving forms of human being, genetically modified to combat disease, using performance-enhancing drugs. Communications age – there will be a genuinely global village, through the Internet and its future developments. Homeworking – may now live up to its long promised benefits, with implications for house design and, boosted by travel taxes, could limit the growth of the car. Disappearing computers and mobile communications – computing power will be incorporated where it is needed, running everything but transparent to users.
- Ageing – this may be highly beneficial for those who live healthily for longer. Medical technology will focus on chronic illness rather than acute crisis management, resulting in a healthily ageing population. Demography – when coupled with declining birth rates worldwide, shifting the balance from young to old, need not necessarily result in problems of funding welfare through increases in the age of retirement. Employees as customers – demographic changes and the booming demands of the knowledge society will lead to skills shortages, and the need to recruit the old. These employees will have to be sold to as 'customers' by designing working conditions which are attractive.
- Lifelong learning – much hyped but little has been achieved. Continuing professional development – skills shortages will require extensive ongoing re-education (90 per cent of the workforce according to the EC), especially of older skilled staff but increasingly focused on individual fulfilment. University of the Third Age – the retired will create informal networks for further education. Generation gap – the proportion of older groups with higher education will grow from less than 10 per cent to more than 20 per cent, and for the younger may come to exceed 60 per cent.
- New economics – knowledge society and personal empowerment will lead to revolutionary pressures leading to totally new organizational forms. New products will be replaced by high value knowledge communications. Intellectual abilities will be used to their full. Most individuals will be involved in communications not knowledge. Knowledge – the speed of growth will continue to increase but rapid uncontrolled innovation will come to an end. Rigid organizations – these structures will become fluid. Networking co-operatives – the organization will have fluid boundaries, inside (networking and self-managed teams) and outside (with new alliances) which favour co-operation with stakeholders rather than competition. Company database management will be one key to controlling anarchy. Network trust issues – with a complexity of offerings and new networks offering a wide range of unknown suppliers, trust by branding and relationship management but increasingly through new specialized intermediaries. Competition – a cashless society based on intellectual capital, superseded by a widespread culture of co-opera-

tion. Small businesses working together in less formal ways – internet developments with telecommunications essentially free, and the computer invisible will lead to massive interconnectivity shaping ideas and ideology.

- New world order – global groupings replace nation-states – with global values. Kosovo and East Timor demonstrate how nation-states cannot maintain absolute sovereignty. The EU has an almost messianic mission rather than nations such as the USA or Russia which will continue their attempts to impose hegemony. The EU will take over global leadership but not hegemony from the USA on the basis of the power of its philosophies rather than armies or financial muscle, though it will be the world's largest economic power. Globalization – the global village will allow resources to be co-ordinated globally. Legitimation – the new values will give rise to problems of legitimation for national government.

These drivers, or others you judge more relevant and significant, will have a profound impact on education, and work and life and the work/life balance.

*How is your school planning for these or other anticipated changes for all those in the school community? How are you planning for your life changes?*

## MAKING TEACHING MEANINGFUL: SECRETS OF THE FUTURE-FOCUSED SCHOOL

Herman and Goia (1998) present the future-focused issues of the work–life balance. This refers to USA companies but can be appropriately applied to the education service in the UK. Survival depends on teamwork, loyalty and vision at every level. Workers are no longer willing to work in an authoritarian and dehumanizing environment. They require meaning in their work, balance in their lives, opportunities to contribute and to be valued as individuals with goals and aspirations. Possibly teachers are not finding this if they are leaving the profession. Response Analysis of Princeton, New Jersey, research found that the three most important aspects of work are:

- 52 per cent to be responsible for their work and the results it produces;
- 42 per cent acknowledgement for their contributions;
- 39 per cent their tasks matched to their strengths.

Companies that hope to attract and motivate enthusiastic and dedicated workers will demonstrate sensitivity to the level of responsibility workers want.

## MAKING TEACHING MORE MEANINGFUL

The key elements for meaningful work in the future, for teachers and other staff working together in partnership, adapted from Herman and Gioia, and putting the work–life balance in a wider context, are:

1) A valued part of the whole – staff must know their work is important, how it

fits into the school strategy, share more information and have access to the information that will enable them to be accountable for pupil performance.

2) Making an impact – staff should know how to improve school processes and the environment. Improving school effectiveness is about successfully using the intellectual capital of the school. Staff knowledge and experience provide knowledge not otherwise available. All staff will contribute their knowledge enthusiastically in school cultures that value them.

3) Responsibility for outcomes – responsibility and authority to make decisions enhance the meaning of work. Staff who are able to recommend and implement improvements increase their impact. They need clear goals and the authority to make things happen. This needs a culture of mutual trust which acknowledges that staff are capable of making the right decisions and trust it is safe to do so.

4) Measuring results – teachers and all other staff need direct and timely feedback so they can make changes and improve their performance as a result of this ongoing evaluation. The feedback will show their effectiveness in making things happen, solving problems and making decisions. Pupils and parents evaluate the service performance, but teachers must be involved in determining their performance ratings. They are encouraged to take the initiative in improving their work and results, supported by ongoing coaching.

5) Meaningful rewards – a direct relationship between job performance and reward makes work more meaningful. The culture needs to emphasize individual responsibility for results and a high respect for individuals, giving them access to information, resources and higher management. Schools and individuals benefit from creating opportunities for every employee to self-actualize. Constantly measuring performance is essential to assure contributions are rewarded.

6) Team effort – everyone is expected to support others to serve pupils and parents. The distribution of additional financial rewards is based on a balanced formula of customer satisfaction and return on invested capital at Compaq. Such rewards acknowledge the contribution of the individual. Future-focused companies are redesigning their compensation strategies to reflect their connection to the importance of the individual.

7) Balancing work and family – teachers will be motivated, stable and productive in schools which are highly sensitive to the personal/professional life/work balance. A sensitivity to concerns outside the workplace through such processes as quality of life programmes has added value benefits.

8) Personal and professional growth – to be marketable internally and externally, staff require opportunities to learn, to increase their responsibility and to implement solutions. The learning opportunities need to be both academic and experiential. Professional development adds meaning to work; personal development adds meaning to the life of the individual, both of which build self-confidence and self-esteem.

9) School–staff relations – prospective staff are reluctant to join a school which treats its people badly. There is an emphasis on making an active use of the varied perspectives that workers bring when diversity is recognized positively.

10) Corporate social responsibility – teachers want to work in an ethical school with a clear set of values. Younger teachers are more interested in the environment.

11) Spirituality in the workplace – staff want to be able express their values, share their hopes and tap into their creativity. There is an increased sensitivity to the human spirit at work. School leaders have strong collaborative relationships with staff.

12) Mission – the more experienced who have weathered the last two decades may well be mistrustful. Companies are now being held increasingly accountable as good corporate citizens as are schools. Both will need to regenerate trust.

*How do you and your school respond to these 12 aspects of meaningful work and their implication for the work–life balance? Is this approach reflected in your school?*

## REFERENCES

Ashridge Management College (1999) 'Work life balance', *Personnel Today*, 26 October.

Buckingham, M. and Coffman, C. (1999) *First Break All the Rules*, London: Simon and Schuster.

Fullan, M. (1993) *Change Forces: Probing the Depths of Educational Reform*, London: Falmer.

Herman, R.E. and Gioia, J.L. (1998) 'Making work meaningful: secrets of the future-focused corporation', *The Futurist*, December.

Guest, D.E. and Conway, N. (1998) Fairness at Work and the Psychological Contract, an IPD survey. IPD.

International Survey Research (ISR) (1998) *Tracking Trends: Employee Satisfaction in Europe in the '90s*, London: International Survey Research Ltd.

*Management Today* (1999) Work–Life Balance Survey

Mercer, D. (2000) 'Six drivers for the future' (Millennium Debate, Future Observatory).

*Observer*, in association with the Department of Trade and Industry (www.dti.gov.uk/work-lifebalance), *Work Life Balance: Redressing an Imbalance*, 3 March.

Pearson, I. (2000) 'Long term drivers in IT' (Millennium Debate, Future Observatory).

# Index